# PRESS BOX REVOLUTION

## HOW SPORTS REPORTING HAS CHANGED OVER THE PAST THIRTY YEARS

## RICH COUTINHO

SPORTS
PUBLISHING

Sports Publishing books may be purchased in bulk at special discounts for sales promotion, corporate gifts, fund-raising, or educational purposes. Special editions can also be created to specifications. For details, contact the Special Sales Department, Sports Publishing, 307 West 36th Street, 11th Floor, New York, NY 10018 or sportspubbooks@ skyhorsepublishing.com.

Sports Publishing® is a registered trademark of Skyhorse Publishing, Inc.®, a Delaware corporation.

Visit our website at www.sportspubbooks.com.

10 9 8 7 6 5 4 3 2 1

Library of Congress Cataloging-in-Publication Data is available on file.

Cover design by Tom Lau
Cover photo courtesy of AP Images

ISBN: 978-1-61321-985-0
Ebook ISBN: 978-1-61321-986-7

Printed in the United States of America

This book is dedicated to my mom and dad, who both helped form the passion for sports that has remained in my soul for last half a century. Mom passed in 2004 but she is always with me and my dad is a constant reminder to me that hard work can bring wonderful things to your life.

I would also like to dedicate this book to the memory of Shannon Dalton Forde, the Mets media relations professional that left this world far too soon but taught us all to always love and care for people first and only then worry about yourself.

# CONTENTS

# Introduction

SPORTS REPORTING HAS TAKEN SO many twists and turns in the past thirty years and my aim in *Press Box Revolution* is to take you on a journey exploring that history and also tell you things you've never heard before, helping you to understand the changing landscape of the sports media.

Press boxes have always been filled with interesting personalities and you will quickly learn from reading this book that far more egos exist in those press boxes than in the clubhouses. So many media members are so jealous of the money the players make, they feel they have the right to criticize every misstep the athlete takes in the course of a season. This book will explore how trite and immature those actions are and how it affects the relationship the media has with these players.

I will also address the many social issues that affect sports reporting whether it is racist tendencies, how women were treated when they first entered the locker rooms, or how the use of drugs was covered differently in the '80s when it was just recreational as opposed to its vocational use a decade later.

Technology has evolved in a multitude of ways since the 1980s, and I will take you through that trip that began with cassette recorders and no Internet to what we have today—smart phones, instant messaging, and multi-tasking so the fans get the inside news as quickly as possible.

Speed sometimes becomes more important than accuracy and I will address that.

Social media and the Internet have drastically changed the way fans get their sports news and I will examine how the print media botched the use of both, which is leading to its demise.

I will briefly take you through the early stages of my life where I was exposed to the love of sports but also saw racism at an early age and fighting it has become such a big part of my adult life. Seeing it in the media when I started in the industry shocked me at first but my childhood experiences helped me deal with it in the best possible fashion.

I will recall many individual events from the past thirty years and I will explore those times taking you right into the press boxes and corners of the clubhouse you've never seen. The crutches that reporters use such as analytics will be addressed as well as how the media sometimes sounds like voices in an echo chamber, never really using their minds to analyze issues—they merely parrot each other's viewpoints.

Two huge issues that have totally changed the way sports are reported will also be discussed—fantasy sports and teams and leagues owning sports networks rather than corporations. This has affected the objectivity for the most part and also created the fan's notion that winning a fantasy league is equal to winning a real championship. This manifests itself in social media every single day.

There are certain athletes that I have enjoyed covering over the past thirty years and we will talk about them but I will also broach the sensitive subject of how racism manifested itself in the way players like Darryl Strawberry and Dave Winfield were covered by, quite frankly, a predominantly white male media group . Diversity began to appear in the clubhouses and I will share with you how much that diversity made a huge positive difference even though many of these new media members were treated disrespectfully by the veteran media.

We will also show how the era of "Los Mets" was covered in a very unprofessional manner and how two big names—Bobby Valentine and Rex Ryan—were disrespected on a number of levels when they led New York teams because the media had preconceived notions they refused to abandon.

The mid '80s Mets will be recalled in an honest fashion as the team that changed how sports would be covered because from that time on reporting on the game itself would not be enough—the player's personalities dictated coverage. The 1980s was a live for the moment decade and that team fit that concept like a glove. But they also came to the view of public when the biggest change occurred in our business— sports talk radio.

Fans would now get a chance to talk about their teams on call-in shows and the game experience now included pre- and postgame shows. This transformed the three-hour experience of watching a game into a five-hour visit complete with hearing the voices of your favorite players or the ones you hated because they lost the game for the team you lived and died with every single day.

These all-sports stations also killed network radio and I will take you through the last few years of the Howard Cosell era at ABC Radio which symbolized the transfer of sports on network radio, to specialized all-sports radio. This not only destroyed the networks but created sports revenue sources that liquidated the advertisers from the daily newspaper's sales portfolio and at the same time, dispelled the notion that having a classic voice was necessary to be a sportscasting superstar. WFAN became the standard for which all-sports stations would be compared and I will take you through that evolution complete with how they almost did not make the grade in their early years.

So sit back and get in the sports reporting time tunnel as I share my experiences and examine how covering sports has evolved over the past three decades.

Rich Coutinho
January 2017

# CHAPTER 1

# The Making of a Sports Reporter

WHEN YOU HAVE AMASSED THREE decades of sports reporting in New York, it begs the question: How did you get started?

Life was pretty simple for me as a youngster growing up in the Bronx in the late '60s and early '70s. It was all about going to school, hanging out with your friends, and visiting family. I grew up in the Northeast Bronx, which was Yankees country, but being a contrary kid, I grew up a Mets fan. In those days, the four athletes everybody talked about were Tom Seaver, Walt Frazier, Joe Namath, and Muhammad Ali, and quite honestly, I loved that quartet very much.

On my block, most agreed with the first three but could not understand why I liked Ali so much. You have to remember I lived in a white, Catholic neighborhood in the midst of changing. I firmly believe my education taught me that this was OK and cultural diffusion would actually benefit us. However, there were members of both my family and my friends that could not understand my stance, especially when I tell you a story that shaped my life.

I went to Cardinal Spellman High School which was the premier high school in the Bronx and remains so to this day. It was located in an area that personified the racial changes going on and each day I would take a bus to and from school. One afternoon when I was on the bus, I was blindsided by a black youth who nailed me with a punch to the face, cutting the bridge of my nose and sending blood everywhere. I threw a punch on the way down but it harmlessly connected with nothing but air as my attacker exited the back door of the bus.

The driver stopped the bus and, although I was feeling the effects of the punch, all I wanted to do was to get home. One of my close friends walked me all the way home as my white dress shirt was covered in blood. My parents were very calm and took me to the hospital to stitch up the bridge of my nose, and when I got home I had a conversation with my parents that I will never forget.

I was only a teenager and my dad knew the worst thing I could do is try to retaliate for this act even though he saw his son covered in blood. He said to me, "Rich, you have every right to be angry as this was a terrible thing that happened to you. Don't overreact to this as this is just a sick person and you need to get it out of your mind especially if you are thinking of retaliating against an innocent black person just to even things out. That would make you as bad as him."

His words resonated with me during my entire career as our world has become a diverse one and the sports world is certainly very symbolic of that concept. And it has allowed me to spot "closet racism" even in the people closest to me in my life. My spirituality as a Christian allowed me to forgive the person that assaulted me but in a sense I also understood that if it had never happened to me those words from my dad might never have been uttered. And the whole experience made me understand that I just can't realize what the non-white person feels every single day.

The guy who nailed me with a punch might have come from a broken family or been abused or possibly a white person had done the same to him that he did to me. It would never excuse what he did to me but retaliating against an innocent black person just to even the score was pointless. As you read this book, this racial concept will crop up again in the reporting of the sports world as well as the way women who entered the business were treated.

Aside from that one incident my childhood was peppered with fun as sports was such a focal point of my neighborhood in the Bronx.

Being a Mets fan was tough, but my best friend Donald was one as well and we held our own with the Yankees majority. I had a cousin on my dad's side that was a huge Mets fan and on my eighth birthday my sister bought me a baseball board game called "Gil Hodges' Pennant Fever" which was a Strat-O-Matic-type board game that really taught me about baseball.

In those days there was no cable TV so we listened to many games on the radio. Mets broadcasters Lindsey Nelson, Ralph Kiner, and Bob Murphy were like members of our family as you could often hear them in the background when cousins were visiting and Mom was cooking up a storm. In those days, my mom would insist we'd all eat together but cleverly timed out her cooking so most dinners were postgame meals.

Listening on the radio taught you so much more than watching on TV because you had to envision the picture in your head. Many times I would hang out in my buddy Donald's garage and we would try to predict if Gil Hodges, the manager of the Mets, would pinch hit for certain hitters. You'd really learn the game having those discussions. We would also listen to the radio for sports reports to get scores and even if we were playing stickball in the street or tossing a football, we'd all stop the game to listen to Howard Cosell's daily report because he usually said something controversial. I would go on to produce that same show later in my career.

The first game I ever attended was at Shea Stadium on August 9, 1967, watching rookie Tom Seaver beat the Atlanta Braves, 5–1. The Mets scored four runs in the first and were never headed as Seaver pitched a complete game. Hank Aaron played right field for the Braves, whose lone RBI came off the bat of Joe Torre. Little did I know that two short years later these two teams would meet in the first ever National League Championship Series.

What I remember most about that day is getting to the stadium really early to watch the teams warm up. That was fun, but and the real excitement for me was seeing my first game in color. To that point, I had only seen Mets games on a black and white TV set, so this was a real treat for me. My dad bought me a scorebook and taught me how to keep score. It was so much fun. When I got home, I took a spiral notebook out and copied the scorebook format so I could keep score of games while watching on TV.

That was not a great season for the Mets. They finished last but Tom Seaver became my hero and I never missed a game he pitched whether it was on TV or radio. Growing up in a Yankees neighborhood all you heard about in those days was Mickey Mantle but Tom Seaver was the first Met you could force into any baseball conversation. For that reason alone, his nickname of "The Franchise" was well-deserved and as a nine year old two years later I knew why.

Nineteen sixty-nine was a very special sports year in New York as the Jets, led by Joe Namath, won the Super Bowl over the heavily-favored Baltimore Colts. My friends and I spent most of that summer following the Mets while wondering if Namath, who actually announced his retirement while arguing with the league about some of his business dealings, would ever play again.

Gil Hodges was hired by the Mets in 1968 and suffered a heart attack late in that season but returned to the dugout in 1969. And I went to a host of games that year as a friend's father had season tickets through his job. I attended so many great contests, like Seaver's near perfect game in July. I was also there the night they went into first place during a twi-night doubleheader versus the Montreal Expos. The Mets became a focal point of my life. My mom used to catch me listening to a Mets West Coast game with the radio muffled under the pillow way after bedtime. I firmly believe she let it slide at times because she was watching it on TV.

Baseball was always a big part of mom's life as her brother, my Uncle Sal, was a great pitcher as a youngster who nearly made it. He was in a tryout for the big leagues but a pitcher by the name of Billy Loes, who would later pitch for the Brooklyn Dodgers, beat him out during that tryout. My uncle always told me that Loes had a little bit more on his fastball and he never got another shot as he served in the Korean War and was never quite the same after that.

Uncle Sal was a very important person in my life. He taught me how to pitch, which helped me in my Little League career transform from a terrible hurler to an average one. He told me if I ever threw a curveball before the age of eighteen he would break my arm but showed me how to throw a changeup, which made my slow fastball look better. He died far too young and, quite frankly, my family has not been the same since he passed away in the early '90s.

When I returned to school in September for the fourth grade, the Mets for the first time became a hot topic as so many kids had shifted allegiance from the Yankees to the Mets—even at a Bronx school. In fact, our teachers let us watch games during class if we finished our homework and behaved ourselves. My fourth grade teacher told me years later that she became a Mets fan because when they won, student conduct dramatically improved.

Attending a Catholic elementary school (St. Frances of Rome in the Bronx) we had half days on Wednesdays so teachers could instruct religion to public school students. I got to watch Game Four of the World Series against the Baltimore Orioles with my mom in the comfort of our living room. The day before, I saw Tommie Agee's two great catches in Game Three because our teachers let us watch the game.

Knowing what I know now, I realize it was such a turbulent time in New York with things changing but also the country was in a period of extreme disharmony as the war in Vietnam was a terrible by-product of poor government decision-making. There was also the issue going on in our neighborhood of homes being sold to minorities, as I described earlier in this chapter.

I was only nine years old when the Mets won it all but that whole experience taught me that the old school thoughts put in my mind by some adults in my life would never be part of my values. I saw Cleon Jones hug Tom Seaver and Joe Namath hug Matt Snell and a few months later saw Bill Bradley hug Walt Frazier. In all of those situations, a white man and a black man played together on a team and succeeded in winning. Once that occurred, the emotion of the situation made color a non-factor. We still live in the real world where racism still exists today but for a brief moment, it was like it didn't exist. And that is the biggest reason I love sports. Color, religion, or wealth does not matter once you get on the field. The scoreboard will give you the final results and the rest of it is just conversation.

I think of the great relationships I've had with athletes like Allan Houston, Curtis Granderson, Larry Johnson, John Starks, Dwight Gooden, Curtis Martin, Wesley Walker, Freeman McNeil, Willie Randolph, and Darryl Strawberry. It has made me a better person and sports opened that gateway for me despite being around people who thought racism was OK and at times even encouraged.

It also taught me how to spot racism and that sticking your head in the sand makes you part of the problem, not part of the solution. So to this day when I hear things like "Curtis Granderson speaks very well" and the voice has a tone of surprise in it I know what they are saying. They are saying how can a non-white person speak well?

The other thing the 1969 Mets showed is that dreaming of a great moment is not only permissible—it is mandatory. There are some who live their life that thinking they can't dream because it will disappoint them, but to me reaching for dreams is the only way to live. From 1962 through 1968, the Mets never won an opening day game and in 1969 they lost their opener to the expansion Montreal Expos. They were 10 games out of first place on August 13 and ended up with 100 wins, making up 18 games in the NL East standings in just fifty days.

They swept a great hitting Atlanta Braves team to win the pennant and upset a heavily-favored Baltimore Orioles team to win the World Series. They were a team that had never finished any season less than 16 games under 500. They were a team that people joked about and categorized as losers. But these twenty-five players led by Gil Hodges (who should be in the Hall Of Fame, by the way) did not get the memo that they would languish in mediocrity at best.

The leadership of Gil Hodges and Tom Seaver just would not permit it and watching that put an indelible mark on my heart and soul. So when people told me I couldn't do something I would merely look at that team and say to myself why let anyone destroy my dream. I knew from that moment on I would never be happy if I wasn't around sports. And there were times where that determination was tested but I did what I had to do to keep it alive.

I also understood early on that I could not do it alone as every winning team needs teammates. And obstacles will *always* surface in the chasing of any dream. For me, the illness of my father in 1971 was a rude awakening to that fact especially after my mom got ill two days later. The day my dad suffered his heart attack, my landlord drove him to the hospital instead of waiting for an ambulance and it saved his life. But my dad was never able to work again and his dreams of owning a home went up in smoke as he told me later we were four months away from having enough funds for a down payment.

It created hard financial times, but my parents made ends meet and put their children's interests over their own. And sing no sad songs for me as my childhood was normal because my parents—coupled with family support—made that happen. I had as much fun as any other young kid on my block and got into the same mischief. And yes finances hurt us in that vacations were less commonplace and we had to wait for things because my parents had to live on a fixed income in their mid-forties.

But those of you who follow me on both social media and on-air, know I am an optimistic person by nature, which is pretty uncommon these days. It was this time in my childhood that cemented that in my soul.

It would have been so easy to grow bitter about things in my family life but it merely created a resolve to understand life is not perfect and God gives us all we need to live our lives happily and at the same time, does not give us anything we can't handle. Later in my life when I converted to Born Again Christianity, this concept was reaffirmed in vivid fashion.

Covering sports has always illustrated to me that for whatever reason, the thought is that to be a great reporter you have to be negative, biting, pessimistic, and jaded. My childhood built a foundation that despite tough times you can't let the world change you. I never succumbed to that "reporter mindset" because it would not be me.

The sky *always* looks pretty dark right before dawn and that concept often shows its face on many a night that I am watching games from press row. Sports very often imitate life better than any form of entertainment. They are no scripts—it is reality television in its purest sense and the fact I get to analyze those events inspires me every single day.

So that's how this dream of being a sports reporter entered my mind. The first two stops: WFUV and Sports Phone—the two best farm systems in the business.

CHAPTER 2

# WFUV and Sports Phone:
# Sports Reporter Farm Systems

DURING THE 1980s, WFUV AND Sports Phone were two prime outlets for the cultivation of aspiring sports reporters. The foundation for my reporting career as well as many others was set at both places. We were all so young and shared some unforgettable experiences while working long shifts and learning our craft. They gave me my first entrance into the press box, providing me with a firsthand view of the business I was trying to break into.

WFUV is the best college radio station in the country, sending out 50,000 watts of power in the tri-state area from the Rose Hill Campus of Fordham University. Its alumni includes the likes of Vin Scully and Charles Osgood. I worked there from 1980 through 1982 while getting my degree at a top-notch university.

I worked alongside a talented group of students that would later make their mark on the sports media. I actually started in the news department, but in short order the News Director, Debbie Caruso, advised me to join the sports department. The staff included names like Mike Breen, Michael Kay, Charlie Slowes, and Jack Curry. People often ask me who the most talented broadcasters were in that group. That's not an easy question to answer but I will say this: In my senior year, Bob Papa came in as a freshman and was, in my opinion, the most ready to become a professional I met there. Charlie Slowes, who now broadcasts for the Washington Nationals, was a close second.

Both Papa and Slowes had a very professional way about them at a young age. Charlie was so helpful to me in my career. He taught me how to sound better and by co-hosting so many talk shows with him, I really learned that craft which helped me later on. Some other WFUV names get more publicity, but Papa and Slowes personify what a play by play broadcaster should be in our business. They both paint a word picture on the radio that leaves no stone unturned, as do Howie Rose and Gary Cohen.

About ten years ago, I co-hosted a reunion show at WFUV with Charlie and it was so much fun reliving those years as well as talking about sports with the young WFUV aspiring reporters. I still visit the station today and work alongside so many of the young reporters learning their craft.

Things sometimes got a bit testy between some of the young reporters at the station. In those days, the Sports Director position was awarded following an election among students and it sometimes got heated. Michael Kay was a dynamic personality even back then and by being elected Sports Director, he also scheduled the talent assignments. I always felt this was a huge conflict of interest since at no station I worked at after WFUV did an on-air person organize the schedule.

For the most part, Michael was fair with the schedule but many of us still complained about it. The irony of that schedule is it rarely placed Mike Breen in a play-by-play role as he was often the color analyst. You could tell Breen had a knack for play-by-play, which he demonstrated by becoming the best NBA play-by-play man in the business.

Kay was an interesting personality to be around and quickly became a leader at the station. He has always exhibited the Pied Piper quality of leading people into his corner.

The thing that makes Breen so special is that when he asks you how you are he really wants to know. One day I ran into him at Madison Square Garden. While we were talking, St. John's coach Lou Carnesecca passed by and Breen made sure I got an introduction and made the conversation about me. He is not only a talented broadcaster but one of the finest people in our business. Another classy WFUV alumnus is John Giannone, who is sideline reporter for the New York Rangers on MSG. John has the 2 H's—hunger and humility—and exhibits those traits every day.

We had many fun social events while at WFUV (the drinking age was eighteen, not twenty-one then) and had what we called called roof parties on top of of Keating Hall, which housed our studio. They were fun nights and nobody ever drove after them as many of the dorms became places where students (even commuters like me) could always sleep off long party nights.

In my senior year, we had a bunch of talented freshmen arrive including Paul Dottino, who is the best Giants reporter in our market right now, and a guy named Harry Miller. To this day, I really do not know what happened to Harry but he was a unique person. Harry was not there to build a career—he merely viewed WFUV as a frat house and he enjoyed every minute of it.

One night I was co-hosting *One on One* with him. In those days, the show aired from 11 P.M. to 2 A.M. each Saturday and Sunday night. Because of the late hour, you had to have the guard shack call the station and someone would let you in. I usually arrived two hours before the show but Harry was always late, often strolling in five minutes before we went on the air.

I was in the midst of editing something so I sent the producer down to let him in, but Harry was not standing by the correct door. The producer came back saying he was not there. A few moments later, Harry walked in but his hands look bruised and bloodied. He said, "You guys never came down so I broke the window and let myself in." Typical Harry.

We had some memorable college basketball moments as Tom Penders did a great coaching job as the Rams received NIT bids in both 1981 and 1982. There were so many great games including two wins over Notre Dame (one in South Bend) and an upset of Syracuse at the Meadowlands.

But the team never won the MAAC postseason tournament until a year after I left the school. Even then, the Rams did not get an NCAA bid because the conference had not yet attained automatic bid status. Still, it was more success than the school had seen in over a decade because Penders was a strong coach and an excellent recruiter. That was further illustrated when he left to man both the Rhode Island and Texas programs that took huge steps forward during his tenure. Fordham's program was never the same after he left. Joining the Atlantic 10 proved to be an awful basketball decision as the Rams are way out of the mainstream of college hoops in New York.

That is sad because the Rose Hill Gym is a throwback and really keeps the fans close to the action. Of course, today money is everything and these small gyms have become obsolete. To me, it is the way college basketball should be, especially in the New York market where it is not the focus in the winter the way it is in places like Kentucky and Kansas.

Towards the end of my WFUV career, I did far more sports talk than play-by-play and I feel that it made me a better sports reporter. Play-by-play was never a great skill of mine and I realized that early on, so I really tried to perfect my sports talk craft. There wasn't a lot of sports talk on the radio anywhere in those days but I truly believed *One on One* proved it would work. I recall when we expanded to both Saturday and Sunday nights we were worried phone calls would diminish or even disappear. But on that first night, phones jumped off the hook, cementing the notion that sports talk was a viable format.

I distinctly remember one show after Jets lost a game in 1981 that put them at 0–3, which made the experts declare their season over. I went on the air that night and proclaimed the Jets would be in the playoffs by the end of the season. I was grilled for that but as the season wore on, coach Walt Michaels turned their season around and by year's end the Jets not only made the playoffs but their 28–3 home win over the Packers in the season finale also gave the Giants a playoff spot.

At the time the only other sports talk show in New York was on WABC radio hosted by Art Rust Jr., who attacked WFUV in one of his shows. Twice a year, we had an overnight show to raise money for the station with callers asking us trivia questions while we asked them one. One night Rust got a call where he was asked a question about the Mets and the caller proceeded to cite something I said on *One on One*. I had commented that I felt Tom Seaver would return to the Mets in 1983 in my one of my last shows in the summer of 1982. Rust responded by saying. "Oh, I know that station and all I can say is I don't have to go on the air and beg for money."

The following week I opened the show by giving a message to Art Rust Jr. I said, "This is very true. He does not have to go on the air and beg for money—good thing." The whole incident gave me a glimpse of what the future would hold: that radio talk show hosts would begin taking on each other once sports talk radio hit the airwaves. But it also revealed to me that *One on One* was not just a college radio talk show. It provided a place for NFL fans to voice their opinions on Sunday nights after all the games had been completed. I am so proud to be part of that and equally proud the show is still on the air and still the longest running sports telephone talk show.

Leaving WFUV was sad for me because I was unsure where my career was headed. I sent out hundreds of résumés but got very few interviews. It was 1982 and we were in a deep recession, which prompted many businesses to curtail or even eliminate new hires. By the fall, I began working three jobs to make money as I worked in public relations at an insurance company, worked seasonally at a department store called Caldor, and did overnight shifts at the other farm system for broadcasters, Sports Phone.

The service was run by Phone Programs, a company that produced a variety of recorded phone services: Dial-a-Joke, horoscopes, and many others, including sports scores. Sports Phone's phone number, 976-1313, was engrained in every sports fan's mind and our job was to update scores every ten minutes for callers. We also had a supplemental line that had contests and audio from athletes about the upcoming games. On NFL Sundays we would employ more talent to give fresh updates every two minutes. We were also responsible for an audio service used by many radio stations including 1010 WINS as well as being the New York stringer roster for AP Radio. To this day, a handful of us still freelance for AP. That relationship was established in the early days of my career and thirty-five years later, they still call on me when local sports stories become national in nature.

Note that this was pre-Internet, pre-Bottom Line, pre-sports talk radio. For most fans this was the only way to get the latest scores. It is hard to conceptualize in today's world, but this company had a monopoly in many ways. Though the pay scale was barely above the minimum wage, the job improved our skills as a sports anchor. We had systems in three cities—Chicago, New York, and Detroit—so we had to tailor to fans of those cities. For example, when on the Chicago system you always led with the Cubs in baseball season, then gave the White Sox score, followed by the rest of the American League scores, and finally back to National League scores. It taught us how to build a proper sportscast and the supplemental line helped us learn how to incorporate sound bites inside a report.

Even during the baseball strike in 1981 (some of us interned at Sports Phone in our college years) we had callers because we ran a Strat-O-Matic baseball game World Series between the 1969 Mets and 1978 Yankees. The Yanks won the first three games of the series but Mets won the next four. Little did we know that would be a view into the future as the Yankees would become the only baseball team to blow a three games to none lead in a best-of-seven series twenty-three years later.

Sports Phone had a roster of future New York and national broadcast talent including Howie Rose, Gary Cohen, Steve Cangialosi, Michael Kay, Charlie Slowes, Bob Papa, Chuck Cooperstein, Linda Cohn, Jim Cerny, Peter Schwartz, Don LaGreca, and John Giannone, just to name a few. The original office was on Third Avenue in Manhattan. P. J. Clarke's was the bar we hung out at after shifts because it was right next door to our building.

Little by little, the changes in the industry started to hurt Sports Phone, but the mid-'80s was a classic time. I still did part-time work for them later in the decade before they moved to Elmont, near Belmont Park racetrack, which was not so convenient, so I took my craft to ABC Radio.

I learned so much at both WFUV and Sports Phone and am better for it. I covered games, improved my announcing skills, made contacts, but above all, worked hard and played hard. In those years, I did some bartending as well and all these things made me ready for the changes that were coming in both my career and my life. I actually made far more money bartending and in advertising sales in those years but would never trade the time I spent at Sports Phone for anything. It no longer exists because of the evolution of our business and that is sad because it helped so many of us grow into the professionals we are today.

## CHAPTER 3

# Electronic Media Enters the World of Sports Reporting

SPORTS REPORTING HAS EVOLVED INTO something very different than it was when fifty-somethings like myself left school to start a sports career thirty years ago. Back then, the broadcast reporter was a fairly new creation and it made newspaper writers a bit uncomfortable. The technology was very primitive, but the characters in place were anything but ordinary.

In the 1980s, there was no Internet, no Bottom Line or score box on the television screen during a game, no all-sports radio, no social media, and ESPN was in its infancy. Electronic reporting consisted of sports reports on local news stations. If you wanted an updated score, you either waited for a sports report or called Sports Phone, where I happily worked with a host of others sports broadcasters to keep fans updated.

Think about that for a minute. Fans in New York couldn't see every Mets or Yankees game on TV so the transistor radio became their best friend. And if you lived in the Bronx like I did, you had to travel to watch a Rangers or Knicks home game because our streets weren't wired for cable television yet.

So that electronic update heard on 1010 WINS or WCBS News-radio 88 or the call to Sports Phone (that lifted phone bills to the heavens) was all that fans had. And as far as being updated by the writers, you had to wait until the next day—assuming the game did not end too late. There were no Twitter updates or online editions of newspapers. Given this, you can see how the writers disliked the electronic media. Of course, many of them have since entered the electronic world because the newspaper business has undergone dramatic change.

A radio reporter's job in those days was all about live updates done over the phone. Not only the local stations in New York but the networks—ABC, CBS, and Associated Press—needed updates whenever the local team became a national story. In the mid–1980s, the Mets, Yankees, Jets, and Giants were always in that fraternity and the networks paid pretty well since these updates aired over hundreds of stations around the country.

Before I get into a typical day in the '80s, I want to explain how the business worked back then and how people in the radio business abused their network power, creating an almost Ponzi scheme-like atmosphere.

In those days, Sports Phone would send me to cover games (mainly Mets home games), but other work would be filtered down by networks, which mainly used their staff to man games during the week. When their regulars were off on weekends, however, they hired many of us on a freelance basis to provide game reports. I received assignments by a radio network producer and, after completing the work, he called me to explain that I had to give him a "finder's fee" for getting me the work. Of course, I refused, and then one of his henchmen approached me at my next game. You might recognize his name—Howie Spira. He would later become involved in a legal triangle involving both George Steinbrenner and Dave Winfield, which makes this all rather comical. He said to me, "Rich, you have to pay a finder's fee because we got you the work. You know we could make sure you never work in this town again." My response was, "You're not getting a dime from me and this conversation is over unless you want to take it outside."

Like any bully, he backed off and irony of all ironies—the guy he was collecting for at the radio network some years later lost his job, which I took over in early '90s. What goes around comes around.

The second part of the job was to gather postgame sound by interviewing players and coaches. This led to some clashes betwen the electronic media and writers. In the pre-digital days, there was only one way to gather this sound—with a cassette recorder and a microphone. And some of those machines were as big as a briefcase, making the area around a player's locker very crowded for all media members. Personally, I always tried to operate from the corners so my microphone was close to the player. We called it a "media scrum" and at times it became downright nasty, especially when TV cameras were added to the mix (usually after midweek day games).

In those pre-Internet days, print reporters viewed radio reporters as stealing their stories because they could electronically get the quote out there six or seven hours before any newspaper hit the stands. There were shouting matches and near physical brawls when the newspaper beat writers felt their leads sweeping away onto the broadcast airwaves.

That's not to say that some of the writer's objections weren't valid and oftentimes, I felt my radio colleagues could have been more flexible. Personally, I had to do both updates and postgame, so I tried to get some look-ahead stuff in pregame access time, especially with the next day's starting pitcher, which quite frankly, most radio reporters did not do. I knew in postgame the writers needed "hard core" game-related quotes so I tried to wait if I had any "feature type" questions until after the scrum was over. In a way, this also helped me develop a relationship with players like Gary Carter, Mookie Wilson, and Darryl Strawberry as they spoke with me one-on-one as opposed to an entire group of reporters.

The other thing that really upset the writers—and I totally agreed with them on this—was the reporter who basically just stuck their microphone in the player's face, never asked a question, and often would not even look at the player. I always referred to these reporters as ambulance chasers and there were so many of them they really made players leery of all the radio people. What most people were not aware of is that some of these radio guys would not even show up until the eighth inning of a game so asking a question about the game was the furthest thing from their minds.

Once you accumulated all of your sound, the laborious part of the day began. You had to rewind the tape and edit your material into sound bites which could be used by the radio station or network. The recorder had a counter on it and you had to mark that counter on a cut sheet so you could preview the cut when you fed the sound over the phone. Remember, no Internet, no email, no digital files being attached to an email, there were no FTP sites you fed the sound into—I am talking mega-primitive.

When you were ready to feed the station, you called them on a box phone, and to feed the clips you had to unscrew the receiver (in those days it was circular area you spoke into) and place a device called "alligator clips" into two jacks inside the phone. One on the other side of the jack was a mini input you inserted into the external jack of your cassette recorder (where you would put an earphone) and that is how you fed the sound. And in the non-digital era, that meant rewinding of fast forwarding your tape between every edited cut using the cassette pause button at the end of each cut.

The producer at your station had it even harder—they had to record the sound onto a reel to reel tape machine and then edit the sound onto a cartridge (what looked like a mini 8-track) which the engineer played from a cart machine. Once the cut outlived its usefulness, those carts had to "bulked" (erased) for future use. Getting it from the reel-to-reel to cart was not an easy transfer—at times you even had to cut the reel-to-reel tape with a razor blade so the cart would play the cut accurately with enough lead time so it sounded good.

Present-day reporters must be laughing right now as the digital world has totally transformed this into a seamless process. There were no cell phones in these days, so sometimes you actually had to feed over a pay phone, which were in every press box in those days.

Even given all of these constraints, radio reporters still got these sound bites out to the public far sooner than the newspapers got stories with quotes delivered to the newsstands. That created a sometimes heated atmosphere in the locker room. I regularly saw reporters shoving each other when trying to access a spot in front of a player's locker.

I operated under the notion I had a job to do and there were times I needed to be a little patient, but there were times, like writers, when I was on deadline and had to be firm with the players.

As the mid-'80s evolved, the press box started to look a little different. Computers made their first appearance, but they were far from what they look like today. Most of them were huge and really crowded the press boxes. As radio reporters, our technology began to improve as well. I was given new equipment, including a smaller recorder—a Sony Marantz—that was much easier to carry around and also had two different kinds of output jacks that would make doing work in a press conference setting much easier. Our recordings were on cassette tapes, but moving around in the locker room became much easier. Still, the postgame clubhouse was getting busier and busier and it was harder to move around as the players' locker stalls became so crowded. Writers insisted on being up front because they were still transcribing quotes onto a notepad and I often read quotes in the following day's newspaper that were different than what I had recorded on tape. It did not differ all that much, but a misplaced preposition could always alter the entire quote.

More importantly, you did not get the player's tone in a quote, which could really affect how the reader would interpret the story. For example, in 1986, Darryl Strawberry was quoted as saying, "I appreciate Keith Hernandez trying to help me with tips on hitting left-handed pitching because I know he is the best at it."

On my way upstairs to the press box, a newspaper columnist told me that he thought Straw was being sarcastic and might slant his story that way. A fan could listen to what the player said and make their own assessment. In print, you can't hear the player's tone but *always* get the writer's tone. And that particular columnist always took black players to task whenever they said something controversial and never did that with white players.

Towards the end of the decade, computers became more commonplace and I got my first machine, which was more of a word processor than a laptop you might see today. It was a glorified typewriter that actually made corrections on a screen rather than having to use white-out on a paper that had words typed on it. It took a little getting used to, but once I got rolling with it I never touched a typewriter unless I was in the sports office typing labels for carts that would play my sound on the air.

As we entered the '90s, we all heard rumblings about a system that housed sound digitally but most radio stations still used carts for the next few years. Cassette recorders were still being used in locker rooms and, for the first time I saw writers (most notably younger ones) also using them to help gather quotes. I also began to see writers from competing newspapers share quotes, which I found to be very strange.

As the late '90s approached, my bosses provided new machinery to both feed sound and deliver live reports. It was a Gentner box which had output jacks for both a headset and a way to connect to the recorder. This allowed me to deliver wraps which are reports in which a sound bite is inserted inside a voiced report.

For the first time in my career, ad sponsors were attached to my name and it proved to be the wave of the future: They called it a club-house report. This was the first time my name was attached to revenue for the station I worked for, proving that content can always create revenue. It is a concept the print business never really understood and when websites began cropping up, the newspaper business dropped the ball big-time.

For TV networks, it is a simple game plan—create initial revenue by bringing in affiliate sales money by selling your network to major cable companies at a rate per subscriber. You keep penetrating that market and at the same time, develop your programming. Once the affiliate number levels off (and it will) the ad sales dollars will take the ball and run with it. Unlike affiliate sales, ad sales can grow with good

Nielsen ratings but more importantly, great pricing and planning of commercial inventory creates spot rate growth by offering in-program embedded messaging viewers will watch because it is in-program. A great example of this is WFAN tailoring clubhouse reports to sponsors or even putting a title on things like the broadcast booth. It gave TV and radio stations the ability to take every piece of real estate and sponsor it. Madison Square Garden has transformed the sideboards at Rangers games to a series of sponsor logos embedded in every broadcast and baseball teams have followed suit, resuming the old school practice of peppering the outfield walls with messaging.

I bring this up because the newspaper business did not have management skilled in this area. They generated their revenue by selling the daily newspaper and some limited advertising. Once the Internet exploded, they made a critical mistake. They offered their web content for free, thinking selling web ads would bring in revenue.

This philosophy was misguided on a number of levels. First of all, once people could get the newspaper online why would anyone buy a physical newspaper? Secondly, the TV model clearly gave them time to build up the ad sales portion of the equation. And giving "affiliate money" out for free clearly kills a plan that in the TV world, proved to be a money-making concept.

There were other problems as well. Writing for an Internet site is much different than writing for a newspaper. The attention span is shorter and it's all about the content.

Giving the content away for free made about as much sense as emptying your wallet into the garbage can every day. At this point, many sportswriters attempted to move into electronic media, which I found amusing since they always said how insignificant we all were, yet now they were venturing into our business to save their careers.

You could readily see that in the technology that the writers began to use. They started to ask us what equipment we used and you could see in their eyes they knew what was coming—the end of being a beat reporter as they knew it. We understood that but I often think what if the situation was reversed. Many of us in the radio business were good writers and what if we decided to try to enter their business because ours was failing?

With a few exceptions, most of the writers were lost when they got on-air gigs. And a big reason is the technology was not as easy as they thought it would be. Plus doing on-air work is not for everyone as the airwaves of sports talk radio proves every day.

As we entered into the new century, cell phones became commonplace and so many radio reporters began to get live interviews for sports talk show hosts, which is now pretty standard in the postgame process. Our cassette recorders were replaced by digital machines and we began to email content, improving the sound quality and speed of which we delivered content.

But there was one final piece to the technology puzzle that would transform our business and further harm the newspaper industry. Social media is quite possibly the biggest change I have witnessed in the past thirty years.

I first noticed the Twitter craze in the locker room during spring training in 2007. It created a new way to break news, but these "tweets" were limited to 140 characters, sending grammar and spelling back decades. In the beginning, the teams limited its use by establishing guidelines when reporters were allowed to tweet.

Twitter can be a great tool to send out information, but I personally *never* send anything out until my employer gets it because, quite frankly, they pay my salary. It has also lengthened the work day by hours because we need to respond to tweets since our bosses demand it.

We now live in a press box world where most writers care more about their Twitter feed and number of followers than they do about their core job description. I can be guilty of that sometimes but I yearn for the days when we talked to each other about storylines concerning the game—not about whether I saw a tweet insulting me and what my reaction was to it.

We've all become very sophomoric in the way we talk about sports. We care more about what players think of their teammates, how accommodating they are to the media, and what their off-field interests are rather than why they threw to the wrong base or how they pitched a three-hitter.

Twitter has also made us all *think* we are celebrities—we are not—we are normal everyday people who get a chance to see the world athletes live in.

Social media has given sports reporters a false sense of security as many of us really evaluate our worth of how many followers we have rather than on the content of our reporting. And when a story is broken, we seem to think the fans have to know who broke it and nothing could be further from the truth. In journalism school I learned it is better to be second and correct than first and wrong. But the Twitter world flies in the face of all that and makes immediacy such a key to evaluating our job performance.

People often ask me what is the best part of covering sports? No question it is the game and I put up with all the pre- and postgame nonsense because the game is what drives me. I know that not all journalists feel that way, so I will share a story to illustrate that. During the 2009 World Series, I asked several reporters, what is one thing they still want to do in their career? I said I wanted to cover something I never covered before—the Indy 500 or Wimbledon, for instance. We went around the room and one columnist said all he wanted was to build up a player and then bring him down and destroy him. We all looked at him like he was crazy but the scary part is I don't think he is the only one that thought that way.

I firmly believe that social media has made us all think of ourselves are far more important than we actually are—yet we think players should only think of the team first and accept less money so the team can win. I do not know one reporter (including myself) who would do that in their career. And when a job opens up in our industry, I've seen many a reporter try to discredit others applying for a position rather than stating what they bring to the table.

Much like the Twitter world, those dispersions to others are likely untrue and they don't seem to be accountable for that immature behavior. We seem to be much more concerned with political correctness than we are with moral correctness.

As Twitter becomes more entrenched in the fabric of our communities, there might be no need for sports reporters. To get the truth, fans might just become followers of their favorite players on Twitter or read the *Players' Tribune*.

But I am an optimistic person and sincerely hope the next wave of technology will drive people away from Twitter and to a more realistic view of sports. We need more analysts that understand the game and do not rely on sabermetrics to analyze everything for them. I also hope our industry learns not to just follow the prevailing notion like a bunch of sheep.

I have tried to take that route in my sports reporting but often I have been criticized for it. Still, I understand that seeing through the trees in life can leave you alone and what the majority thinks is not always the way to go.

The changing technology has been a mixed bag. The platform we live in makes sports reporting quicker and more accessible to the fan. But the intricate analysis that makes sports great is generally ignored and that makes our work far too simplistic and often far too reliant on statistics.

CHAPTER 4

# Are Beat Reporters Becoming Obsolete?

GROWING UP AS A METS fan in New York, all I ever wanted to do was be a reporter who covered the team. Reaching that goal continues to be all that I envisioned it would be, but the job has evolved as the world of social media has made it a shell of what it used to be. I will address social media in more detail later in the book but in this chapter I will take you through a typical day in the life of a beat reporter and highlight some of the best I've observed over the past thirty years. We will also explore what the future holds for beat reporting.

Radio beat reporters were nonexistent at the beginning of my career in the 1980s as most of my radio colleagues concentrated on getting postgame sound, which angered the beat reporters and I could understand it since many of them demonstrated an ignorance of the game they were covering. One funny story illustrates this. Bill Gullickson, who pitched a majority of his career in the National League, was traded to the Yankees during the 1987 season. A veteran radio reporter entered the room after he joined the Bronx Bombers and he said to him, "Oh my god, are you in *this* league too?"

It was a notion many players had about radio reporters and quite frankly, those feelings were not totally off base. I worked to change that perception, but the credit for the advent of radio beat reporters belongs to two people: Suzyn Waldman and Ed Coleman of WFAN, who paved the way for radio beat reporters to become an essential part of sports coverage.

They also created the platform that radio reporters should travel with the teams and paved the way for beat reporters like myself and Sweeney Murti. Players and team ownership appreciated that both Suzyn and Ed were ardent students of the game and provided the plasma for the body of sports radio in New York by constructing a direct connection to the listeners each and every day.

So what is a typical day like for a beat reporter? It varies by sport and to me baseball beat reporting is by far the most difficult. Covering the national pastime is a long day. For a night game you should get to the ballpark around 2:30 P.M. to prepare your pregame strategy until the locker rooms open around 3 o'clock. The manager meets the media around 4 o'clock, usually in a press conference setting but it was not always that way. Years ago the manager's office was the place to talk with them both before and after the game.

I don't want to sound like an oldtimer here, but I preferred that setting as you could really get to know the manager personally. After the session some of us could stick around if the manager was in a good mood and talk about everything—not just baseball. I had great chats in the manager's office after the standard questions with guys like Dallas Green, Bobby Valentine, and Buck Showalter.

This allowed us to talk to the managers about topics that they might not discuss with every member of the media in the room and it actually disarmed them even when you had to ask tough questions. Today, that just does not happen. Terry Collins is an exception to that rule as he always makes time even if it is just when walking down the hallway after his media session. He has always done that since the day he was hired as Mets manager.

The other big change is that years ago players would hang out at their lockers and access was much easier before the game at the older ballparks. Today there are so many places for players to hide with lounges in the clubhouses where players can unwind without the media watching them. In fact, the total access time has diminished in the past few years as once batting practice starts, the locker room is closed and does not reopen until the game is over. In the past, the locker room generally reopened after batting practice and stayed open until an hour before the game.

The way around this is to talk to players when they complete batting practice in the dugout and I will do that before just about every game I cover. This schedule also means you have far greater access when covering a team on the road because the visiting team takes batting practice last and that means that clubhouse stays open longer.

There are certain stadiums where this access is especially helpful like Citizens Bank Park in Philly or Nationals Park in DC, where there seems to be fewer hidden rooms. Over the years the Mets have generally been far more accessible than the Yankees, especially over the past fifteen years.

Once the locker room is closed, the beat reporters migrate back to the press box where they begin writing their stories. Keep in mind that there are many different types of stories and radio reports that the beat reporters send to their editors or broadcast control rooms. In the radio business, we send manager and player quotes that our stations can use in previewing the game. But we also put together any preview sound that could be used the next day from various sources such as the next day's starting pitcher, for instance. Personally, I always hesitated sending too much of that as the game could affect how you carve out the next day's preview pieces.

Newspapers that cover the team on a daily basis normally have more than one writer (especially for home games) and that second writer generally writes a "sidebar" piece that complements the game story. Columnists also play a huge role in game coverage.

You can get a bite in the press room when you have a free minute for a very small fee, and I remember the days when the meals were free and most stadiums had a bar serving alcohol to the media. However, those days are long gone. I do remember completing my postgame work and having a beer while listening to Ralph Kiner talk about the old days and it was so much fun hearing him talk about everything from his days as a star with the Pirates to the night he dated Elizabeth Taylor—yes, Kiner was a real rock star.

I can also recall the time during my early years covering a game at Yankee Stadium when Billy Martin strode into the press lounge demanding a drink on a Sunday morning right before that day's game. He was not managing the team at the time as he was serving as a TV analyst and I've never seen anyone drink six beers in such a short time. He proceeded to do his TV work and we had the sound up in the press room. I must say you could not tell he was impaired and he made some great points late in the game regarding setting up hitters. Whenever I saw Martin, I thought of the story my mom told me about meeting him at a nightclub while he was playing for the Yankees in the 1950s and he asked her to dance. While dancing with him, she told him that she could not believe how short he was. He asked who her favorite player was and she said, "I have two and neither of them are Yankees. One is Gil Hodges and the other is Jackie Robinson—the best second baseman in baseball." He replied, "You know I'm a second baseman." She responded, "You're pretty funny, but Jackie is a star." My mom loved telling that story and every time we'd hear a news story about Billy's drinking escapades, she would merely say that she was not surprised.

The press room is also a great place to hear the rumors of the industry and to do some networking, especially with visiting members of the media. Over the years, I have obtained a great deal of freelance work after out-of-town beat reporters recommended me to their local radio stations who wanted their teams covered while on the road.

Once the game starts, you return to the press box and this is where I have seen the biggest change over the years. There used to be a time when the game was watched intently with every media member keeping score and not multi-tasking. Today, you see very few beat reporters watching the game continuously as most are tweeting, on Instagram, or complaining about their jobs to anyone who will listen.

This is where I differ from them in that I really love what I do. Even when I am having a rough day I know most people listening to me or reading my work would trade places with me in a heartbeat. They are not interested in my travel issues unless it results in a funny *Seinfeld*-like moment we might share with them, but I always keep in mind that we live the lives they really want to live.

Now don't get me wrong—being a beat reporter has a profound impact on your personal life but it is a choice you made because at one point you loved doing this. Whenever I start feeling negative (and we all do at some point), I look at these jaded beat reporters and I snap myself out of it because I have far too much respect for sports and feel so lucky that I do this for a living.

As the game wears on, the story begins to write itself but a baseball game can take a sharp turn at any moment, rendering your story or broadcast report useless. It is something that you have to get used to and actually view as a challenge because in these times you learn so much about yourself. There is a great feeling when you overcome this obstacle and actually do a better job with this new result than you would have done if the game did not take a 180-degree turn.

Moments like this inspire you and make you a valuable employee to your company. And believe me, word gets around in this business because it is a small fraternity. When I landed a job at ESPN, I was told by Pete Silverman, my boss at 1050 ESPN, that one of the reasons I got the job was my ability to do live reports in a setting where a game instantly changes. It was not a skill I always had but learned from great bosses like Eric Spitz and Mark Chernoff at WFAN. They worked so hard at helping me to get better at it in my years there.

Once the game ends, the postgame process begins and even this has changed in recent years. First, the manager has a press conference and then the locker room opens. The players are asked about the game and in this new setting, it is very hard to get anything other than politically correct answers and that's because the players know every single thing they say will be totally dissected. First, on the team's postgame shows . . .

then on the shows after the postgame shows, and then on sports radio, social media, Internet sites, and it goes on and on.

In my opinion, this is overkill and eliminates the human factor in sports reporting. It also makes every reporter repeat the same take everyone else has and to me that has made sports reporting very boring. Back in the day, there would be divergent views in competing newspapers or radio stations and fans would have time to digest those takes. Today, everything happens with the speed of light and is so cliché-driven.

For example, when a player shows individuality the media runs to slam them but to me that is the greatest thing about sports. Some players flip their bats after a home run. Some do not. Some players dance in the end zone. Some do not. So what? The diversity of those emotions make sports great and personify that we live in a country where different opinions live and coexist.

The best beat beat reporters understand this and I've seen quite a few over the thirty years I've been in this business. Two of the first I ever met stand out as among the best I've ever seen. Marty Noble and Bob Klapisch are very different personalities but would both be on my short list if I ever ran a newspaper. Both are worthy of Hall of Fame consideration.

Noble, then with *Newsday*, spent time early in my career helping me understand that my job is to get a story—not have a player just deliver it to me. He was adept at getting players to open up to him and demonstrated that the end of an interview session is just as important as the beginning of one. Time and again, Marty worked the corners of the locker room and knew the meaning of what off the record meant and always honored that concept.

Marty, who now covers the Mets form MLB.com, showed me that once a player said something in confidence, you could only use it if he recanted that request. But even if he did not, you could use it as deep background to get another player to conceptualize the issue. By being around him, I came to understand that no story, no matter how important, was ever worth betraying that trust.

Klapisch, who has written for both the *Daily News* and the *Post* and now is a columnist for the *Record*, goes about his job in a different manner but achieves the same results. His relationship with the '86 Mets taught me that some players are easy to bond with while others are challenging, but not impossible to get a story from. Bob thinks like a ballplayer (in fact he was a pretty good one at Columbia) and players respond to his approach. I can't tell you how many times Klap and I have talked baseball and to this day, he often sees something I miss. Sitting next to him at games in the press box is always a great time, but also a time when we see off the field issues blend into results on the field and he connects them so well.

During the '86 season, we openly discussed our observation that something was amiss with Doc Gooden. I will never forget seeing Bob at the championship parade and we both knew Gooden's absence was chilling. We did not say a word to each other but just nodded.

Both Marty and Klap have been such a huge part of baseball coverage in New York and have been pioneers on how this sport was covered. They both taught me so much and helped me understand my areas of development that made me a better reporter.

Another pro who was royalty to me was Bill Shannon who served a beat reporter for AP from 1984 until his tragic death in 2010 after being trapped in a burning house while trying to save his mother. In addition to his reporting, he was an official scorer for both Mets and Yankees games. Bill saw it all and shared so many stories with young reporters like myself and was very honest about how stories should be reported.

I fondly remember talking about historic baseball moments with him like how the '69 Mets transformed New York into a small town and how the Tom Seaver trade happened in 1977 complete with M. Donald Grant stories in which two competing columnists in town took sides like you would in a gang fight. In a way, that struggle gave us our first preview of sports talk radio.

Those were the days when print and broadcast reporters had a daily struggle to coexist and Bill truly understood both sides, constantly trying to help us all get along together. Many talked about it but he did something symbolic that would help bridge that gap. Howie Karpin, a longtime radio announcer, wanted to become an official scorer and most writers scoffed at the notion, but Bill knew Howie was qualified and also knew the time had come to pioneer this move.

He worked with Howie and told him that it would not be easy and he would have to turn a deaf ear to the nonsense he might hear. To his credit, Howie also knew how important this would be to all the radio reporters as this would add legitimacy to their presence in every press box. Karpin made us all proud that first night and each and every game he has patrolled that seat as official scorer. He has over 1,000 games under his belt as scorer, including many postseason games.

Bill Shannon saw something special in Howie and to me he's the best official scorer I've ever seen next to Shannon. Howie is like the brother I never had—we talk baseball even during the offseason. He was my supervisor at Sports Phone and believed in me when many did not. He has authored numerous books and gave me the idea that I could actually write one as well. Bill, Howie, and I could always find time to talk about the game we love. We both miss Bill, who always made the press box a better place.

Present-day baseball beat reporters who personify what the position should be are Anthony DiComo (MLB.com), Kristie Ackert (*Daily News*), and Marc Carig (*Newsday*). This trio all work long hours and do a great job getting the story to their readers.

I met Anthony early in his career and you could tell he was a future star not only because he wrote so well but understood the dynamics of the clubhouse like a veteran. DiComo really melds the social media aspect of his job as well as anyone without being facetious or condescending.

Kristie Ackert is relatively new to the Mets beat having joined the group in 2013 and she is terrific at her job. In my opinion, she is old school in that she works so hard at developing relationships with players in the Mets locker room. You can tell that Matt Harvey, among others, has a tremendous amount of respect for her. I've had great chats with Kristie on a myriad of topics and she is one of the most genuine people in our business.

Marc Carig has patrolled the beat for both New York baseball teams and does it with a hard-working mentality that all young aspiring reporters should emulate. He is never afraid to take an opposing view but at the same time listens to you with the utmost respect. Marc and I have disagreed on some baseball-related topics in casual conversations but it is always a healthy exchange. He also shines on his WOR radio segments and I wish I was his agent because I'd have no problem finding him a full-time radio gig.

On the football side, there are two beat reporters that give fans everything they need to know about the Jets and Giants: Paul Dottino (WFAN) and Rich Cimini (ESPN New York). I've known Paul for over thirty years as he was a WFUV alumnus and the Giants were always his passion. But it was not a blind passion. He always breaks down the game very objectivly and never skirts an issue. A friend of mine who now works at CBS Interactive went with him to the Broncos-Giants Super Bowl in 1987 and got tickets to the star studded Super Bowl gala, which I can tell you first hand is an event that is unique and it is impossible not to have a good time. Paul declined to go because he said he had to prepare how he would cover the game and really sounded like a coach, not a reporter.

Rich Cimini has covered the Jets for well over two decades. He has seen it all but treats every day like a new experience helping Jets fan understand not only what happened but why it happened.

I honestly feel bad for Adam Rubin, Rich Cimini and all of the writers ESPN hired to organize a roster for ESPNNY.com, which now for all intents and purposes no longer exists. Every writer on that site worked so hard to put it on the map, but the management team there really turned their backs on all of these talented beat writers.

The leadership there really missed the boat because they overpaid senior management and they abandoned the project when times got tough. I am amazed that a company like ESPN, rich in ad sales personnel, could not make the site a success, and sell the personalities on this site as brand representatives of ESPN.

When I worked there on the radio side, I gave their sales managers leads and contacts for advertisers that were slam dunks. Not only were those deals never made—they never contacted the people I hand delivered to them. These were New York-area clients that I knew for years and wanted to place ads on ESPNNY.com or at worst, run trade deals that curtail travel costs for ESPN reporters.

Poor management decisions always make the wrong people suffer. It is unfortunate that so many of my friends and colleagues at ESPN have felt the heat in the past year. My contacts tell me the next couple of years might even be worse. Decisions like starting the Longhorn Network as well as exorbitant rights fees will spell even more layoffs.

So what is the future of beat reporting? From a national standpoint, they will exist for the short-term but not in the numbers they have in the past. Companies will continue to cut costs and may even use freelancers to cover their team. Travelling with a team may have to come out of the reporter's own pocket, which might drive many of them to become independent contractors.

Many said the newspaper business would never die and beat reporters would always be needed. Right now, the print medium is dying and unless reporters have a broadcasting gig connected to their writing, they could be in deep trouble because bloggers might take away their paycheck.

# CHAPTER 5

# The 1986 Mets: Decadence and Power—An Illustration of the Times We Were In

THE 1986 WORLD SERIES CHAMPION New York Mets had a plethora of personalities: the likable Gary Carter, the aggressive Lenny Dykstra, the shy Doc Gooden, the intellectual Ron Darling, the tell-it-like-it-is Keith Hernandez, and players like Mookie Wilson and Ray Knight, who always gave thoughful answers to our questions. Kevin Mitchell and Rafael Santana had their hot and cold days, while Roger McDowell could always make you laugh. It was the most varied group of twenty-four people I have ever been around in my life.

But I always had a special place in my heart for Gooden and Strawberry because they were rookies around the same time I was a rookie reporter. Doc was very shy in his rookie year and in his awesome Cy Young Award year of 1985 every client I worked for requested audio from him. I quickly found out I either had to get him to say more or my assignment would not be satisfactory to my bosses. So I worked hard at talking to Doc about other things—the weather, other players, TV shows—anything to get him to loosen up. It was a slow process but our relationship improved in that 1985 season.

That season (my first full year on Met beat) had plenty of drama as Strawberry got hurt early in the season but the Mets hung in the race and entered the final month battling the St. Louis Cardinals for the NL East crown. The teams played a key three-game series at Shea Stadium beginning September 10. In the first game, Cards pitcher Danny Cox hit George Foster (remember him as a Met?) after Howard Johnson had crushed a grand slam. The Mets led 5–1 and held on for a 5–4 win and part of my assignment that night was to get reaction from both locker rooms, so I headed to see Cards manager Whitey Herzog.

Herzog had spent many years working for Mets and felt slighted by the team after Gil Hodges passed away during spring training in 1972 when the Mets hired Yogi Berra to replace Hodges. Herzog's bad feelings towards his former organization heightened this rivalry in the mid-'80s. I entered Whitey's office and asked the question I thought everyone wanted to hear, "Whitey, do you think Cox threw at Foster on purpose?" He looked my way and asked me to repeat the question, which was likely his way of saying *Don't ask it again*. There was a heavy bookend on his desk and to this day I think if I asked it again he might have buried it in the back of my skull the way he was looking at me. The other reporters got a chuckle out of it.

That month was nonstop reporting for me as I traveled to St. Louis late in season to cover the next meeting between the teams. The Mets entered the series three games back of the Cardinals and in the opener Ron Darling pitched a gem with the game going into extra innings before Darryl Strawberry settled things with a mammoth homer off Ken Dayley that to this day is the most impressive homer I've ever seen—hitting the digital clock behind the bleachers in the massive old Busch Memorial Stadium.

The Mets proceeded to win the next night but the Cards won the series finale, effectively eliminating the Mets. Their 98-win season was not enough for a playoff appearance, further enhancing my theory that if the present playoff format had been in effect back then they may have done exactly what the Yankees did a decade later.

It was the first time I covered a clubhouse where a season was ending and dreams had faded. As a twenty-five year old it was a worthwhile experience. It taught me as a reporter that you had a job to do, but you also had to respect the player's space and it was a tightrope you had to walk. I endured it and got what I needed, but more importantly, this helped me years later when I tapped into this experience when I covered the '94 Knicks and the 2006–2008 Mets. I even used it when covering the 2015 World Series. It is an important part of the job and one that is easy to do incorrectly. You have to be objective but you still need to show you understand what the players are going through.

While eating dinner earlier that night in 1985, I asked Marty Noble, then with *Newsday*, how he handled a losing clubhouse. He said, "You have a job to do, never forget that, your tone is important because players in these situations know you *have* to ask the question, but some notice how you ask it." It was great advice and not the last time I picked the brain of someone who has always treated me so well.

The following offseason was spent tracking Mets player moves, and in those days the Winter Meetings weren't televised or covered like they are today. Still, reporters had to keep in contact with the team because we knew they were looking for another pitcher and a right-handed compliment to Wally Backman at second base. It meant working the phones and other than primitive voice mail, you just hoped general manager Frank Cashen would return your call. There were no text messages in those days, but he generally returned calls—not right away—but he gave you his time.

Everyone was taken by surprise when the Mets had traded for Gary Carter the previous winter, but this year we had a pretty good read that Boston's Bob Ojeda was available and knew the Twins were peddling Tim Teufel. Both proved to be very important players for the team as well as good interviews.

The first spring training I ever covered was in 1986 and I discovered that traveling with this team was like being with a rock and roll band. In those days society was all about overkill—drinking, clubbing and, quite frankly, drugging. As a twenty-six-year-old man, I knew I had to be careful around them. You could see they were a by-product of the times they lived in and exhibited that every single day.

Spring training is a very challenging assignment in that it really has three stages: players reporting, then working out, and then playing meaningless games. In those days, the Mets trained in St. Petersburg, Florida, sharing facilities with the hated Cardinals. This location had been the spring training home of the Mets since their inception in 1962 but would be the next-to-last year they would train there as they would be moving to Port St. Lucie in 1988.

One thing I noticed right away was almost every writer wrote the same story every day, especially before the games started. In those days, players used those seven to eight weeks as time to get in shape compared to today, when they arrive in camp in much better shape after working out all offseason. The workouts still look the same but they seemed longer in those days, especially the fielding drills.

From a work standpoint, much like today, you were always able to get better material before the players finished because once they ate after the morning workout, they all went home. In those days, not as many fans showed up for spring training, especially before the games began, so occasionally you could walk with a player from the workout field to the main complex. That could never happen today since fans seeking autographs would preclude that.

But the biggest thing that must be accomplished in spring training is formulating the relationships that will make your job easier all year long—and that means away from the ballpark as well. Think about it—you are all eating in the same places, filling your cars with gas at same stations, and you see players in a different setting. It is your job as a reporter to take advantage of that situation.

That spring, I really got to know Gary Carter, who was nice to everyone and it was always baseball-related, but that year we really began to chat about other things. Forging that relationship helped me during the season as did speaking to both Ray Knight and Mookie Wilson regularly during that spring. You are never going to bond with all twenty-five players but you must have a solid base of "go to guys" or quite simply you will fail as a sports reporter.

I don't think today's reporters fully understand that. I learned a great deal by being around writers such as Bill Madden, Bill Shannon, Bob Klapisch, and Marty Noble. They did not always have nice things to say about us radio reporters, but I could understand it to some extent. Even though I did not agree with most of their opinions about my fellow radio brethren, it did not mean I couldn't learn from them by observing their skills and using that in to enhance my own.

There are twenty-five players in a room and I can assure you that about twenty-one of them are normal guys—three are incredible people everyone loves to talk to—and two are loners that want no part of the media. But that's the way every group of twenty-five people in the world is—so why should a group of twenty-five baseball players be any different? The challenging part is getting to a point where you can go to those two loners and make them understand you just need a quote or two and then you will leave them alone. That's because you have twenty-three other people to round out your story. With a basketball team it is tougher because you only have twelve players, but the percentages are the same.

One of the real strange dynamics in that '86 Mets locker room was that the beat writers treated Darryl and Doc very differently. Doc was well-liked, but Darryl was treated very poorly by the media and to this day I do not understand why that was the case. I remember a veteran beat writer complaining that Straw never gave him any interviews and I told him that I found that not to be the case. In fact, Darryl always spoke to me while Doc only spoke the day before he pitched and after that game. That very night we all talked to Straw after the game and he was energetic and answered tons of questions. As we traveled back to the press box on the elevator from the clubhouse I said to him, "See, like I said, he talks to us."

He responded to me, "Rich, you always love those people." I asked him to explain what he meant and he replied, "You know—inner-city people." At that point, I had an incredulous look on my face and he responded, "Is something wrong, Rich?" My response was, "Closet racism is sometimes more scary than blatant racism." And I never spoke to that particular reporter again because he made my skin crawl.

Around that very same time, the press was also treating Rickey Henderson very badly as he was leading off for the Yankees and showing why he was a future Hall of Famer. I firmly believe he never got the accolades he deserved because quite frankly, the old school "white media" was simply not ready to cover a black man who did not just blindly agree with them. If black players showed personality they would label them militant. As a result, quiet black players like Doc got so much more leeway. To be crystal clear, I would *never* blame Doc for this. He did not ask for special treatment—he was just a shy kid trying to perform on the world's biggest stage.

Rickey played across town so I rarely covered him, but so many Mets reporters were critical of his personality from afar. When he joined the Mets in 1999, I expected to be covering an aggressive guy who was very difficult to speak to after the game. To my surprise, he was not like that at all and I enjoyed talking baseball with him.

To further illustrate the point, when Yankees teammates Don Mattingly and Dave Winfield were battling for the American League batting title in 1984, I don't know one Yankees writer who credited Winfield with a having great year while they were all extolling the virtues of Mattingly. Don deserved all the credit that came his way, but Winfield was cast aside as a casual participant in the race much in the same way Roger Maris was treated during his home run race with the more popular Mickey Mantle in 1961. But there was one basic difference here: People were gravitating to the white Yankee as opposed to the black Yankee. And judging by the Yankees owner George Steinbrenner's later suspension after it was revealed he paid $40,000 for information in an attempt to discredit Winfield, maybe there was an ownership impact on what was written orchestrated by the Yankees front office's relationship with veteran sports columnists in New York.

When it came to covering the '86 Mets, Carter, Knight, Teufel, Wilson, and Backman were the guys you could always go to every time.

I'd add Darling and Ojeda to that list as well. Some players (Sid Fernandez) were shy, while others such as Mitchell, Hernandez, and Santana had hot and cold days. Dykstra was very hard to deal with and, unfortunately, had a lisp that did not play well on the radio. George Foster, who was released before the season ended, was aloof with a capital A and got real angry with me on a number of occasions.

Covering this team also involved their off-the-field activities, not to the level they are covered today, but in my opinion, this squad began the transformation of media into a group that cares as much about backstage stories as they do about the game. Part of that was the cocaine-driven world of the mid-'80s where you could walk into any bar in New York City and routinely see cocaine being ingested in full public view. Bathrooms became public drugstores in restaurants and I was at the Limelight one night where a customer had cocaine delivered there by a courier so it could be sold to patrons.

I always say this about these years—think about the wildest drug stories you heard about the '80s and multiply it about 100 times—and then and only then will you get an accurate picture of the society these players lived in. I am not defending what these players did because we are all accountable for our own lives but living in that society while in my mid-twenties, I can readily understand how someone of my age who all of a sudden was earning more money than they ever thought possible might fall into the wrong crowd.

As a reporter, you had to cover it but you had to be careful because any accusations could end your career if you got the slightest detail wrong. That's why I laugh when I hear tweeters today commenting on what they *think* is going on. In those days, even if you had a source, unless you had a confirmation, nobody would let you go with the story. Today, some do not even have a source when they pontificate on social media.

Once in a blue moon you had to go to Finn McCool's in Port Washington because that is where many players hung out after games and it was a scene emblematic of the era. There were nights I left that bar with women who merely left with me because I covered the Mets and *might* introduce them to a player. Of course, I never did but the ends justified the means if you get my point. I was a twenty-six-year-old living in the decade of the '80s and knew that every once in a while an opportunity would arise.

This is where my experience as a bartender prior to my reporting days helped me immensely. I worked in some real high-end clubs and saw the decadence first hand. The funniest story in those years was when mob boss John Gotti and his entourage entered a bar I was working at one night and ordered drinks for about forty minutes. This was a high-end club and very rarely did a bartender buy every third round like they do in a small neighborhood bar, but I figured it might be wise for me to do that even though the tab for those drinks would likely come out of my pocket. I also decided to walk as far away from the group as I am sure they did not want their bartender to hear anything.

After four or five rounds, Gotti called me over by pointing his finger at me which made me think I had to have done something wrong and this could be my last night on earth. He simply said, "You're a good bartender—you kept your nose clean and gave us space." He then proceeded to put eight one hundred dollar bills on the bar as a tip and left.

My point is, if I could handle John Gotti and disarm him to be nice to me, would I ever have a problem with a ballplayer? I called that night a success not because of the eight hundred dollars but because it taught me about myself and how I can handle tough situations.

Putting all of this off-field activity aside, that team came to play when the bell rang. As a reporter, I was mainly concerned with covering what happened between the lines. I was not a lifestyle expert and, quite frankly, I got into the business because I loved the game—not the off-field nonsense. Many modern-day reporters care so little about the game I often wonder why they chose this profession.

During that 1986 season, you could readily see that the media was taking its first steps into the future. First of all, the technology was changing as we began to see more and more laptops in the press box and fewer typewriters. The advent of laptops made writing stories easier and would provide the foundation for the massive changes we would see in the following decades. Even us radio reporters were getting better equipment as box phones were replaced by slimline phones that eliminated the need for alligator clips. I even purchased something called a "voice-ac," which attached to the box phone directly.

In the locker rooms, the older writers still used paper and pen to transcribe quotes but the younger ones started using recorders or even asked us to play them sound from our machines to validate what they wrote on their pads. Little by little, technology was making the job easier in a year in which the Mets would reach the promised land.

The Mets got off a great start and swept an early season four-game series from the Cardinals in St. Louis, establishing the fact that they planned to run away with the division title. Their pitching was incredible with Bobby Ojeda and Sid Fernandez having great first halves while Ron Darling pitched like a bulldog in every big spot he faced. Doc Gooden was solid, but you could tell something was amiss. Reporters were rumbling about his off-the-field activities, but everyone (including myself) turned their head a bit.

What made the 1986 team interesting to cover during the regular season was despite making a mockery of the National League East, the team had many moments where their aggressive lifestyles filtered onto the field. Ray Knight, of all people, showed superior boxing skills in two separate brawls—the most dramatic one occurring in Cincinnati where he floored Eric Davis. That was a strange night as pitchers Roger McDowell and Jesse Orosco both had to play the outfield and Gary Carter manned third base because of players being ejected following the fight.

Despite their huge lead, some media critics doubted them and I believe the players caught wind of that notion, which made some postgame interview sessions challenging. I remember having a pregame conversation in the press dining room with a veteran writer who questioned their championship credentials. He admonished me for questioning his opinion, calling me a loser radio ambulance chaser. When I realized he was the same columnist who took on Tom Seaver in the 1970s, I told him, "This ambulance chaser might be chasing a parade come late October." Bill Shannon, a great columnist whom I deeply respected, told me later, "Rich, for a young guy you have spunk and you just might be right."

By September, it was clear the Mets would walk away with the NL East, and we began preparing our coverage of the Mets clinching the division. The team had three chances to clinch in Philadelphia against the second-place Phillies, but the Mets played their worst three games of the year and then split a two-game series in St. Louis, meaning Mets fans would get a chance to celebrate at Shea Stadium with the Chicago Cubs in town. That night, while driving to the park, I thought this was one of those nights Mets fans could really enjoy because although they wanted to clinch, this was really a no-pressure party night. Little did I know there would be more than enough pressure come the postseason.

Upon arriving at the ballpark, we found out Keith Hernandez was not in the lineup due to an illness and Dave Magadan, who was a September call-up that year, would be playing first base. The rookie had three hits and drove in two runs and Doc Gooden had an early lead, which prompted a night-long party atmosphere at Shea Stadium. The clinching would occur and the locker room scene typified the team as they partied long and hard while Mets fans tore up the field just like many of their dads had done back in 1969.

As I entered the victorious clubhouse, the first player I encountered was Wally Backman. He said to me, "This is great, but anyone that thinks this is it is badly mistaken. We want more." It was a scene I had never covered before—a locker room with champagne flowing. Not one member of the media escaped being doused with the bubbly, including me.

They had a game the next afternoon, which nobody really remembers very well. I recall the Shea infield looking like a war zone but I didn't give it much thought. I was now preparing to cover the postseason, which is so different than covering the regular season. Many of the veteran reporters that befriended me during the season advised me to rest up because covering postseason baseball is so different and intense.

Starting the National League Championship Series in Houston was not supposed to happen—but an Astrodome scheduling conflict with football forced Major League Baseball to switch it, giving the Astros the home-field advantage. In those years, home field alternated—it wasn't based on which team had the best record. As luck would have it, this switch hurt the Mets two years later in the NLCS against Los Angeles because the sequence was altered.

The games at the Astrodome were interesting for me in that addition to my core work I was asked by ABC to help with their telecast, tracking pitch speed and using a walkie-talkie to relay the info to announcers Keith Jackson and Tim McCarver in the broadcast booth. Watching Nolan Ryan and Doc Gooden from right behind home plate was really eye-opening and I wondered how their pitches were able to get hit at all. And by the way, it also made it crystal clear that Mike Scott was indeed scuffing baseballs. But I will get back to that later.

Coming into this series, the Mets were installed as favorites, but all of us in the media thought the Astros would have more than a puncher's chance because the trio of Mike Scott, Nolan Ryan, and Bob Knepper would pose a stiff challenge to the power-laden Mets lineup. In a playoff setting, there is no pregame clubhouse access, so it was hard to gauge the confidence of the Mets. This was new territory to most of them with the exception of a few players with postseason experience. Much like the Mets, that night at the Astrodome was my first exposure to reporting a postseason game and it was worlds different than the regular season. I had covered a Jets playoff game against the Patriots a year earlier, but that was just one game and not a series.

Even though the locker rooms are closed before the game, players are made available in a conference room. Getting a one-on-one interview, however, is almost impossible. You are called on by an MLB media relations executive, so developing a relationship with them is very important. These sessions almost become branding time for reporters as they introduce who they are working for before even delivering the question.

There was one radio reporter during the 1986 postseason who made a point of asking controversial questions to make himself look tough. Sometimes he would even wear sunglasses to make himself look sinister.

After these press conference settings, the media is given a written transcript of the entire session, which greatly assists the writers in framing quotes in their stories and helped the broadcasters locate that sound bite on their cassette recorders that captured the essence of the press briefing.

The drawback to these sessions is that it is very often staged by both the press and the players and resulted in "politically correct" answers. I usually get better quotes inside the clubhouse because players tend to be more honest at their lockers than they are sitting at a table in front of tons of reporters in a press conference setting.

In my opinion, the 1986 postseason was the most riveting in baseball history as both the Mets and Red Sox emerged with terrific late-game comebacks. Boston trailed the California Angels three games to one but pulled out an extra-inning win in Game Five after being down to their last strike and then enjoyed two blowout wins in Fenway Park to advance to the World Series.

The road for the Mets was very different as they lost a tough 1–0 game in Game One behind Mike Scott, a former Mets pitcher whose career blossomed when he joined the Astros. Before the series, several Mets players indicated to me they thought he was illegally scuffing the ball before throwing it to the plate.

During the series opener, Scott's fastball was fluttering like a butterfly in and out of the strike zone and he bested Gooden before a wild crowd at the Astrodome. The next night, Bobby Ojeda took the mound and I ran into him hours before in the hallway by the Mets locker room. He was set to face the ageless Nolan Ryan and I asked him how he felt. He looked at me and said, "Nothing will stop us tonight."

I always felt Ojeda is an overlooked player on this '86 team as he pitched so many big games during that postseason and they sorely missed him (out with a freak injury to his finger) in the 1988 NLCS because he was such a great big-game pitcher. Three times the Mets needed big performances from him—not only in this game but in Games Three and Six of the World Series when the Mets trailed the Bosox. He was one of the most cerebral pitchers of that era and current day Mets fans saw that when he served as an analyst for SportsNet NewYork.

Ojeda pitched well in that key Game Two victory and even made a great defensive play by tagging a runner out at home in unassisted fashion. So, the Mets came home with the series even at one game apiece and I was getting ready to cover my first Mets home playoff game. As a youngster, I was at the last Shea Stadium postseason game in 1973, when Jerry Koosman and Tug McGraw shut out the Oakland A's in Game Five of the World Series.

Driving to the ballpark before Game Three in '86 it dawned on me the Mets and their fans had waited thirteen years for that moment, which to this day is still the longest stretch in franchise history without a home playoff game. I often laugh when I hear present day Mets fans lament their losing seasons, not having lived through the worst years.

Shea Stadium was rocking on this day despite the Astros taking an early 4–0 lead and then in the bottom of the ninth inning, the Mets did something they had never done in team history. Lenny Dykstra hit a two-run homer to give the Mets their first postseason walk-off win but hardly the last. A few days later they would do it again as Gary Carter drove in the game-winning run in a game that featured an epic pitching duel between Gooden and Ryan.

Those two moments were very memorable but for some reason people tend to forget the two big homers Darryl Strawberry hit in those games. In Game Three he hit a three-run homer off Bob Knepper to tie the score and then in Game Five he hit a low tracer of Ryan that gave the Mets their only run of the game until Carter's heroics. When I talk to Mets fans, very few remember Straw's exploits but it must be said without those home runs there is no parade because the Astros would have been in the World Series.

In between those two Met wins, Mike Scott once again baffled the Mets and the ball-scuffing theme came full center as the Mets started to keep baseballs that were fouled off, which they claimed Scott had scuffed. It seemed to me that it was the first time all season the Mets seemed affected by an opponent and it was so unlike them. I remember asking Gary Carter about it and he told me, "He may indeed be doing it, but we have too much at stake to cry about it."

As we traveled back to Houston for Game Six, the Mets to a man seemed affected by Scott and given that he would be the Game Seven starter, they all viewed Game Six as being like a Game Seven. I felt for the first time all year they were feeling the pressure. Little did I know I was about to cover one of the greatest games in baseball history.

Astros starter Bob Knepper was on top of his game and when the Astros scored three runs in the first inning, we all thought a Game Seven would be a distinct possibility. The contest rolled into the ninth inning with the Mets still trailing, 3–0, and then they put together a ninth-inning rally that was emblematic of their resolve to win. Sitting in the press box as the ninth inning began to evolve, all I was thinking about was if the Astros brought in Dave Smith the advantage swings to the Mets. For whatever reason, the Mets had Smith's number dating back to a July game when the they lit him up like a roman candle and again when Dykstra hit the game-winning home run against him in Game Three.

And we saw that in this game as the Mets tied the game up against Smith in the ninth inning, sending it to extra innings. Remember these were the days before the Internet, cell phones, and instant messaging. There was no Bottom Line on ESPN and New Yorkers did something we will never see again.

While on the phone with my boss, he told me the streets of New York City were packed with people looking through front windows of electronics stores catching a glimpse of the game together. And since this was a late afternoon game, nobody was leaving the city.

The Mets took the lead in the 14th inning but Astros center fielder Billy Hatcher, who misjudged a fly ball that helped the Mets tie it in the ninth inning, hit one off the screen attached to the foul pole to tie it back up. While Hatcher circled the bases, I saw the greatness of Keith Hernandez as he walked to the mound almost shielding Mets pitcher Jesse Orosco from seeing the Astrodome go insane. To this day I think his calming influence got Orosco through that inning.

The Mets put three runs on the board in the 16th but the Astros, as they had done all series, fought back to score twice and had the winning and tying runs on base as Kevin Bass stepped to the plate. Orosco was running on fumes and both Carter and Hernandez kept him focused. With Jose Cruz on deck, Jesse made Bass swing at his pitches because he knew the left-handed Cruz was a great matchup for him.

Bass struck out and the Mets won their first pennant in thirteen years. As we entered the clubhouse the Mets looked elated but exhausted. Lee Mazzilli came right up to me and said, "You're a New Yorker like me, Rich, and you know what this means." At that precise moment, I thought back to his first stint with the Mets and how hard is was for him to be the *only* player people cared about. Trading him away netted two key components in Ron Darling and Howard Johnson (who the Mets received for Walt Terrell, who came in the original trade) but Lee returned just when the Mets became the center of the baseball world. I saw that in his eyes and it was an image I will never forget.

They were so many unsung heroes on this day and the one I remember most is Roger McDowell, who pitched five innings of scoreless relief for the Mets. The second-year righty gave them an impeccable performance in a crucial game and did it with the poise of a grizzled veteran.

The postgame celebration in the clubhouse was loud but not nearly as loud as the night they won the division because this series was exhausting both physically and mentally. I do remember Randy Niemann, a little-used Mets pitcher dousing Frank Cashen with champagne so aggressively his famous bowtie fell off. Frank did not look happy and complained, "Why do the people who contribute the least do the most celebrating?"

That night I flew back with the ABC crew but had to wait an hour or so at the hotel to get everything put together to leave. Tim McCarver, who was broadcasting the game for ABC, graciously bought food and drinks for all of us, knowing even the reporters had a long day. Of course, the story of what happened on the Mets team plane was legendary and so '80s.

The Mets trashed the plane in celebration and the way people described it to me it made *Animal House*'s toga party look like an insurance seminar. But it typified this Mets team's persona—work hard on the field so you can play hard off the field.

Upon returning to New York, the Mets organization was told by the airlines that the damage needed to be paid for and sent a memo that manager Davey Johnson proceeded to tear to shreds in front of the team.

The Red Sox and Mets were set to square off in the World Series, but on media day the Mets appeared to be exhausted and were still talking about the NLCS. Meanwhile, the Red Sox had to field questions about their history and inability to win a World Series title since 1918 with the overriding theme of "The Curse of the Bambino." There were Boston writers who actually believed in it (Boston had not won the Series since selling Babe Ruth to the New York Yankees in 1920) and were convinced that that curse was not only real but irreversible.

The 1986 World Series had so much media covering it that we were forced to move our press box seats to the Shea Stadium picnic area beyond the outfield fence, far from the field of play. The good thing is we were a short run down the corridor to the clubhouses which proved very helpful after Game Six. My seat was in the second row of the picnic area, and I sat next to Carl Beane, a longtime Boston radio reporter. We knew each other casually but we sat together for all seven games, developing a lasting friendship that was very special to me. Carl later became the public address annnouncer at Fenway Park and his voice could be heard in the movie *Fever Pitch*, which culminated with the team ultimately breaking the curse in 2004.

This ten-day stretch occurred over three decades ago, but I remember it like yesterday as I was covering the team I rooted for growing up playing in the World Series. Looking back, I am grateful there were no cell phones in my life because my house phone was inundated with ticket requests. For the most part, I ignored them, but one of my best friends, John Pezzullo, an Emmy Award-winning sports producer who now works for CBS Interactive, got tickets. John was forced to sit with my then girlfriend, Barbara, who actually liked sports so I was happy that two people who would really appreciate the moment got to sit in those seats.

Here's a funny story about John's tickets. After the Mets lost Game One, we drove to ballpark together the next day and were walking towards the stadium gates. John had to enter at Gate A while I had to enter through the press gate and he said to me, "Rich, you are not going to believe this, but I lost my ticket. I must have dropped it somewhere." We traced our steps back but had no luck finding his ticket and I had to enter the press box so I told John I'd see what I could do. Remember this is before the age of cellphones, so I told John to stand by a pay phone outside press gate and I would call him. In the meantime, he was trying to talk his way into the stadium. I called the pay phone and John told me no luck but a ticket taker was trying to help him get inside. My girlfriend had her ticket so she would see if anyone was in the adjacent seat but John would have to wait outside until the third inning.

As it turned out, the seat was empty and they actually let him sit there. John offered the man (his name was Artie) a tip but he refused saying people might think he benefited from sneaking him in. So, John actually got into the World Series without a ticket.

Roger Clemens faced Doc Gooden in Game Two that night but the Mets starter was tagged for six runs in five innings and Clemens was not much better, only pitching 4 1/3 innings as the Red Sox won, 9–3. After the game the Mets clubhouse was very quiet at first but then the team leaders spoke up. Gary Carter said, "This is far from over. We've won four of five tons of times and that is what we have to do."

Upon returning to the press area, many writers thought the series was over and one national writer said, "Teams don't come back to win a World Series after losing the first two games at home." I could not help saying to him that the Kansas City Royals had done it the previous year, beating the St. Louis Cardinals in seven games after losing the first two at home. He replied, "Well I meant it won't happen again." I call that the Pee Wee Herman school of reporting—"I meant to say that." That was his famous line from the movie *Pee Wee's Big Adventure* that came out a year earlier.

In any event, we headed to Boston and it was my first trip ever to Fenway Park, which was a real treat. What an awesome ballpark, but the clubhouses were really tiny and that proved challenging in the post-game setting. Monday was an offday, which the media generally uses to get interviews since there is no pregame access during the Series.

We all got a rude awakening when Davey Johnson decided to make practice non-mandatory, limiting our access to players. I think this was a stroke of genius as the Mets were in a very tense mood in the club-house after Game Two. The media was saying the series was over in the papers. In fact, the *New York Post* was running a column written by Yankees owner George Steinbrenner saying that the Mets now know about life in the American League East.

Davey, in his infinite wisdom, knew his players would react adversely to being ripped by the media and he wanted their entire focus on Game Three. He took all the blame for it upon his shoulders and that relieved the pressure his team was feeling upon arriving in Boston.

We saw the results from that immediately as Lenny Dykstra led off the game with a home run and, after a botched Red Sox rundown, they plated four first inning runs and were never headed as Bobby Ojeda kept the Bosox bats silent with his "dead fish" changeup en route to a 7–1 win. In the Mets clubhouse following the game, you could sense a huge pressure lifted off them as they knew Game Four would pit Ron Darling against Al Nipper, who several Mets told me they felt confident hitting against.

Their faith was rewarded as Carter slugged two homers while Dykstra once again went yard as the Mets knotted the series with a 6–2 win and had their ace Doc Gooden set to square off against Game One winner Bruce Hurst in Game Five. For the second time in the series, Hurst stymied the Mets, this time with a complete game win, 4–2. Many point to these two Series losses as the beginning of Gooden's demise but I honestly think on these two nights his curveball was just not as sharp as it was in the NLCS. Doc's drug issues have been well documented but I feel this was not the overriding factor in these games.

Gooden had a great 1985 season and that's hard to duplicate. But his 1986 season was solid and in the NLCS he threw 17 innings of two-run ball but hindsight forces everyone to make connections based on the events surrounding him missing the championship parade. To me those are two mutually exclusive events and any media member who says otherwise is wrong. We all knew Doc the baseball player but none of us really ever knew Doc the person.

The Mets returned home down three games to two, and felt returning to Shea Stadium would be all they would need to win it. Carter told me after Game Five, "People say we have to win two games but my feeling is we have to win one game and then both us and the Red Sox need to win one game." Carter did not say it but he meant to say if the Mets won Game Six, the pressure on the Red Sox would be enormous, given their history.

Game Six—it's funny when you bring this up to any baseball fan, they only think of Game Six of the 1986 World Series. In fact, a movie was produced in 2005 starring Michael Keaton called *Game 6* depicting a man's obsession with the Red Sox winning that game. Driving to Shea that night, I was thinking I might be witnessing baseball history if the Red Sox won but at the same time knew a Game Seven would be an awesome event to cover.

I again sat in of the outfield press box with Boston radio personality Carl Beane, who was as nervous as I have ever seen him. He relayed to me that the city of Boston is a different town than New York in that their sports fans always prepare for the worst but hope for the best. He told me the town felt the Celtics (who had won the NBA champion-ship that year) and Red Sox were opposite organizations as one has collected numerous titles while the other has very few of them. Celtics fans expect the best to happen while Red Sox fans expect the worst. He said that Celtics fans are like Yankees fans while Red Sox fans are like New York Rangers fans. And he told me if the Red Sox won tonight, then you know there is hope for the Rangers, who at the time hadn't won the Stanley Cup since 1940.

With the score tied, third baseman Ray Knight's error gave the Red Sox the lead, which the Mets erased with a Gary Carter sacri-fice fly in the eighth inning, sending us to extra innings. In the tenth inning, Dave Henderson nailed a homer and the Red Sox added an insurance run to lead, 5–3. Looking at my scorecard, I was lamenting that Davey Johnson had double-switched Darryl Strawberry from the game, knowing that that spot in the order could represent the tying run if the Mets got a runner on base.

Sitting there watching both Wally Backman and Keith Hernandez make outs, everyone in the park thought it was over. Don't let anyone tell you otherwise. All I was thinking when Carter stepped to the plate was *Please don't let him make the last out* and he drove a single to left. Now here comes the worst nightmare for Davey: Can you imagine if pinch-hitter Kevin Mitchell makes the last out of the season after dou-ble-switching Straw out of the lineup?

Mitch made that a moot point as he singled to center and then Knight singled, scoring Carter and leaving runners on the corners. At that moment Beane turned to me half smiling and said, "The next five minutes will prove to you what being a Red Sox fan puts you through."

Bob Stanley came in the game to replace Calvin Schiraldi on the mound and as Mookie Wilson stepped to the plate, Shea Stadium got loud but not insanely loud as many patrons had left and those still there were as nervous as an expectant father. Stanley hurled a wild pitch and a couple of things came to my mind: catcher Rich Gedman made a halfhearted effort to stop the ball, and to this day I have no idea how

Mookie twisted his body so the ball did not hit him, which would have sent Mitchell back to third base.

Right after the wild pitch, Mookie hit a hard line drive foul down the third-base line and then the moment occurred the baseball world will never forget. Wilson dribbled a ground ball that went through first baseman Bill Buckner's legs, allowing Ray Knight to score the winning run. Buckner's life would never be the same and I feel bad for him for that. I was gratified that the Red Sox have recently reached out to him so the honor of his career would not be ruined by this moment. As a teenager, my parents took me to a Mets game around the time my cousin tried out for a number of teams including the Dodgers and got to know many players, one of them being Buckner. I got to meet Buckner after the game and he told me as I was preparing to try out for my high school team as an infielder to always remember to keep my glove close to the ground.

Once Game Six ended, I made a mad dash to cover both clubhouses and thought briefly about that moment. I had just seen history but not the type I thought of when the game began. In the Mets clubhouse, Ray Knight looked as though he was totally spent while Mookie talked for a long time to us about how proud he was of his teammates.

Despite the win, Darryl Strawberry was clearly unhappy about being pulled from the lineup. Although he tried hard to hide his emotions, you could see this might become an issue. Still, the Mets survived with some help from the Red Sox and the Bill Buckner jokes were already starting. One columnist said to me, "What does Bill Buckner have in common with Michael Jackson? They both wear a glove on their right hand for no apparent reason."

To me, this criticism of Buckner was misguided because he was someone who was very responsible for the Red Sox being in the Series. John McNamara had lifted him for a defensive replacement in many other games and decided not to do so in Game Six because he wanted Buckner to be on the field to celebrate. That questionable decision made McNamara a public enemy in Boston. What I remember most about covering the Red Sox clubhouse was Buckner sitting there and answering every question and never losing his cool even when reporters asked stupid questions like did he feel the Curse of The Bambino put the ball under his glove? The Red Sox clubhouse was not particularly downcast as they believed Game Seven was still there for them to win.

Driving home that night at about 3 A.M. after my work was completed, I fully realized I saw a historic moment and it was likely I would never see a World Series game like that again. It was an amazing night but there was more to come.

The Sox got a big break the following day. A rainout pushed Game Seven to Monday night and McNamara properly replaced Oil Can Boyd with Bruce Hurst, who had pitched so well against the Mets in Games One and Five. Boyd was livid about it and some Red Sox writers staying in the same midtown hotel as the Red Sox could visibly see his disappointment.

For the Mets, the offday helped them because I truly believe they needed it since Game Six was so emotionally charged—even though Bruce Hurst was now standing between them and a world championship.

The night of Game Seven also featured a huge Monday night NFL game at Giants Stadium between the Redskins and the Giants but New York's attention was totally focused on the Mets. To their credit, the Red Sox jumped out to a quick 3–0 lead and Hurst was dealing like he had earlier in the series. But he was only working on three days' rest and he tired in the sixth inning as both Mookie Wilson and pinch hitter Lee Mazzilli singled while Tim Teufel worked out a walk, loading the bases for Keith Hernandez.

In my opinion, Keith Hernandez is one of the best clutch hitters in baseball history and he proved that point with a two-run single, making it 3–2. Gary Carter drove in another run with a force out and the game was tied after six innings. Four years earlier when Keith was with the St. Louis Cardinals, he had a similar bases-loaded hit in Game Seven of the World Series against the Milwaukee Brewers.

Ray Knight homered in the bottom of the seventh inning and RBIs from Rafael Santana and Hernandez made it 6–3. But Dwight Evans cracked a two-run double in the eighth to make it 6–5 before Jesse Orosco entered the game to get the Mets out of the inning with a one-run lead.

In the bottom of the eighth inning, Darryl Strawberry crushed a solo homer and the Mets were on their way to a 8–5 win, securing the second World Series championship in franchise history. The Mets clubhouse was a madhouse with so many backstories. One was the fact that Darryl Strawberry and Davey Johnson embraced despite the fact Straw was angry after being double switched out of Game Six. The reconciliation was made possible by both Gary Carter and Ray Knight intervening, demonstrating the leadership skills of these two veteran players.

The media asked good questions for the most part but a few of them kept harping on the fact that the Mets were lucky to win due to Red Sox failures in Game Six, which I thought was rather astounding. In a championship locker room, punching holes in a win like this was pointless. It was also a glimpse into the future where the media always tried to poke holes into winning teams.

Years later, many media members call the mid-'80s Mets a disappointing story and I could not disagree more. You build a team to win a championship and that mission was accomplished. This organization built a franchise that averaged 95 wins a season from 1984 through 1990 and two years after the 1986 season, they won 100 games. In the present-day playoff format, they would have been a playoff team in six of those seven seasons.

I think the media focuses too much on their off the field issues and almost think it overshadows the success of the organization in the 1980s. Simply put, Frank Cashen came to New York in 1980 promising that he would build this team into a winner and many at the time said it would never happen. Not only did they become champions but they made the Yankees an afterthought despite the fact they had star players like Don Mattingly, Dave Winfield, and Ricky Henderson on their roster.

The off the field events are well documented and recently Doc Gooden has been open about his addiction to drugs which first came to the forefront prior to the 1987 season, but we all thought something was wrong when he missed the parade the day following Game Seven.

Covering that parade was something I will never forget and I've been at plenty of them since then, but none come close to this one in terms of raw emotion. The Rangers parade after winning the 1994 Stanley Cup was riveting, but this one was special because of the way this team gripped all of New York.

I arrived at the media checkpoint around 6 A.M. and the way it works from there is that media members are put on a truck on the parade route. Each press truck generally follows a truck with members of the organization. There were ten members of the media (mostly radio broadcasters) in my truck and most of them were from news, not sports, so they were asking me what certain players looked like.

The view from the truck was unlike anything I had ever seen before. The raw unloading of emotion from the fans was obvious—some even in tears—as the Mets waved to them from the streets of New York. I began to feel what a grip this team had on everyone, even casual sports fans. I remember interviewing fans and the most memorable was with a husband and wife who where there with their two children. They told me they were at the 1969 parade (in fact they were wearing jerseys with Tom Seaver's name on the back) while the children were wearing jerseys with Keith Hernandez's name on the back. They told me that they were at the '69 parade as a recently married couple and today wanted to share that moment with their young children. It dawned on me at that moment that sports is the ultimate generation gap connector and can help families bond in a way that nothing else can. I lived in a home where sports always connected my family, even in times where there was disagreement on social issues. To this day, my ninety-year-old dad and I can always bond through sports, even though his memory wavers on a myriad of other things. And my mom, God rest her soul, knew I was passionate about sports and even in her last days asked me in 2004 if I thought the Mets would land Pedro Martinez.

I also realized during the '86 parade I was a different sports reporter than most in that these are the moments why I got into the business. While others were writing about whether the Mets could repeat or why Doc Gooden was absent, I concentrated on the joy of the moment. I am not saying I am right or wrong about that but that is how I felt.

I loved reporting on the game and with the advent of sports radio just around the corner, things would change but it would not change me and October of 1986 proved that. It may have cost me jobs in the future as I refused to talk about personal lives of players like others did. I refused to be a sports talk nerd who is making every player pay for the fact he was never picked to play or was taken last while choosing up sides in the playground.

My experience covering the Mets in October of 1986 made me the reporter I am today and I am proud to say that foundation has never changed. I wanted to be a sports reporter from the time I was young because I loved the game. My sense is some media members picked up the idea in their twenties that sports reporting might be a good career. And that is why passion is missing from their reporting. That might make them better reporters in the current state of the media than I am.

But as the great Bill Shannon once told me, "Rich, you would have been an ideal reporter in the '50s and '60s because you fit the very definition of that era."

# CHAPTER 6

# The Demise of Network Radio

WHEN I STARTED IN THE broadcasting business, sports radio did not yet exist, ESPN was a newly launched television network, and ESPN Radio was years away from launching. I was freelancing for a few small stations when my big break came—in a very bizarre way.

I was working as a bartender in Manhattan when a man came in to drink a few and talk sports, which the two of us did for hours. He told me he worked in the human resources department at ABC and said he was impressed with my sports knowledge. As the night wore on, he continued drinking and proceeded to get pretty wasted.

I made sure we called a cab to get him home and before he left, he gave me a business card and told him to come see him the next day and to bring a résumé. I also prepared a demo tape that I edited in the middle of the night at Sports Phone, where I was also working at the time.

The next day, I got dressed in the best business suit I owned and headed to 66th Street and West End Avenue, where the ABC Radio Network was located. After my interview, I was sent to meet Shelby Whitfield, the head of ABC Radio Sports, who told me he could offer me a producer position and I could also cover games on my nights off. The shifts were very intense as I worked every weekend (12 hour shifts plus an overnight shift on Wednesday nights). But the money was not really good enough to pay the bills, so I held on to my full time gig at Lifetime Television as a sales assistant.

I was married at the time and made the choice that my career was important to me. In some ways, it ended my marriage, which I regret. But to this day, I know I made the right decision. My wife, Melissa, was a beautiful Midwestern woman but had trouble understanding why I worked so much and I agreed that it was unfair to her. I enjoyed the three-plus years we were together, but deep down in my heart, I knew I could never give her 100 percent and also realized having children would only exacerbate the issues we had in our relationship.

My time with her made me a better man and I've had many relationships since but always knew when push came to shove, I could never make that commitment again.

When I got there, ABC Radio was clearly the best of the three major national radio networks. They were a finely oiled machine that was broken down into three sub-networks to accommodate all the radio markets across the country. The Information Network was devoted to ABC affiliates in big markets. The Entertainment Network was designed for secondary stations in bigger markets or primary stations in midsize markets, and the Direction Network catered to the smaller markets.

In my position as the weekend producer, I was responsible for the sportscasts on all three networks—making sure the scripts were accurate, master controlling the casts, and producing soundbites for the anchors to use in their casts. This was a key time in my career as I came to the realization that by being a sports reporter in New York I was provincial in nature and my knowledge of college sports was deficient. I saw firsthand that the nation loves baseball, football, and basketball but sports like NASCAR and golf were big-time in most of the country.

Saturdays in the fall were filled with college football parties in places like Lincoln, Nebraska, South Bend, Indiana, Ann Arbor, Michigan, Columbus, Ohio, and Norman, Oklahoma. I visited many of these places and I saw Americana at its best. It opened my eyes to the fact that what New Yorkers loved was great but the country had so much more to offer. That is why I begged my boss to let me cover Big East basketball in addition to my baseball responsibilities at Shea Stadium. I wanted to round out my sports knowledge.

Covering the Big East, I had the opportunity to cover stars such as Patrick Ewing and Chris Mullin, who were great players, but I also got to see firsthand how unfairly the media covered Georgetown. John Thompson coached that Hoya team and protected his players by keeping them away from the media, which he was openly criticized for but I never subscribed to that notion. I grew to respect Thompson and started to understand how difficult life is for a black person in the spotlight.

The Big East tournament was a huge money maker for reporters. I picked up freelance work from many stations around the country as this event became a showcase for college basketball leading up to NCAA tournament.

There were some years I was able to make thousands of dollars in a three-day stretch by doing live reports, exclusive one-on-one interviews, and even appearing on pre- and postgame shows on ABC affiliates around the country. On the network, thousands of ABC listeners heard my reports on the same station I listened to as a youngster, which brings me to working alongside the great Howard Cosell.

I spent so much of my childhood listening to him but the first time I met him, I faced a moment in which I had to decide if I would cower in a corner or if I would stand up to him. I had heard he was a tough person to deal with and he could undress people in a moment's notice. I was sitting at a desk working on revising some scripts on a typewriter as Howard walked into the room.

He immediately asked me, "Who the hell are you?" and I quickly responded, "I'm Rich Coutinho, who are you?" He shot back by saying, "Who am I? Who am I? I am the most recognizable sports voice in the world." So, I held out my hand and said to him, "It is a pleasure to meet you, Mr. Musburger."

We both stood there in silence for a few seconds and then both laughed. Now, I was taking a real chance as Howard could have eaten me up and spit me out, but he did not. In fact, he enjoyed introducing me to people by telling them the story of our first meeting.

My boss, Shelby Whitfield, told me I indeed took quite a chance but said I showed him I had stones. It also gave me a great resource in Cosell, who always helped us getting guests like Joe Namath, Muhammad Ali, and Pete Rozelle at a moment's notice.

When I joined ABC, the industry was beginning to transition. Our company was downsizing, which played to my advantage as a free-lancer, but full-timers in our news department were being terminated left and right. The sports department was pretty lean and I developed a great relationship with the three anchors I produced shows with: Fred Manfra, Mike Harris, and Chip Cipolla.

I grew up listening to Chip on WNEW Radio and he was so nice coaching me on my delivery plus I loved to talk sports with him. He was old school in many ways, but he really understood the pulse of sports and he anchored on the Direction Network. Chip was quite a ladies' man as well, generally dating women half his age.

He knew all of the 1969 Mets and when I told him I grew up a Mets fan he brought in a jacket that Tom Seaver actually wore in the '70s and gave it to me as a way of thanking me for producing his casts. I still have that jacket.

A few years into my stay at ABC, Shelby Whitfield was looking to part ways with Chip and started to make it personal, which was my first taste on how brutal this business could be. We were preparing our Olympic coverage and he was demanding all anchors work double shifts while only getting paid for single shifts. Chip was furious at this but kept quiet about it until Shelby tried to berate him in a staff meeting. It made me so uncomfortable I left the meeting.

Chip was clearly on the 18th hole of his career by then, but to me he deserved respect because of what he had accomplished in the business. He was one of the voices of New York Sports and always had time to help youngsters like myself. I left the meeting because I just did not want to see a retiring sportscaster treated like yesterday's garbage. Shelby admonished me for leaving the meeting and told me I embarrassed him and my response was crystal clear. "You've done a great job today at embarrassing yourself."

After the Olympics, he suspended me without pay for two weeks unless I publicly apologized to him. I refused, telling him I'd take the two weeks without pay. When other anchors heard, they offered to pay me themselves, but I refused. I appreciated the thought but did not want a handout. We were fine after that and in fact, I believe in a weird way he respected my stance. I stayed at ABC for seven years.

It was sad to see Howard Cosell became increasingly bitter as time went on. He was only on radio by then as his TV gigs at ABC had dried up because he made many enemies there. While we were working, he would often come in and disparage his former colleagues like Frank Gifford, Al Michaels, and even Keith Jackson. This should have been a time Cosell became a voice for the business much in the way Vin Scully has in the past decade, but Howard's limitless ego, which had propelled him to success, made him a defiant old man.

He still performed his daily show. But the local station WABC refused to air it, so he was not heard in New York. Producing his shows became a real chore as he no longer did it live because he would constantly stumble over his words. I never complained about it because I honestly loved Howard and the impact he had on the business was profound. Howard's health was deteriorating, so ABC put a studio in his home to do the shows remotely.

When his wife Emmy passed away in 1990, Howard really changed and grew increasingly introverted. As much as he was a confident ego-driven man, I've never met anyone in my life (aside from my own dad) that loved his wife more than Howard did. Without her, he was like a lost soul and I genuinely felt bad for him.

He was diagnosed with lung cancer in 1991 but fought it bravely, having surgeries and he also had a few strokes until his death in 1995. I remember my last conversation with him, asking him about many things, including his devotion to Ali, which I intensely respected. We talked about his recollections covering the '69 Mets, specifically Gil Hodges. Howard said to me, "Gil was a great manager but an even better person. He would have loved you, Rich." That brought tears to my eyes and I will never forget it.

Howard and I did not talk every day but I learned so much from him. He is the reason *Monday Night Football* is the institution it became. He was not perfect and trashing his colleagues in his acid-dripping books did not endear him to the industry, but he was the first broadcaster to ask tough questions as none of his interviews were puffball sessions. He supported the rights of Ali when most broadcasters refused to even call him by his correct name.

Columnists like Dick Young always took shots at him and refused to acknowledge he was a star that crossed over from the sports world to the non-sports world. What people like Young failed to realize is Cosell made our broadcasting jobs matter because he was the one of the true pioneers in our business, and quite frankly, deserves Hall of Fame status.

We worked long hours at ABC and the thing I remember most is the team atmosphere that existed there. The engineering staff was top of the line but management was trying to decertify unions in our place and I saw people who had worked so long lose jobs in their middle-aged years, wrecking their lives. It made me stop and think and I tried to keep my career like a stock portfolio. By that, I meant diversify myself: I began to work both in sports and ad sales because I knew if I developed ad sales skills, my life would always be financially safe. And I learned a lot of that at ABC where Shelby was so adept at creating revenue, especially around major events. In those days, the cost of owning broadcast rights had begun to skyrocket and ABC decided it would cover it as a news event and sell sponsorships by getting exclusive interviews and hiring analysts that would appear on affiliate stations rounding out the packages.

We also performed a nightly feed known as *Sportscall* and we added feeds for special events. Those special deliveries of sound would only go to stations that cleared our shows, giving the sponsors more people that tuned into their spots. I took the premise with me to Bravo and IFC and used "the Olympic Plan" in our coverage of Film Festivals like

Cannes and more recently, to FiOS1 in our coverage of the 2015 Mets postseason run.

As the years wore on, Shelby became increasingly volatile, which did not bother me much because I worked on weekends, but he was an old-school manager living in a world that was changing. He was the type of manager that came in at 10:00 A.M., made a few calls, went to a liquid lunch, berated employees in the afternoon, and then went home. And he thought it was OK because that's the way his managers treated him early in his career.

He was a member of the Friars Club—an old-school place where he took me to lunch quite a few times. I firmly believe when Donald Trump talked about "locker room talk" he had this club in mind. Shelby would have five or six drinks at a lunch and you could see him getting more and more vociferous as food was served. To be honest, it made me uncomfortable and I almost wished he would not ask me to lunch. I was brought up in a house where women were respected and the way he talked about female ABC employees was downright frightening.

Shelby was different than any boss I have ever had, but he taught me about the business. Quite frankly, I also learned from him how *not* to manage employees. With him, it was all about control—when he had it, he made life impossible for his employees. When you had it, you could write your ticket, but he never cared about the quality of life of his employees and I hated that, vowing never to be that way.

In my last few years at ABC, things started really changing as we started cutting our reporter budgets and began planning for the launch of ESPN Radio, which signaled the end of ABC Radio Sports as we knew it. Our team of stringers around the country started to be used less and more affiliates began leaving ABC Radio for greener pastures. Our nightly *Sportscall* feed began to be packed with play-by-play calls rather than sound from the athletes because "play-by-play" was free.

Sports radio really became a staple in our markets around the country and ABC Radio Sports was just a fraction of what it was. Anchors began to leave and it was time for me to take my skills to sports radio.

In the '80s, network radio was everywhere—ABC, NBC, and CBS with plenty of work and jobs for everyone.

Those days were long gone by the end of the decade as network radio people were looking for exit strategies—something we never imagined at the start of the decade. Shelby lost his job because of a memo that got into the hands of the wrong senior executive. Sports became a non-factor at the network with the advent of ESPN Radio.

Times were changing as on-air jobs were no longer always union positions and producer salaries were cut in half. In the old days, I could make hundreds of dollars on any NFL Sunday. Now we were lucky to make $100 a day.

I had a simple choice—move with the times or be buried in the past. Great memories would always be there but I decided memories are there for when I am old and retired. I had the skills to make it in this new sports radio world—and my time at ABC would make that happen.

Sports talk radio became a staple in New York as we entered the '90s, so I decided I would actually be better off taking less money to freelance at a radio station than work at a network. It was a tough decision because WFAN had already become a force. I was way behind in developing the next stage in my career—local radio and becoming a beat reporter in the pure sense of the word.

From a network perspective, sports at major networks were decreasing while sports-oriented networks began blossoming all over the place. Some succeeded and others failed but it created so much freelance work, especially with NFL coverage.

Technology was changing and so was the way sports was reported as that network classic sound where the sportscaster enunciated every word properly would be gone forever. The guttural sounds, which previously had no chance of being on the radio, were now commonplace.

Local sports talk radio was in full control of the sports reporting marketplace—and the business would never be the same. There was a time ABC Radio Network housed the greatest sports coverage in the industry but it never adjusted to the new marketplace and is now just a shell of its former shelf.

By being there during their demise, I learned a lot about what to do and what not to do. Much like our fathers talk about sports stars of yesterday, I look back fondly at people that made network sports happen. We would not be where we are today without them.

## CHAPTER 7

# Sports Talk Radio Takes Over the Airwaves

It is impossible to overstate the impact the advent of sports talk radio has had on the media landscape over the past thirty years. Social media and the Internet have also been played a large role but sports talk radio has been responsible for providing the impetus that has shaped our changing sports world.

I remember distinctly where I was when I heard about WFAN taking over the signal of country music station WHN (1050 AM). I was eating lunch with some of my Sports Phone colleagues and we were ecstatic because we thought it would be the perfect place to take the next step in our careers.

But all of our hopes were dashed rather quickly when we found out that WFAN's parent company, Emmis Communications, would not hire any current Sports Phone employees. Officially, we were told all positions were filled but we knew better as we head rumblings from the inside that station management felt our company was a direct competitor. I had a couple of problems with this. First, we were not nearly as direct a competitor as a radio station was—we were a phone service. Also, why wouldn't they want to hire competitors? It made no sense.

By doing this, they passed over talented broadcasters such as Bob Papa, which is ironic when you consider he now does the play-by-play for Giants football games for the station. In fairness to the current management team, I firmly believe had they been in charge at he time, both Mark Chernoff and Eric Spitz would have handled it differently. Their predecessors hired mostly out of towners and the problem with that was they lacked a feel for the pulse of the New York sports fan.

Jim Lampley and Greg Gumbel are fine broadcasters but New Yorkers did not gravitate to them. Pete Franklin, the afternoon show host from Cleveland, didn't really understand the give and take with the New York sports fan. They were flying in talent on a weekly basis, spending tons of money and not getting much in the way of ratings or revenue. The weak 1050 signal was an issue as well and the first eighteen months of the station's existence was tough. Many experts felt they would not survive.

There were some positives, however. Mike Francesa, Ed Coleman, and Howie Rose were a trio of solid pros that would help shape the future of WFAN. In addition, Emmis inherited the right to broadcast Mets games from purchasing the 1050 real estate and that gave them live sports every night during the summer.

Looking back, a number of things went wrong from the start. Franklin was just the wrong guy at the wrong time. He signed a two-year pact worth $600,000 which in those days was a pretty steep price tag for a radio host, even in New York. He was gruff with the callers and never quite understood that New York, unlike Cleveland, has multiple teams in every sport, and you should at least try to give fair and balanced reporting. He used sound effects but only to demean callers and his act wore thin very quickly.

Jim Lampley and Greg Gumbel were far too stiff to appeal to the listeners and quite frankly, advertisers were not flocking to WFAN aside from the clients they had on Mets broadcasts.

But that big trio of pros I mentioned earlier helped keep the ship afloat.

Howie Rose was a big contributor in those early years as Mets broadcasts were making money for the station (one of the few things that did) and Rose hosted *Mets Extra*, a pre- and postgame show that was far ahead of its time. The show originally debuted on WHN during the 1986 postseason with Dave Cohen and Rusty Staub co-hosting but Rose took over on WHN at the start of the 1987 season. Once Emmis bought the station, Rose gave WFAN listeners an inside look at the team and played psychiatrist with unhappy fans after a tough loss.

The show was produced on-site at Shea Stadium after home games but was done at WFAN studios, which at the time were in Astoria, New York, when the Mets were on the road. Kenny Albert, son of the great sportscaster Marv Albert, served as the primary associate producer, in one of his first jobs in the business. Of course, Rangers fans came to know Kenny as the radio voice of the team, as his dad had been years earlier. He would go on to a great career, becoming a national voice as well with FOX Sports.

Ed Coleman is perhaps the most versatile sportscaster I have ever been around. Eddie can do an update, a sports talk show, a pre- or postgame show coupled with a solid ability to do play-by-play. Successful companies in any business always have unsung heroes that allow management to better utilize their entire staff and Coleman has always done that for WFAN. The only other talent I have been around that carries this level of versatility is Don LaGreca, who in many ways does for ESPN New York what Ed does for WFAN.

Mike Francesa originally turned down a producer spot on the station but his persistence paid off as he was given a weekend show that featured college football and basketball analysis. Francesa had spent many years as a researcher and his command of the college scene was second to none.

Despite this talented trio, the station floundered for a year and a half until they received the gift that vaulted them into success. General Electric, which at the time owned NBC, sold their New York station, WNBC 660AM to Emmis, which moved WFAN down the dial. The move, which occurred on October 7, 1988, improved the station's signal. That night, the scheduled National League Championship Series game between the Dodgers and Mets was rained out but listeners got to hear the difference in how WFAN sounded on their new powerful 50,000 watt signal.

I remember driving to Shea Stadium to cover the game that night and was blown away by the difference in the sound on my car radio. The deal with NBC also brought Don Imus to the station and this saved the day. The morning show WFAN had been airing was hosted by Greg Gumbel and I knew this change was just what the station needed as I was an intern when both Don Imus shared the spotlight at WNBC with Howard Stern.

This was a huge coup for WFAN and I have to laugh when I hear people say WFAN proved all-sports radio works. In all honesty, had Imus not arrived in 1988 I am not sure we'd be talking about how successful WFAN became because he bridged the sports fanatic with the casual sports fan in a way that no other person was capable of doing.

The greatest illustration of this was Imus utilizing Mike Breen for early morning sportscasts. I went to Fordham with Breen and always knew his sense of humor coupled with his sports knowledge provided a great listen. Breen did an incredible job, showing he knew how to capture an audience even if Imus constantly interrupted his reports. In fact, so many talk show hosts try to do that now but nobody has ever done it as well as the combination of Breen and Imus.

There were other changes on the horizon as WFAN began branding their updates as 20-20 sports flashes. I could often be heard giving live reports from events on those updates. I freelanced for a bunch of stations, including WFAN, and that is where I first met Chris Russo. We sat together in the press box one night and talked sports for the entire game. He was doing a sports show at WMCA at the time and invited me on quite a few times to provide updates during his show while I was covering the Mets.

You could tell right off the bat that he was a real go-getter. His on-air style was different and many of my colleagues thought his voice was very irritating, but I enjoyed listening to him from the beginning.

Something which impressed me right away was his vast knowledge of sports history. He could recall even the most minor detail that would connect a point he was trying to make on the air. Years later, he still does it as well as anybody.

In the meantime, Don Imus and afternoon show host Pete Franklin began taking shots at each other, which made for great radio. You could see Don was just having fun but Pete was getting heated in his discussions, referring to him as "Minus" while the morning show host called Franklin a dinosaur, among other things. I think it soured Franklin on WFAN and both sides had enough of each other so they parted ways in August of 1989.

This was important because Russo had since joined the station as a part-timer while Mike Francesa parlayed his WFAN weekend gig into a daily show with Ed Coleman. The station was searching for an afternoon sports show duo, and I am sure Don Imus was heavily involved in the decision to pair Chris Russo with Mike Francesa. By this time, the nickname "Mad Dog" starting to grow with the help of *Daily New* columnist Bob Raissman, who coined the phrase and Don Imus, who drove it into the heads of WFAN listeners.

On September 5, 1989, the duo was paired on an afternoon talk show that would be like no other. Here were two guys that would change the way we talk about sports and the show started at a time when the New York Mets had become a team you could find on both the front page and the back page.

The Mets were in the news constantly in those days, good and bad. There were court cases, police incidents, off the field fights, and Mike and the Mad Dog took listeners through it every step of the way while pulling no punches.

They also put some radio stereotypes to bed. Neither host had the classic radio sound but their success made that less important. They also refused to parrot the popular take and were not afraid to take guests to the mat when interviewing them. To this day, they both remain the best interviewers in our business by asking the questions we all want answered.

Another stereotype that they put in the grave was you couldn't be both a fan and a talk show host. This is one that is a pet peeve of mine because any talk show host that tells you they are not a fan of a team or a player is either lying or they don't have the passion to do that job. The people that call in to these shows are fans because they listen to hours of sports talk per day and they don't want to hear "politically correct" drivel—they want passion and point of view. If you are totally objective, passion tends to get lost and they understood that better than anyone.

The combination of *Imus in the Morning* and *Mike And the Mad Dog* were the main reason that WFAN was the highest billing station in the country during the 1990s. From a reporter's standpoint, you could not be in the press box without hearing the media talking about what they said on their shows.

I worked at WFAN as a reporter and production assistant during the '90s when they were going though some tumultuous times. There were long stretches when they did not speak to each other off the air but still performed compelling shows. I did not have too much direct interaction with Francesa since my shifts were usually at night, but he was always pleasant to me even though I saw him big-time others. Honestly, I kind of understood it.

When Mike first landed the gig, there were actually people who said that he lucked out and did not pay his dues. Nothing could be further from the truth. He was at CBS during the heyday of *The NFL Today* and was instrumental in the production of that classic NFL pre-game show. Brent Musburger, Jimmy The Greek, Irv Cross, and Phyllis George relied on Francesa, whose research was complete, accurate, and he always found something the viewers did not know.

He moved up the ranks at WFAN and deserved everything he was given. He took the opportunity and ran with it. If there ever was a star that paid his dues, it would be Mike Francesa.

Russo, unlike Francesa, never big-timed anyone but sometimes I wish that he would have because the media was so phony to him. I knew him before he got to WFAN and he always had time for me.

He was exactly the same off the air as he was on the air. There is not a phony bone in Chris Russo's body.

Of course, he's struck it rich but in many ways he's still the same guy he was at WMCA. Sports is in his soul and he will have a debate with you all night and then go out for a beer to give you advice on your career. Mike and Chris are two very different personalities but together they were picture perfect and if they ever reunite they are still the best duo that has ever been put together in the history of sports talk radio.

Mike and Chris had their show simulcast on the YES Network starting in 2002, allowing them to reach a wider audience around the country, which further enhanced Mike's weekly football show heard around the country on every NFL Sunday.

I often hear veteran writers telling me they are no longer sports fans and invariably, they are the ones who tell me they also hate their jobs. I do not think that's a coincidence. Baseball will always be in my soul because when I pull up to the park, I'm a little kid again. That's the same reaction Chris Russo gives when he opens his show by yelling into the microphone.

There are people that contend you must always be objective and I think that's true if you are a news reporter but sports is a recreational tool people use to forget their problems and part of that is being a fan. And Mike and the Mad Dog brought that into the mainstream when most others were afraid to admit their fandom. Some are still very afraid of it.

Another WFAN show host that is never afraid to show his fandom and has become a big star is Joe Benigno. His first taste of radio came about in 1994 when he guest hosted a show after winning a contest held by WFAN management. His skills were raw but his passion for sports was obvious as he brought his heart to every broadcast after he was given the overnight shift on WFAN in 1995.

I became close friends with Joe because we both worked weird hours and he wore his heart on his sleeve for the teams he rooted for: the Mets, Knicks, Rangers, and Jets. But the Jets were his most special team and he openly rooted for them on the air while at the same time being their harshest critic. To this day, I say Joe's best shows came after Jets losses because his panic and grief came right to the surface. He was never afraid to show it and bonded with his fellow Jet fans on an overnight show, which was actually therapeutic for the fan base after a brutal day watching their team.

I remember working the last Sunday of the NFL regular season in 1997 when a Jets win would have put them in the playoffs in Bill Parcells's first season as Jets head coach. It was a tightly contested game with the Jets trailing 13–10 late against the Lions in Detroit. Parcells was not a big fan of quarterback Neil O'Donnell and many felt it affected his fourth-quarter game calling as a failed halfback option from Leon Johnson and an interception from second-string quarterback Ray Lucas ended the Jets' playoff hopes.

I will never forget Joe entering the studio that night reeling from the game and cursing up a storm in the newsroom regarding Parcells. He felt Parcells' hatred for O'Donnell clouded his judgment and he pinned this loss at the feet of the head coach. I did not disagree with him but I knew someone at the station that would—Mike Francesa, who was very close friends with Parcells.

Joe was getting more and more testy as he prepared for his overnight show and I tried to calm him down, but he was ranting and raving like a caged prisoner. I actually began to get him more upset by sharing in his angst. When he hit the air, he let loose on Parcells and simply would not stop.

At this point, the phone rang and an intern answered it. It was Francesa, and he and Joe went at it over the phone. It filtered onto Joe's show as Mike demanded air time and a fierce debate ensued that got personal. To his credit, Joe stayed on topic but their debate went on for close to forty-five minutes. Poor Sam Ryan, who was doing updates, lost air time not knowing when she would go on as Francesa made it seem like he was executing a Senate filibuster about the issue.

This was great radio by two impassioned people who were not afraid to show their fandom for a team or an individual and it had the attention of every sports fan listening in New York. That is the very definition of sports talk radio.

The one show that seemed to be a revolving door for The Fan was middays. After Francesa left that slot for his show with Mad Dog, the station tried a number of different combinations. Ed Coleman and Dave Sims had a very entertaining show through the mid-'90s but the station hoped that Len Berman and Mike Lupica could co-host that slot. I had issues with that idea from the start as neither was a radio guy and there is a dynamic to a radio show that is sometimes difficult for writers or TV broadcasters to grasp.

Before it even began, Berman had second thoughts but WFAN would not let him out of his contract so they each did a separate two-hour show beginning at 10 A.M. That did not last long, and then Russ Salzberg was teamed with overnight host Steve Somers (which made Benigno's overnight show possible) and was coined "The Sweater And The Schmoozer." Russ was known for wearing all different kinds of sweaters while Somers really enjoyed conversing with people.

Steve began his career in the early '70s and came to WFAN at its launch in 1987, manning the overnight shift until this opportunity presented itself. He really began to popularize his brand on this show using humor to talk about sports. But people fail to realize Somers was also a great resource for reporters as he personally helped me by giving us airtime on his show to help perfect our skills.

In 1999 the midday ratings were tanking so WFAN decided to fire Salzberg and Somers, but after fans starting complaining they re-hired Somers and gave him a prime-time show that would be pre-empted on most nights by a game as the station was carrying a Mets, Jets, Knicks, and Rangers broadcasts by this time.

The next midday show was handled by Suzyn Waldman, who did a great job of covering both the Yankees and Knicks for the station, and Jody McDonald, who, like Suzyn, was an original WFAN member and hosted weekend overnights in the very beginning. This was a great partnership as Waldman knew so much about what was going on in the team clubhouses while Jody was one of the first pros that actually acknowledged the popularity of fantasy sports. He also understood the passion fans had for wrestling as Rich Mancuso often appeared on his shows to talk about the WWF (before they changed their to WWE).

In 2001 Waldman left the station to join the YES Network and was replaced by Sid Rosenberg, whose offbeat personality sometimes overshadowed his outstanding sports knowledge. Sid and Jody McDonald tried hard to boost ratings, but to no avail. McDonald was let go and Joe Benigno was moved into to the slot, leaving the overnight show a revolving door to this day.

Joe and Sid were able to mesh well and they captured the fan's need for sports talk around lunchtime. But Sid had a bunch of demons that he has bravely fought off in the past few years. At that time, he was very talented but reckless with his on-air responsibilities resulting in his being removed from the show, forcing Joe to fly solo for over a year until the station found the answer to their prayers in Evan Roberts.

With the exception of the Francesa/Coleman duo in the early years of WFAN, Roberts and Benigno are the best duo in this time slot I've ever heard. They are years apart in terms of age but are a shining illustration that sports bridges those gaps. They appeal to a plethora of demographic groups because they never scold listeners—they listen and will debate them but always treat all of them with a respect level rarely seen.

As WFAN continued its growth in both ratings and revenue, sports stations started cropping up all over the country, but the FAN flew solo in New York for a long time. There were some brief competitors such as Sporting News Radio, which existed in some form on 620 AM in New York from 2001 through 2011. Aside from Scott Wetzel and Bruce Jacobs, who formed a great morning show that actually brought in some listeners, most of the programming never caught the ear of the New York sports fan. Sporting News Radio was formerly One on One Sports but neither organization effectively cut into the listenership of WFAN in any meaningful way and is now called SB Nation Radio.

I spent a most of my time in the early '90s working at ABC Radio and lived through a transition of that organization as most of the network's sports resources were being directed towards ESPN Radio, which launched on January 1, 1992 as Sports Radio ESPN.

By then, ESPN had become such a big part of the sports fan experience especially once their *SportsCenter* program began to change the way fans looked at sports. The sports anchor had always been defined as a person who gave the scores and big news of the day but rarely inflected their own personality in those reports. The one exception to that was Warner Wolf, who delivered a nightly sports report complete with highlights.

Warner gave us a look at the future with his catchphrase "Let's go to the videotape," as he clearly understood his personality was important in developing a brand. This is a concept that ESPN employs to this day as SportsCenter is more than a highlight show—it is a place where segments like the Top 10 highlights of the day were born.

Anchors such as Keith Olbermann, Stuart Scott, Rich Eisen, and Kenny Mayne each had a distinct personality. To me, the greatest of these stars was the late Stuart Scott, who brought hip-hop culture into his delivery. His catchphrases became legendary, and my favorite was "Just call him butter 'cause he's on a roll," which described a player on a hot streak.

The combination of the migration of the nightly sports report courtesy of SportsCenter coupled with evolution of sports talk radio brought about the genesis of ESPN Radio. The channel's signature show for many years is *Mike and Mike*. They have spent more than seventeen years together in the morning and prove that not every sports morning show needs to be a shouting match. They have their fierce debates but really began to perfect the biggest revenue grabber in the business—embedded messaging in program for advertisers and many have tried to copy that concept but few have done it as well. A shining example of this is how they used everything on their show, including the very broadcast booth they worked in, as a sponsorable piece. Greenberg is so great at putting sponsor mentions out there but never disturbing the content of the show.

Sports Radio ESPN only aired on weekends at the start. It provided updated scores and talk shows but did not take calls from listeners, which I think was a huge mistake. Those weekend shows pulled in good ratings during football season, but I learned a valuable lesson seeing the birth of this network up close.

You can accumulate as many affiliates as you want but if you do not have real estate in New York, Chicago, and Los Angeles, your revenue model falls apart. ESPN attempted to get around that by clearing programming in New York as WFAN ran some ESPN programming especially after they gained NBA broadcasting rights in 1995 and MLB rights in 1997. They cleared many of those games for ESPN here locally but the worldwide leader needed clearance in New York for other programming after they expanded to a 24-hour, seven-day a week format in 1996.

This became a pressing issue for them even though some of their radio shows began to be simulcast on ESPN2. Ad sales dollars began to level off, and the revenue model was shaky at best. In 2001 they made the move they needed to make—entering into an agreement with New York station WEVD, which was ironically located in the same position on the dial where WFAN first entered our lives.

The first all sports day on 1050 was September 2, 2001, just nine days before the 9/11 attacks. The station began running the ESPN national feed and was hoping to filter in local programming to give WFAN a run for their money. But to this day, the station's impact on WFAN has been pretty negligible and I am telling you that as someone who still does work for them.

They never quite understood that to do sports talk in this market is impossible if you are not going to dive into the pool. There have been times where the local angle was played up but they never kept it on a consistent basis. In fairness to management, Bristol, not New York, runs the show there.

Still, they have always reached out to me to help with their coverage of the Mets. In 2006 they approached me to cover the postseason for them and followed it up by asking me to be a beat reporter in the same way Ed Coleman covered the Mets for WFAN. The problem was they had no money to send me on the road so I brokered a trade deal with an advertiser that paid for all the travel. I broke some stories and appeared nightly on a show called *New York Baseball Tonight,* which previewed the night of baseball from both the Yankees and Mets perspectives.

Andrew Marchand and Larry Hardesty covered the Yankees while I covered the Mets. The show was a great alternative to the Mets pregame show on WFAN. It featured a one-on-one interview with both a Yankees and Mets player plus pregame sound. In fact, we aired the Met and Yankees manager pregame sessions way before anybody aired it as we played excerpts on *The Michael Kay Show.*

The station faced many obstacles but the back room production team was not one of them. I worked together with pros like Ryan Hurley and Andrew Gundling whose main goal was to get content on the air and they did it so well. Both of those producers would be on a short list of people I would give the keys to if I ever owned a radio station.

*New York Baseball Tonight* was the brainchild of Pete Silverman, who had spent years at MSG and to this day remains someone that gave me so much in terms of coaching.

ESPN Radio had the chance to put a crack into the WFAN ratings in 2008 when Chris Russo left WFAN to join SiriusXM. The two satellite companies brokered a merger earlier in the year and they offered Chris Russo his own channel known as Mad Dog Radio. Many suggested it happened because of a falling out between him and Francesa. I do think there were times they fought about issues, but this move was about money and not much else.

They did their last show together on August 8, 2008 from the Giants training facility in Albany. Six days later, WFAN and Russo officially decided to part ways, leaving Mike Francesa alone to keep the program alive.

The previous year Don Imus was forced to leave the station after he referred to the Rutgers women's basketball team in a derogatory manner both sexually and racially. It was an issue that forced WFAN to fire him after they thought a two-week suspension would be a just punishment. CBS, which picked up ownership of WFAN in 1997, felt the public outcry was too much and so they severed ties with Imus.

In a mere sixteen months, the two biggest revenue sources of WFAN had left the station. It could have signaled a changing of the guard in the New York sports radio market.

Many 1050 ESPN executives pontificated that this was the opening they were waiting for, but their actions illustrated that nothing was going to change much in the near future. I never quite understood why ESPN did not take the ball and run with it, especially with the fact that an ESPN New York website was on the horizon. The simple fact was they were not equipped to handle the conversion.

A managerial switch brought Dave Roberts to the station in 2009 and many of the moves that would provide a local flavor to the station went out the window. I got the sense that Dave was a nice guy but did not understand the flavor of New York radio. And across town, WFAN had two absolute pros at it in Mark Chernoff and Eric Spitz. Quite frankly, Roberts was no match for them.

Boomer Esiason, the former Jets quarterback and Craig Carton had taken over Imus's slot and immediately provided listeners with a sports show that considered no topics taboo. It was almost as if these two had been together forever and Carton knew how to play an audience. Boomer Esiason is a brilliant host whose command of the business goes far beyond the sport of football. He is a true sports expert in every way and Carton is an indispensable part of WFAN because he connects directly to the fans and provides one of two emotions—you either want to hug him or strangle him. Jerry Recco's interaction with Boomer and Carton is the closest thing I've ever seen to the Mike Breen/Don Imus connection.

In my opinion, Imus was the best morning host I ever heard on a sports station and although I'd put Boomer and Carton behind Imus, I'd have to place every other morning show well behind this duo.

At the same time, they explored giving Mike Francesa a co-host but he demonstrated he could do a great job as a solo act. I firmly believe the split up benefited both Francesa and Russo. They have both proved they can breed success in any setting. WFAN was able to survive the losses of Imus and Russo that most thought would bring them back to the pack.

That's not to say 1050 ESPN lacked for talent. *The Michael Kay Show* is a superbly produced property and both Michael Kay and Don LaGreca form a duo that would beat 99 out of 100 sports shows in the world. They bring a real personal touch to what they talk about and have a great way of interviewing guests as well as allowing fans to speak their mind in a respectful and open forum.

They have never had a lead-in show that brought in anywhere near the listeners that *Joe & Evan* pull in for the FAN. They also do not have local baseball broadcasting rights for either of the New York teams, which would provide inventory that could command high revenue. Getting a YES simulcast was a great start but they need to get the sales team to sell every inch of real estate on their shows. Kay and LaGreca's names on embedded in-show messaging carry a lot of weight and sales management needs to demand their account executives understand that. These two are the face of the franchise.

In many ways, *The Michael Kay Show* is on an island there and I firmly believe nobody could do more with the limited resources they possess than they do. I have appeared on that show a number of times and from my experience, I can tell that Kay and LaGreca are both true professionals in every way.

With Francesa leaving WFAN at the end of 2017, I sincerely hope ESPN will put the money and resources into this show by providing better lead-ins and the capital to get them No. 1 in their time slot. Kay and LaGreca are capable of it but management needs to step up and support them so they can reach the heights we all know they are capable of achieving.

Aside from the local sports stations, satellite radio has blossomed in the last decade to be a major player in the sports media marketplace. There was a time when some felt satellite radio would never catch on. Two things pushed it along—a loan from Liberty Media and an increased penetration into the automobile satellite installation business.

If you want to pinpoint one thing that saved the day, it was Howard Stern. Every person working there today owes him a debt of gratitude. He could generate money if he uttered three words and then left for the day because the three words would spike subscribers. I briefly ran into him when I interned at NBC years ago and he was entertaining then but is ten times more entertaining now. When I worked at News 12 in Westchester, I served as a production assistant on one of his pay per view shows and it an indescribable experience. He was super nice to all of us and in many ways should serve as an example for people that don't know how to make their brand profitable.

I worked at Sirius XM in a sales and programming senior management position while I was between ESPN gigs and I must say there were issues right off the bat. The merger was still in its infancy stage but instead of consolidating things they treated it like Noah's Ark—they had two of everything. Two sales software systems, two automation systems, two control room facilities, two totally different master control processes, and an ad sales team that had trouble making the grade.

I tried to persuade them to use Wide Orbit, a sales software system that was quickly becoming state of the art in the industry. I begged them to use it but they resisted. They finally installed it five years after I urged them to do it. Sales-wise, they sold out Howard Stern, but little else. I never quite understood how the NFL Channel, Mad Dog Radio, and even the Martha Stewart Channel were undersold. These channels should have sold themselves—they had Stern and could then force customers to buy other channels if they wanted Stern but somehow that never happened.

They also had a large amount of live sports and very rarely sold it—events such as the World Cup, World Series, Super Bowl, and the NBA Finals were grossly undersold not to mention college bowls and even the NCAA Basketball Tournament. I would never blame the salespeople because they were not given the proper direction. I also found it astounding that inventory sellout levels were never used to spike pricing. The sad part was the programming was outstanding and more channels were cropping up like the Sports Fantasy Channel that should have been a cash cow. I worked in sales for companies that had far less brand recognition than Sirius XM and they brought tons more ad sales revenue than their Sirius XM counterparts.

The sports division is manned by Steve Cohen, whom I always respected for his sports knowledge as well as his honest approach to managing people. The Mad Dog Channel is armed with pros such as Steve Torre and Scott Wetzel, who have paid their dues and can attract listeners the moment they speak into the microphone. Wetzel is one of the few people WFAN missed the boat on as he's a talk show host that took a single concept like "opposite picks" and made it a recognizable characteristic of his brand. He picks games by taking the opposite team he chose initially which sounds silly but spikes conversation from callers.

Following the SiriusXM merger, Mel Karmazin became CEO of the company and had very mixed reviews. There is no question he is an adept businessman who knows how to make money but I never thought he let ideas ferment and grow. Oftentimes, he would make changes just for the sake of making them and brought in a head of ad sales who had no broadcast experience at all, making process implementation impossible to execute.

I was not surprised that Sirius XM became more successful after he left because his successor, James Meyer, understands that quality employees bring a value that should never be underestimated and at the same time, subpar employees must be shown the door. The two go hand in hand. The old management would rarely fire anyone; they would just make their lives so miserable they would voluntarily leave the company.

I only stayed at SiriusXM for a few months, but I learned in that time how *not* to manage people and how to spot great managers like Steve Cohen or Steve Torre.

So how has sports radio and satellite radio changed the business? It made reporters rely on reaching fans with instant messaging as well as topics to debate until the games got underway. It also furthered the demise of the print industry because tomorrow's newspaper would never have the clout that sports talk radio or satellite radio could provide. But it also eliminated so many full-time gigs as independent contractors and freelancers have become more plentiful these days than staff positions.

Don Imus, Mike Francesa, Chris Russo, and Howard Stern stand alone as the voices that shaped the foundation of sports talk radio as we know it today. It is important to note that two of them really do not have much to do with sports but they were able to connect the casual fan with sports.

# CHAPTER 8

# Pre- and Postgame Shows Take Center Stage

DECADES AGO, THE GAME WAS the only thing we ever cared about, and with the exception of *Kiner's Korner*, postgame shows rarely existed. So how did we get to the point where pre- and postgame shows have become so important?

The biggest reason these shows were constructed by broadcasters was a simple one: Follow the money. These shows allowed additional inventory and sponsorship opportunities to help defray the increasing cost of acquiring the broadcast rights to live sporting events.

For my money, two people were the real pioneers of these shows and one came to the forefront in the late '80s, while the other pro set the standard for TV pre- and postgame shows in New York about a decade ago. Those two pioneers were Howie Rose and Kevin Burkhardt, who were the best I've ever seen executing this job and I compare all others to the high bar that they set during their time behind the microphone.

I was around both of these guys every day when they hosted these shows—Howie early in my career and Kevin later on—but both of them did things that many try to emulate but very few duplicate.

Howie Rose is the consummate professional who spends countless hours preparing. So many younger fans have only been exposed to him as a play-by-play man, which he excels at, but from 1987 to 1991, he hosted *Mets Extra*, a pre-game show on WFAN before every Mets game, followed by a postgame show in which Rose interviewed the star of the game, took phone calls, and analyzed the game as well as anyone had ever analyzed baseball in that setting.

The shows were put on the air primarily to promote revenue but quickly became a news source as fans got to hear Howie's pregame conversation with then-manager, Davey Johnson (and later Bud Harrelson)—something we had never had access to in the past. At first, Johnson seemed a bit nervous but as time went on, he embraced the value in the segment. This became a stage for him to state his opinion on anything from an umpire's call from the night before to whether curtain calls by Mets players following home runs were offensive. This became must-listen radio.

Back in those days there were no batting practice shows or any team-owned stations like SNY and YES. This was the first time fans really got inside the pregame clubhouse and as these segments became popular, advertisers flocked to buy sponsorships inside these segments almost as much as they desired in-game sponsorships.

The great thing about Howie Rose, which we see to this day, is he really knows the game and not because he just studies stat sheets—it is in his heart and soul and you could readily see that in these shows before and after each game. Darryl Strawberry and Doc Gooden were stars Mets fans loved, but Howie was never afraid to address their off the field issues and unlike most journalists, didn't back away from negative stories, knowing he had a responsibility to the fans to report them.

The phone-in sessions with Mets fans after the game were lively. Howie would serve as a therapist after a loss and after a win he would reiterate that baseball is a long season with many twists and turns. These shows were a peek into the future as a baseball game was now a four-to-five hour experience rather than the two-to-three hours they had been when I was younger.

The other thing *Mets Extra* did for WFAN was the bridge it provided for nighttime programming as Rose got the phone calls started, heating up the listeners to keep calling all night and, more importantly, to keep listening. This provided a template for future programming and opened up ideas to push viewers and listeners to the game. It also made baseball fans get a "football mentality" in their evaluation of games. In a 162-game sport that meant one thing—revenue took a quantum leap and as a result, made teams understand they could charge exorbitant sums of money for broadcasting rights, and even own their own channels.

On the television side, Kevin Burkhardt is as much responsible for the success of SNY as anyone who has ever worked there. When the Mets launched SNY in 2006, they struggled with the pre- and postgame positions. In fact, most nights I started the questioning with then-manager Willie Randolph as ESPN's beat guy because Chris Cotter never really performed the role for SNY the way it was defined.

That all changed a year later when Burkhardt was hired to serve as their in-game field reporter as well as an important contributor to both the pre- and postgame shows. I saw the difference from the first day of spring training in Port St Lucie as he bonded with players in a way I had never seen any TV broadcaster bond and did it in an understated way that made the players feel comfortable.

I had first met him a few years earlier as I covered all sports for ESPN while he did the same for WFAN. We got along very well from the beginning and always had fun during the game even though we were working for competing stations. More than that, we both felt comfortable enough with each other to exchange constructive criticism and I must say Kevin's perceptions of my work helped me become a better reporter, which is something I will always be grateful for.

We shared some basic views on sports. The most important thing we both understood was that baseball may look easy on TV, but it was our job to tell fans that it's very hard and the amount of time players and coaches spend on preparation needed to be illustrated. And in a way fans would be able to grasp.

In Kevin's first spring training with the Mets, we shared an experience that would bond us forever. In those days, Kevin travelled to all the spring training games (even the road contests) and the Mets had a game in Winter Haven against the Cleveland Indians. The field was a long drive from Port St. Lucie, so we left early. We encountered what was an unbelievable traffic jam—later it was coined by police as the "worst traffic jam in Florida history."

We drove on the Florida Turnpike for hours and at times were at a standstill for over thirty minutes, not moving an inch on the road. In fact, it was so slow that I was able to get out of the car, buy us lunch, and get back in the car before it moved. Obviously, there was a large amount of downtime and we shared so much about our lives, how we grew up, and why we loved the game of baseball. We also shared so much about how deeply we respected Mets television voice Gary Cohen, who in my estimation is the best TV baseball play-by-play voice anywhere in the nation aside from the great Vin Scully.

We also laughed a lot as we exchanged stories of the past. He wanted to hear all about my time with the mid-'80 s Mets and I wanted to get his take on how big SNY would become.

We talked about more than just sports as I shared with him how ill my dad was and what a big part of my life he was in getting me to this stage in my career. As the years grew on, Kevin would always ask about my dad and he quickly became one of his favorite announcers. The stardom that Kevin has attained with FOX does not surprise me, but the great thing is the way he went about becoming a star.

When we finally got to the ballpark, I had to do a live report on 1050 ESPN (now 98.7 FM ESPN) and our seats were in this antique press box that you had to climb into and find a phone line. Kevin was sitting next to me as I performed this report and in the middle of it, a snake crawled up under the press box hissing at me while I was on the air. I completed my on-air update and to this day don't know how I did. A maintenance man arrived and said to me, "Oh here is where the snake went today," as if he were talking about the family pet. Kevin and

I laugh about this to this day as I still do not know if that snake was poisonous or not.

Being around Kevin you quickly got to see that he built relationships in an old-fashioned way. By that, I mean before the game he would always interview the player in a relaxed setting—sitting in the dugout or in the locker room and would never just do the interview and leave. He would end it and then chat with the player about their life, interests, or just even the weather. He has a way of disarming the player so much and that is something very few reporters do.

I see so many interviews to this day that are stiff and sound so scripted, asking questions like "What were you thinking when you hit the ball?" Kevin always understood the basics of a player—their skills are so developed that instincts always take over. He also did not ask long-winded questions because the viewer wants to hear from the player, not the reporter, we are merely the bridge.

Another thing that impressed me about him is that he always listened to his producers both in the truck and on-site and never big-timed them even after he became successful. The Kevin Burkhardt I talk with to this day on the phone is the same guy I talked to when we sat next to each other at Shea Stadium or Madison Square Garden. He has a knack of making you feel good about yourself no matter what mood you are in and taught me that making the player feel comfortable was easy to do and resulted in much better interviews.

Kevin worked for the Mets' network but he never lost his objectivity in analyzing a player or a team decision and some of that credit should go to the Wilpon family who stood clear of the issues on-air—unlike YES, the other team-owned channel in New York that has always been a voice for team ownership. There were sensitive issues that Kevin never danced around, including the Bernie Madoff scandal as well as the firing of Willie Randolph.

Kevin's in-game interviews were always interesting as he would chat with everyone from political figures like John McCain to baseball legends about the game. He would always make it about them and never about him.

SNY also covered baseball's winter meetings better than any regional sports network because Kevin was able to get players, agents, and management to trust in him. The basis of that is why we got along so well. Both of us got so much stuff "off the record" and kept it that way. Betraying that trust for one story no matter how big that story is never worth it.

There are other hosts that define the best in what the position should be and each of them do it in a very different way. Don LaGreca at ESPN New York is so versatile in that he can do these shows in any sport and does them in a way in which the listener gets the most complete rundown you can imagine. LaGreca and I met while at Sports Phone and also worked together at both WFAN and ESPN. In many ways, ESPN New York has no performer more important to their business. Every station needs a Don LaGreca but very few possess one. He would be on my short list if I were hiring for a new station. He has not forgotten what being a fan means and brings that to his broadcasts every day.

The Mets have had three hosts in addition to Rose and Burkhardt who deserve to be recognized as well—one did it as long as anybody while the other two are new additions that have performed at a very high level.

Eddie Coleman is someone I consider one of my best friends even though we have worked as competitors for most of our career. In fact, when I was between jobs at ESPN, Eddie helped broker a deal for me with WFAN writing a blog which kept food on the table. Eddie demonstrated to me that relationships are not just with players or owners because there are individuals like security guards and elevator operators whom you need to show respect for because they possess information and sometimes only share it with people that show them respect.

Eddie hosted a midday talk show on WFAN with Dave Sims entitled "The Coleman and The Soul Man" but once the show was cancelled, Eddie served as Mets beat reporter and the pre- and postgame host while WFAN broadcast Mets games through 2013.

I got to know Eddie well in my travels with the Mets, and I have never heard a bad word said about him from anyone in the business. While I worked at WFAN, Eddie always introduced me to people inside the organization that would become contacts later in my career and did it without hesitation. He does terrific work but he is particularly adept at his sessions with ego-driven talk show hosts who don't spend any time in the locker room, yet think they know it all.

When WOR Radio took over the Mets in 2014, I felt the one mistake they made was not retaining Eddie C. on the broadcast team. They hired Seth Everett instead, but replaced him after one season with Wayne Randazzo, who has done a first-rate job. He is an avid student of the game, has a great voice, and really reminds me a lot of Howie Rose in his years doing *Mets Extra*.

Wayne has a great relationship with Terry Collins and also has the best relationship of anyone in the electronic media with Matt Harvey and I respect him so much for that. Wayne worked on that from day one and when he interviews Harvey you can tell there is genuine trust there.

Wayne might not be here long because his play-by-play is so solid there will either be a team in this market or another that will scoop him up.

I also think Kevin Burkhardt's successor, Steve Gelbs, has a bright career ahead of him. He was put in a tough spot having to replace Burkhardt, but he has set his own course and much like Randazzo developed a great rapport with Matt Harvey, Gelbs has done the same with Noah Syndergaard. And he does it in such an understated way.

When Steve asks how you are he really wants to know. As I have struggled with my dad's health issues, Steve has been a great listener especially on the road when we have so much downtime. But the greatest thing Steve does is when he is off camera sitting with players, he really tried to get to know them as people, not just as athletes.

I got to know Steve very well before he got the Mets gig because we both covered games at Madison Square Garden and we talked so much Rangers hockey sitting next to each other. There are just times you meet somebody and you know they have that "it factor" that will translate well on the air. And I felt that way the first time I met him.

In his final year as host on SNY, Kevin Burkhardt, who worked alongside Steve Gelbs in 2014, confided in me that he really liked Steve because he asked the right questions. When you consider that in his first year he had to cover several locker room celebrations, Steve had to do something right off the bat that took some skill and quite frankly, Cotter could have done better in 2006.

Steve did an excellent job with those interviews that coupled elation with questions that needed to be asked. I have been in my share of champagne-soaked locker rooms and Steve handled them as well as anyone I have ever seen.

He has also been in quiet, season-ending locker room nights the past two years and handled that like a seasoned veteran as well. You need to ask tough questions but also need to understand what he players are going through and give them space to collect their thoughts. Gelbs understands that better than most of the beat guys.

No list of hosts that have contributed mightily to the last three decades of sports reporting in New York is complete without the names of Suzyn Waldman and Kim Jones. I will go into more detail about Suzyn in a later chapter, but she is a shining example of how the evolution of the business has made reporting better.

I have spent far more time covering the Mets than the Yankees but it must be said that Kim Jones handled those postgame interview sessions so well because she understood the nuts and bolts of the game while also portraying the emotion the sport possesses.

She is such a great professional for young people to emulate in that she served her time learning her craft, never stepped on anybody's toes, and whether she covers football or baseball, the listener or viewer is always on her mind—giving them the info they need in an unfettered and unbiased way.

Other hosts that deserve mention are John Giannone, Tina Cervasio, and Bill Daughtry.

Daughtry is a seasoned pro who has hosted pre- and postgame shows throughout the time I have been reporting and his work on the Knicks especially stands out. He and I always shared our respect of Patrick Ewing, especially when he was being bashed by some other members of the media. Bill always taught me in my early days not to follow what everyone else was reporting, and make my own assessment and stand by it. I live by that advice to this day.

John Giannone is another member of my WFUV family and joined the station as a freshman while I was a senior. He always had the nose for the story and told it in writing and by voice in the most elegant way possible even as a teenager. His work on the Rangers in the past few years has been outstanding.

It is hard to believe John has been doing this for over a decade. He has the rare skill of talking to both the casual hockey fan and the diehard hockey community so both can understand it all in the same report.

Being around him in the locker room, he asks the best questions and oftentimes I ask myself why do I even need to ask a question since John has covered everything so well.

Tina Cervasio did a great job covering the Knicks. The way she was let go by MSG was one of the most classless moves I've ever seen. She was let go after covering the NBA draft and was advised of it so late in the offseason it made it hard for her to hook on elsewhere.

Tina had great chemistry with the Knicks players and was always much more concerned about the player's answer than her question. Her ability to bond with star players like Carmelo Anthony simply can't be overstated and this is a person who did the same great job here that she did in Boston while working as the Red Sox field reporter. More than that, Tina did her job with the highest level of integrity I've ever seen from anyone holding the MSG mic flag in the Knicks locker room. She asked tough questions not because she wanted a confrontation but because she knew she had to service the Knicks fans with a pipeline inside the clubhouse. She was rare talent and one not usually seen by a Cablevision employee.

# CHAPTER 9

# Is Play-By-Play Announcing Becoming a Lost Art?

BEING FROM NEW YORK, I was fortunate to have the opportunity to hear some of the best play-by-play announcers in the business in my formative years as a fan. In those days, we listened to games on radio as much as we watched them on television. New York fans listened to the tones of Lindsey Nelson, Ralph Kiner, and Bob Murphy if they were Mets fans while Frank Messer, Bill White, and Phil Rizzuto were the voices Yankees fans came to love. If you were into the Knicks and Rangers, it was the voice of Marv Albert that took you through the basketball and hockey seasons while Merle Harmon, Marty Glickman, and later Jim Gordon patrolled the football broadcast booths.

In those days, radio was king in my Bronx neighborhood, as fifty to sixty Mets and Yankees games weren't televised and Jets and Giants home games were victims of the NFL blackout policy in effect until 1973.

This era was a golden age of play-by-play in the classic sense as all of these announcers had tremendous "radio voices" as well as great command of the game. Today's media police would find issues with their affinity for the home team but I honestly found that rewarding. These voices became part of your family and I could attest to the fact that Lindsey Nelson, Ralph Kiner, and Bob Murphy were always in the background at every family event and there is something so cool about that. Sundays were big family days—eating, playing sports, and being with those I loved but that trio was always there—like three best friends you simply could not live without hearing from every day.

Me and my friends all mimicked the voices of these great announcers and those of us like myself that wanted to become sportscasters followed their every move. When I entered the business I was able to meet Bob Murphy and it was quite a thrill. He had seen it all with the Mets from the very beginning as did his broadcasting sidekick, Ralph Kiner, who always treated me so well.

Ralph had the greatest stories but also had a knowledge of hitting that was so enlightening. In those days, the Shea Stadium press room had a bar and after we finished our work and he completed his post-game show, *Kiner's Korner*, Ralph would tell story after story. Today, most play-by-play guys leave right away and I feel bad that young journalists don't get the same chance I did to learn from them.

When I think of Kiner, I also think of Tim McCarver because in many ways he resurrected Ralph's career. Lindsey Nelson left the broadcast team after the 1978 season and shortly after that, Bob Murphy moved to the radio side only, leaving Ralph with partners that did not meld with him in any way. Tim knew how to reach Ralph and extract those great stories that Ralph loved to tell the fans. McCarver also broke the game down very well and he had pet phrases that became part of the baseball vernacular. "When you think long, you think wrong" and "You run through the base not to the base" became staples for Mets fans, but it also explained when a player was not fundamentally sound.

When the Dodgers would come to town, Vin Scully would arrive with them. I met him for the first time in 1982 while covering a Mets-Dodgers game for my college radio station. When Vin saw that I was affiliated with WFUV he came over to me and introduced himself. He asked me to sit down and have lunch with him. I was absolutely floored and he made me feel so comfortable as we talked about his Fordham days, the Dodgers, and of course, the art of play-by-play. He gave me solid advice, telling me to follow my dreams but always have a back-up plan. That plan will always allow you to keep chasing that dream. It was advice I'd never forget.

Vin also illustrated how much he prepared for his play-by-play. This is a man that had done hundreds of games but prepared like it was his first game. Years later, I saw that same philosophy when I watched both Howie Rose and Gary Cohen prepare for their games.

Lindsey, Bob, and Ralph were the voices that took me through my years as a Mets fan. Gary Cohen and Howie Rose have that role with the young fans of today and Mets supporters are in equally good hands—these are two Hall of Fame-worthy broadcasters in my opinion.

During the early days of the Mets, the duties were shared by three announcers—there were not separate teams for TV and radio. So, for instance, the first three innings Bob Murphy and Ralph Kiner would be on the TV feed and Lindsey Nelson would do the radio. And every three innings they mixed and matched. That would never happen today as the two mediums are separate but it makes me wonder—couldn't teams save money that way? Of course, that would mean three voices that all had play-by-play acumen and they would have to do every game.

Gary Cohen is simply the best everyday play-by-play voice in New York right now because he calls the game perfectly and has an impeccable knowledge of Mets history. But he also has an incredible rapport with any analyst that he works with because they immediately respect his commitment to excellence.

Bob Murphy was able to create words on the fly that perfectly described signature moments such as when he used the word *trickling* to describe Mookie Wilson's grounder that eluded Bill Buckner in Game Six of the '86 World Series. Cohen has that same skill and has exhibited it on many occasions. For example, describing the Mets' division-clinching moment in 2015 at Cincinnati as "tears of joy" put into words what every Met fan was feeling. His sense of the moment is absolutely flawless.

What I appreciate the most about Cohen is that unlike other announcers, he does not need to promote his own individual brand. He has let that evolve over time much like the great announcers in the profession have always done. Yankees radio man John Sterling, on the other hand, has taken the opposite approach.

He has branded home run calls to individual players and his "Yankees win" ending to a game has become a trademark. There is nothing inherently wrong with that but sometimes he sacrifices accuracy for his branding and that is when he gets into trouble. But Sterling was sharp enough to understand the business was changing and play-by-play calls were being taped and played over and over again on sports radio stations around the country. And that would get his name in the limelight—even if the hosts and sportscasters were making fun of his call.

That's been the biggest change in play-by-play—announcers now actually practice how they would call a certain historic moment and to me that's just not play-by-play—it is scripted entertainment. Another significant change is that "classic" radio voices are no longer needed on the airwaves and some of that has brought guttural-sounding broadcasts.

I do think, however, that New York at least has been more resistant to that transformation as broadcasters such as Mike Breen, Bob Wischusen, Bob Papa, and Sam Rosen still fit the classic definition of play-by-play and make their broadcasts both informative and enjoyable.

Breen is the voice of the NBA and he provides basketball fans with an absolutely perfect broadcast each and every game because he has the sense of letting the game play out and never dominating the sound of a broadcast. He also knows how to defer to the analyst so the fan can hear the take from a player's perspective without being overloaded with fancy X's and O's.

On the football side, both Papa and Wischusen do a fine job of painting the word picture for their radio listeners. Papa replaced the popular Jim Gordon, and has all the important characteristics of what an announcer should be—he anticipates the progress of a play like a coach and if you listen carefully on the radio, his call of a touchdown sometimes comes before you hear that final crowd roar or groan, whichever the case may be.

What does the future hold for play-by-play? I am not so sure. When I talk to aspiring play-by-play wannabees, they often ask me what their signature phrase should be, how they could get their college PBP calls on Twitter, and how to compile funny phrases they could use on a broadcast.

Questions like that make me want to scream but at the same time makes me realize I've been around a long time and how resistant I've become to change. Play-by-play announcers should be a part of the listening or viewing process but never bigger than the game. Guys like Cohen, Rose, Papa, and Breen totally understand that concept but others seem to have forgotten that. I don't totally blame them because social media and sports radio give everyone a chance to brand themselves as stars.

But you have to always remember that the athletes are the stars and as much as the play-by-play men are admired, if fans had a choice between keeping their star player or their announcer under contract, they would pick the player.

## CHAPTER 10

# The Role of Media Relations and Team Ownership

EVERY PROFESSIONAL SPORTS TEAM HAS a media relations department and they provide the access that allows us to connect the players to their fans. With the advent of social media that interaction has evolved in a myriad of ways.

Thirty years ago reporters dealt with one or two contacts in the team's media relations department, but now there are so many layers to those departments with many of them separating into media relations and community relations. When I was first starting out, that was all done by one department and in some cases, one person.

Covering the Mets back then involved dealing directly with Jay Horwitz who remains the best in the business to this day. Prior to the Internet, all requests had to be done via the telephone or a fax machine but the relationship you made directly with the head of public relations provided the road to the access of the players. I sometimes laugh when I hear reporters today complain about equal access because in those early days you made your road to access and each reporter had to carve that out for themselves. It was not a birthright—it had to be earned.

Season credentials were only given to members of the media who covered the team on an everyday basis and you had to prove you covered the team either by electronic air checks or articles that were printed in newspapers or magazines. Today there are so many people who get season credentials who I firmly believe should be denied access because they are fraudulent to the extent I have no idea what they are doing in the clubhouse. The biggest issue is in NBA press boxes where I routinely see people with press credentials getting autographs in the locker room, which makes working a postgame NBA locker room an absolute nightmare at times.

I feel for media relations departments because denying credentials has to be validated with more evidence than you need in a court room and even then the energy they need to keep on top of this aspect of the job complicates their day to day work. The best illustration I could ever remember is with a guy named Mark Sabia who patrolled the locker rooms for years before his fraudulent ways were uncovered.

Sabia was a guy who appeared with a credential through UA Columbia Cablevision and would use his access to get credentials for aspiring camera people whom he would ask for money in return for that credential usage. I've lived most of my life in Westchester County and knew of UA Columbia Cablevision and even remember the storefront where it had existed but it closed when Cablevison acquired the cable franchise in all of Westchester County in the early 1990s. To this day I believe they used to legitimately cover games but their credentials ended up getting into Sabia's hands by, let's just say, unorthodox means.

And this guy was everywhere—even on the road during the Yankees postseason run in 1996—and he came to be known as "Doogie Howser" because of his youthful appearance. I called him Vinny DelPino—because he actually looked more like that character from the *Doogie Howser* program than the aforementioned protagonist.

One night in the Knicks postgame clubhouse, he was called out by Allan Houston, who has to be one of the most down-to-earth New York athletes I've ever interviewed. Houston looked at his credential and asked, "Where do you work?"

Sabia responded as he did to everyone, "UA Columbia Cablevision of Westchester, where I do live sports reports." At that point Houston responded, "I live in Westchester and I channel surf all the news channels and I've never seen you." Sabia quietly left the room and Houston asked me about him, knowing that I lived in Westchester County. He saw my reaction and said to me, "Rich, I know you well, the look on your face told me all I needed to know."

Sabia continued to work and began piling in so much money from young aspiring camera people who were desperate to work. Most of us in the media knew about his scam and some even suggested that the teams should look into this situation. One day Sabia, who never spoke to me before this came up, said that he was hearing I was making waves about him and he did not like it. My response was that he should prove me wrong but perhaps he wasn't aware how tied in I was to TV production in Westchester County, having spent time working at Cablevision of Westchester as both a sports reporter and political correspondent. I guess he checked that out because we never spoke again.

A few weeks later, prior to the Mets home opener in 2005, Sabia was arrested at Shea Stadium for scamming press credentials dating back to 1998 and for falsifying business records. He was charged with five counts of felonies. He was holding his camera with that infamous Mark Sabia Sports Zone mic flag and instead of getting his season passes, he was taken away in handcuffs. Give credit to the Mets PR team for finally being the lone team to stand up to this fraud.

The day to day relationship between reporters and media relations is a constant flow and has its good days and bad days, but to me the Mets and Rangers stand ahead of the class in how they deal with the media. Both teams give pretty much unlimited access to the players and both Jay Horwitz and Jon Rosaco, who head up media relations for the Mets and Rangers, respectively, are two of the best to deal with.

And I must say when Rick Cerrone and Rob Butcher ran the Yankees PR team in the '90s, the experience there was superb as well. Butcher, in his infinite wisdom, built a radio press room for us in the old Yankee Stadium by converting an old closet into a working space we used for years. And Cerrone did a marvelous job of organizing the postgame clubhouse, a room that had so many stars.

When I got the beat reporter job at ESPN covering the Mets, both Horwitz and Cerrone gave me congratulatory phone calls—something I will never forget. Rick told me he'd miss me in the Bronx, knowing most of my time would now be spent covering the Mets, but he credited me with working so hard to get the gig. It was a phone call I will never forget.

After ten years with the Yankees, Cerrone left the team and I barely got to know know his replacement, Jason Zillo, because these days I really cover very few Yankees games.

On a typical day covering the Mets, reporters arrive at the ballpark at about 2:30 P.M. for a night game and Horwitz's staff has already provided both background info we need and a schedule of players available to interview. I have found that you could always ask Jay for a special favor and he and his staff have always come through.

Early in my career, I asked Jay for helpful advice on the best way to act with the veteran writers. In those days, there was a contentious relationship between broadcast and print and I wanted to become a better reporter but not one who did not understand the mechanics of the clubhouse, including respecting the pecking order of the group.

I was a relative nobody but Jay took the time out to educate me about it and even went beyond that. He spoke to some of the veteran beat reporters about me and some of them responded in not only co-existing with me but also pointing things out to me I could do better. Some ignored me but guys like Marty Noble, Bob Klapisch, and John Harper always made me feel welcome. I knew Jay brokered that for me with the help of the great Shannon Dalton Forde.

No chapter about media relations would be complete without paying homage to Shannon, who left us in 2016 after a battle with breast cancer. I say left us but in reality she will never leave us. I met her the first day she was on the job back in 1994. The Good Lord is so infinite in His wisdom in that He places people in our lives that not only make our lives better but teach us the things we need to better at so we can serve Him.

From the moment I met her, she always was so helpful with all the things we needed, giving us the resources to provide our listeners or readers the most up-to-date information on the team. It was a ton of little things like making sure we had our parking passes early in spring training so it gave us less to worry about.

In her first year, I remember a long rain delay when Shea Stadium's Diamond Vision was showing *1986: A Year to Remember*, which highlighted that championship run. We watched it together and I shared with her some of the inside stories covering that team. I proceeded to tell her this film was the Mets fan's version of *Gone With The Wind*. And every time the Mets played that during a rain delay we'd look at each other and say, "*Gone With The Wind* never gets old—does it?"

But the true strength of Shannon was she created an environment where competing people all got along. The press box is a very unique work setting in that you sometimes sit alongside competitors with whom you are battling to get a story and if you don't get it, your boss will never let you hear the end of it. And if that happens, you have to face them every day, sometimes travel on the same plane, and eat in the same press room.

I've seen how tense that could be in other places, but there was something about the Shea Stadium press box that made those tense moments go away. That something was Shannon, who always trusted and treated everyone equally and when she talked to you about your life, she not only really wanted to know about it, but she wanted to help you in every way.

There was one spring training where my dad was so ill we thought he would not make it and Shannon spent countless lunches with me where I confided in her the struggle I was having with all of it. She not only listened but gave me such good advice in that she knew covering the Mets was a way I could take my mind off my issues for a few hours. She met my dad that summer at Shea Stadium and treated him so well, listening to his corny jokes and later confided in me I was just like him—telling corny jokes but always saying the right thing to make people feel better. The truth is I learned that from watching her do her job.

When we found out she was stricken with breast cancer, we were all in shock but her strength and courage never wavered and she always changed the subject to baseball when you asked how she was feeling. None of us could ever conceptualize what she was going through, but her sense of humor coupled with her love of the Mets always shone through.

She cared so much about other people and always made what she was going through seem minor even though we all knew it was far from that. She also did a wonderful job of bringing to the forefront what a terrible disease this is and spent countless hours helping the research cause with time and money. As time wore on, you could see how the disease began to spread but she always had a smile on her face and spent the time she had left making others happy—most notably her beautiful family.

The 2015 World Series was a great moment for the entire organization and you could see Shannon was struggling, but at the same time she was so elated her team had returned to the fall classic. There was no place in the world she would rather have been at than Citi Field at that moment. I remember standing with her in the dugout before Game Three and she looked at Citi Field and said to me, "Rich, you and I both saw this at Shea but seeing it here makes the world feel right."

I was covering the team in spring training when I got a call about her passing while I was driving to cover a game in Kissimmee, Florida. It hit me like a ton of bricks and I had to stop the car because my hands were shaking. Forget about baseball—*the world* lost a great person on that day but one who will be remembered forever.

There are times when I am covering a game at Citi Field and my mind wanders to something Shannon said to me or did for me. And it makes me think about what good I can I do for someone today and do it only to help them, not to help the way people perceive me. That is what Shannon taught us all in her own way and why she will *always* be with us at Citi Field.

The loss of Shannon was devastating and in Port St. Lucie both Joel Sherman of the *New York Post* and *Newsday's* Dave Lennon gave stirring speeches about how much we loved her. They are both seasoned journalists but on this day we also saw the human side to them. And Shannon brought that out in all of us—some of us got it brought out easily, others it was a more arduous task, but Shannon did it for everybody. It was impossible not to smile after talking with her no matter how tough your day had been.

The media relations departments are also the direct link to team ownership and in the Mets' case, Jay Horwitz links us directly to the team owners, the Wilpons. I know Fred and his family have been frequently criticized by the media but I must tell you Fred has always treated me well and I genuinely get along well with the ownership. I know that I receive much criticism with my peers on this but to tell you the truth I evaluate people on how they treat me—never on what I hear second hand.

The Bernie Madoff scandal was something we covered but the thing I think people fail to understand is that the Wilpons felt victimized by Bernie Madoff. He took tons of money from both the Wilpon family and others associated with them. And he was their lifelong friend. For a brief moment, just consider if your best friend did it to you, how would you feel?

The Madoff situation gave media members a way to take potshots at the team when their financial acumen could not conceptualize the issues at hand. To me, a sports reporter had every right to be critical of baseball-related decisions the team made but this Madoff situation was far off my plane because I did not have all of the information.

As time has worn on, the story is no longer the Madoff scandal—it is how this organization, despite that obstacle, built a pennant-winning team with shrewd moves and an excellent player development process that has produced a winning team. One that right now is the team in New York—something the so-called experts never said would happen. But you see that does not fit the narrative that the Wilpons don't care.

I can tell you for a fact this family wants nothing more than a world championship but the plan was *always* to build a solid foundation, and then add key pieces to finalize the picture. To me, doing this through the Madoff fallout is a success story. And a process I think the cross-town Yankees are beginning to embrace as well.

It would have been so easy for me to follow the media sheep in this town and pile on the Wilpons. And when they made a bad baseball move I would be critical. For instance, how they handled the firing of Willie Randolph. In over thirty-five years of owning the team, the Wilpons have reached the postseason seven times, which is certainly better than many organizations in the sport. But again it does fit the narrative.

The other thing I want to get straight here is that the Steinbrenner family is looked at so differently, yet George was suspended twice by baseball—once for illegal contributions to Richard Nixon's presidential campaign and the other for paying a known gambler $40,000 to dig up dirt on Dave Winfield. Still, today many think George is a certain Hall of Famer, which I don't necessarily disagree with because he did have a significant impact on the game.

Still, I think you have to look at George's entire report card, not just the championships. The two suspensions are rarely mentioned. But again don't let the facts get in the way of the narrative. In the early days that I covered baseball, George was a story of his own and there was never a dull moment.

When I started covering the Yankees, the radio press box housed about twelve to fifteen spots but there was a loud voice that always greeted you as you sat down. I asked people who this guy was and all I was told is he was Bill the Baker. He not only spoke loudly but would generally recite Yankees stats ad nauseam as you were trying to do live updates. Eventually I got used to it but learned that talking to him was like putting a nickel in a never-ending jukebox playing the same song over and over.

Apparently, he delivered doughnuts to George and the owner took a liking to him, giving him credentials only to the press box—I never saw him in the clubhouse. He would openly root for the Yankees and oftentimes he could be heard cheering over my live updates on the radio. But as time went on, I understood his charm and he almost became part of the press box experience.

He even started attending Mets games at Shea and he would take on anyone who was the least bit critical of Steinbrenner. One day, Lloyd Carroll, a reporter for the *Queens Chronicle*, had written a scathing story about George's abuse of power. Bill, who was using a cane at the time, confronted and threatened Carroll. At that point, Wally Matthews, a renowned columnist, stepped in and told them both to sit down unless they wanted to deal with him. Knowing Wally, that would have been a quick sit down for both parties.

Bill the Baker continued as a press box regular for some time even though his health began to deteriorate. He became a frequent caller to WFAN until he died at the far too young age of sixty-seven in 2014.

The owner that gets the most grief in New York is Jim Dolan whom I worked for while at AMC Networks owned by Cablevision. Jim is loyal to his friends to a fault and I must say from personal experience, not afraid to spend money to make money. While I worked there, I ran ad sales ops groups for him and I must say he paid me well but at times the organization was mismanaged.

When people ask me about my time there they often ask about the differences between Chuck Dolan and Jim Dolan as I attended meetings moderated by both of them. Chuck was a brilliant idea man who conceptualized the concept of HBO before it became a reality and was very open to exploring heavy spending if the five-year plan warranted a surplus for the company. Jim wanted immediate return and often would turn his back on concepts that could take some time to ferment.

But Jim Dolan's notion of a need for instant gratification coupled with his disdain for the media is his biggest weakness and had his dad run things at Madison Sqaure Garden, I have a feeling both the Knicks and Rangers might have a few more championship trophies in the Garden trophy case. He is blindly loyal to people in his inner circle and that explains why both Glen Sather and Isiah Thomas got years of security in a time where both should have been escorted out the door.

But make no mistake—Jim Dolan spends tons of money on the Knicks and Rangers and deserves credit for that, but the way he spends it is an entirely different issue. To me the poster child for this was the day Patrick Ewing was traded for Glen Rice, creating years of salary cap hell. Simply put, the Knicks should have paid Ewing through the end of his contract and then get the salary cap relief that presented instead of carving out deal after deal that put the organization years away from respectability.

And the Knicks became so paranoid about the way the media covered them, it actually put their public relations staff in an impossible situation. Player access to the Knicks became more and more limited and Dolan made them text him questions being asked by the media, which to me is the ultimate illustration of paranoia.

If a reporter took potshots at the team, he was branded an enemy of the organization and I can tell you when ESPN Radio got the broadcast rights things began to get sticky for us. We were never told not to speak our minds but it was inferred. For me it made covering the Knicks very challenging. In the Ewing years, I generally felt the media treated him very unfairly but to me the whole dynamic made a 180-degree turn after he left and I know why.

I worked ten years at Cablevision, including managing sales operations at both Bravo and IFC and was exposed to the decision making of Jim Dolan, who was as unpredictable as any owner I was ever exposed to during my career.

His ego was enormous but he also was one of the most insecure CEOs I've ever come across. Often you could tell he was not listening or focusing on the issue at hand. He had two methods of conversing— talking and waiting to talk—he never had a listening mode. At one meeting I attended, I was taking copious notes and he looked at me with a perplexed grin saying, "You are really taking a lot of notes." His tone was bordering on angry and I said, "I just want to make sure I am processing the correct info."

At that moment, I realized that every MSG executive had an impossible task as they were being micromanaged by an ego-driven man who changed corporate goals at the drop of a hat. Most reporters theorized that was the case but I knew it for a fact because I lived it for a decade.

Knowing all this, it still amazes me how well the Rangers PR staff treats the media and that has been a constant no matter what is going on in the MSG boardroom. Player access is so organized as everyone gets a shot at every player they need and the staff orchestrates that progression. And the coach does an interview session after that to really round out the postgame process. The Knicks do it exactly in the reverse—the coach talks first and then you wait a long time for the players.

A Rangers postgame can be completed in twenty to twenty-five minutes while the Knicks process takes forty-five minutes on a good day and that makes deadlines an issue every single time. It is very puzzling how two teams owned by the same company can treat the media so differently. And don't get me wrong—I never blame the players—they are being told what to do. That is why covering the Rangers and Mets is so much easier.

Football differs from the other sports as in-season reporting is very structured. Following a Sunday game, Monday is post-mortem day, Tuesday is off limits, Wednesday is media day, Thursday is quarterback day, and Friday is game prep day while Saturday is usually designated for travel if the game is on the road.

The coach addresses the media every day and that session becomes like a court interrogation, especially if the team is struggling. I have always tried to understand the coach's perspective because they are subjected to questions that they must answer to merely try to simplify a game that is so complex.

I remember being at ESPN headquarters in Bristol, Connecticut, listening to Jon Gruden break down a series of plays and at that moment I realized how much smarter these coaches are than anyone in the media. They construct a game plan with hours of studying film and then have to answer a question like "How could you run the ball there when the pass was working?"

Gruden explained to us that during the course of a game a coach often calls plays that may not be the best at the time because the team needs a "rest down" since their wide receivers have been running fifty yards down the field for five straight plays. We can't see that because we don't live in it the way they do. And when coaches have to hear question after question throughout a long season I can totally understand when they snap at reporters.

The famous Herman Edwards quote, "You play to win the game" was prompted by a reporter asking him if his 2–5 Jets team had to be reminded not to give up on the season. He responded with his now infamous quote and I don't blame the reporter as it was a reasonable question.

But Herm's response was simple, "You have an obligation as a player—as an athlete at any level—and it doesn't matter what sport it is. When you sign on, you sign on. You prepare that week to go win. I don't care about your schedule, or how many people got hurt, it doesn't matter. You owe it to the people in the building and guys in the huddle to prepare yourself to win. That's the most important thing that week. My dad was in the service for twenty-seven years. He used to tell me, 'It's not about tomorrow—it's about today. What are you going to do today a little bit better than what you did yesterday?'"

I was in the room that day and could feel the emotion in the voice of a coach who lived this life and could not believe people really thought his team needed to be reminded of something so simple. But more than that, he knew how complex this game is and trying to dumb it down is something reporters do because most people don't care about the complexities of the game.

I might sound old but I do care about it and I still try to learn more about the game every day. Sure, I have a job to do—get the story of the day out there or even break a story. But you can learn so much from listening—which should be a mandatory skill for reporters.

Dealing with ownership and media relations people can be a challenge and, as I mentioned, some do it better than others. There will always be negative stories but those "grey area" stories can be handled much more fairly if the reporter's relationship with team management is a healthy one.

# CHAPTER 11

# Recreational vs. Performance Drug Culture

DRUGS HAVE UNFORTUNATELY BEEN A debilitating force in our society in a variety of ways over the past few decades. Sports have always been in the center of society and naturally drugs have affected it in a number of profound ways.

Growing up in the '60s and '70s, I saw it firsthand as many young lives were ruined due to drug abuse, affecting friends of mine, killing their dreams, and in one case was responsible for a death while I was in high school. My support system both at home and at school educated me about what was happening but it was plain to see. While I was in the tenth grade, the police came into my school one day to expose a drug ring and arrest students for selling drugs to fellow classmates. It was a rude awakening for me to witness such an event but would pale in comparison to what I saw when covering sports a decade later.

I observed that the drug use in that time period was far more out in the open than it was in the '70s. Nightclubs became a place you could easily obtain drugs and you could see cocaine being ingested out in the open—you could see it at tables right next to someone's drink.

In my travels with the Mets in the mid-'80s, I never saw a player doing drugs out in the open but it was all around them and the dealers knew these were young men who had tons of excess money. Dwight Gooden's drug abuse has been well documented, and we all suspected it in the media at various times in his tenure with the team.

This recreational culture was very visible even in the clubhouses where cans of beer were plentiful and some players would drink three or four beers after the game while talking to us in the clubhouse. Young reporters in the business are amazed when I tell them this because the only time they see alcohol today is in championship celebrations but it was a daily occurrence in those days. Alcohol abuse was rampant, and in some cases, was combined with drug abuse.

Star pitcher Vida Blue had to spend three months in jail for cocaine use as did a trio of his Kansas City Royal teammates—Jerry Martin, Willie Wilson, and Willie Aikens. If that was not bad enough, Mark Liebl, who was serving time for drug trafficking, started naming players he snorted cocaine with and those names included Dennis Eckeresely, Ron LeFlore, Steve Trout, and Mike Torrez as well as the aforementioned quartet of Royals players.

The drug abuse story really took off in 1985 when the Pittsburgh Seven drug trial hit the sports pages. This brought so much out in the forefront as players like Tim Raines and Keith Hernandez testified at the trial involving Curtis Strong and other drug suppliers. Hernandez indicated that he thought 40 percent of major league players used cocaine. He would later backtrack on that number but I thought it was pretty accurate in the numbers I encountered in friends of mine who had far less money than players did.

Hernandez called cocaine "the devil" and shared the story about how he used the drug before he was traded to the Mets and had to be jolted into realizing he had to stop when he woke up with a nose bleed and had lost ten pounds. He also had the shakes and wound up throwing a gram of cocaine down the toilet.

Hernandez also testified that Cardinals manager Whitey Herzog held a meeting during the 1983 season where he stated that he had knowledge three players were using drugs and wanted them to come clean or they would be traded off the team. The defense tried to use this testimony in examination as the reason Hernandez was traded to the Mets. Herzog said a few days before the testimony that he was not surprised by the players who were testifying. But he added that Hernandez did not have a drug problem at the time he was traded to the Mets.

This part of the testimony got huge play in New York as many wondered how Frank Cashen got him for so little in return. We sometimes forget that Neil Allen was a prominent reliever at the time and the Mets felt the emergence of Jesse Orosco provided the ability to deal Allen. The trade worked out much better for the Mets but that's hindsight as I felt the Cards got a quality reliever they needed at the time. But as the trial went on it certainly made us stop and think that this recreational drug culture was continuing and intensifying in the sport.

Montreal Expos outfielder Tim Raines, who was elected to the Baseball Hall of Fame in 2017, testified that he slid head first while stealing bases because he carried a vial of cocaine in his back pocket and he did not want to smash it. John Milner of the Pittsburgh Pirates, a former Met, said that he purchased drugs in the bathroom stall at Three Rivers Stadium in Pittsburgh and it was also revealed the mascot, the Pirate Parrot, was knee deep in drug distribution as well.

Dave Parker, Gary Matthews, Enos Cabell, Al Holland, Jeff Leonard, and J.R. Richard also testified at the trial. The backlash from fans was intense. The defendant's attorney, Adam Renfroe, claimed the players who testified and were granted immunity were nothing but hero-criminals who were still distributing to other players. In March 1986 baseball commissioner Peter Ueberroth suspended eleven players, who had their bans lifted by donating 5 to 10 percent of their salaries to drug programs and agreeing to be tested.

As a young reporter, the trial certainly made me think that this would become a storyline I would have to follow and little did I know that it would intensify over the next few years. When the drug culture exploded into the Mets clubhouse, we were surprised but not shocked.

And the day that was supposed to be one of the greatest in team history proved to be the harbinger of things to come.

As New York was celebrating the Mets' World Series victory, Doc Gooden never made it to the parade and the next spring he entered the Smithers clinic after a voluntary test showed cocaine in his system just a week before opening day.

Many reporters had mentioned to me the previous winter that there were rumblings of issues as Gooden had brawled with police in Tampa and was given three years of probation. Shortly after that, Gooden's girlfriend, Carlene Pearson, was picked up for carrying a loaded handgun, which she tried to bring through metal detectors at LaGuardia Airport. In that pre-9/11 world, you could meet people right at the gate. Gooden's plane landed thirty minutes later and there was some question as to why she would meet him with a loaded handgun.

All of this provided back drop to the twenty-eight day stint that Gooden served in Smithers but so many people failed to see, myself included, this player was in peril and needed help. Looking back, the last thing he needed was to go back on a baseball field so soon. I'm clearly not a doctor but my thought here is that this was a young man who had such pressure on him to perform and while returning home, all of his old friends had their hands out asking for favors. This does not excuse the drug use but makes me understand it.

This all needed to be explored in an in-depth period of therapy, not in a four-week window that would get him back on the field satisfying the needs of everyone aside from the patient. Doc was always pleasant to be around but very guarded in what he said and would never get past all of the demons that lived inside him as a young Mets player.

The media had put Doc on a pedestal after that 1985 season in which he garnered the Cy Young Award just one year after winning Rookie of the Year. His starts were block parties at Shea Stadium as everybody expected a shutout complete with 15 strikeouts every time he took the mound.

This meant Doc was getting his drugs from outside sources and in those days it was fairly easy as hotels had far less security than they have today. This was the world these players lived in. They had more money than they ever imagined, had women throwing themselves at them, drugs as accessible as chewing gum, and the world validating the star status the media had given them on a daily basis.

To their credit, some players resisted every time they were tempted by any of these things. However, most did not and some did drugs, some drank too much or caroused with women. Some even did a bit of each. Years after his career, Gooden revealed that he melded all of it together and that shattered all of his dreams. He loved baseball as much as anyone I have ever been around and could have been one of the great pitchers in the history of the sport.

That notion is one I hear from talk show hosts all the time but remember he lived in an era where recreational drug use was rampant. Decades before, alcohol abuse was prevalent and players such as Billy Martin, Whitey Ford, and Mickey Mantle were made out to be folk heroes by the media who covered the sport during that time. I must say my media contemporaries did a much better job of reporting off the field issues than those who covered baseball during the earlier era.

Writers such as Bob Klapisch and John Harper dealt with it head on while some of the veteran writers took a different approach, choosing which athletes they would attack while others they would turn a deaf ear to, much in the way writers did with Mantle.

Recreational drug culture was rampant in the locker rooms in the '80s, but if you think that culture did not also exist in the press box as well then you are clearly mistaken. The press could not afford the cocaine price tag as frequently as the players, but I did see it—especially when traveling on the road. When I viewed that, I would think these were the very same people who criticized the players for it. They all demanded regular drug tests for players but I wonder how many would submit to that themselves.

The Gooden drug case was handled very differently by certain members of the media as you could see that the younger reporters were more understanding while the veteran writers took potshots at the drug users. When Gooden returned to the mound after his rehab, columnist Dick Young demanded that the fans boo him.

That night, I remember sitting in the press dining room at Shea Stadium and a well-known columnist said to me that he disagreed with Young on this issue. He reiterated that booing him didn't serve any purpose.

As a young reporter my take was simple. I had been exposed in the corporate world to people I worked for who abused both alcohol and drugs. And I saw them enter rehabilitation with mixed results but also knew these problems were diseases—no different than cancer. Part of that rehabilitation was support—not serving as judge and jury. I don't blame columnists like Dick Young because they lived in a far different world than me and did not have the benefit of seeing the rehab process. But in the back of my mind, these columnists were the same people who thought drinking excessively was OK and even glamorized it. It was a shining example of "do as I say but not as I do."

It was a decade complete with decadence and for every ten people I knew, I would say about half did drugs with one or two of them having serious drug problems. If those numbers existed in society, why would a baseball locker room be any different?

I firmly believe that MLB began to police recreational drugs better as we approached the mid-'90s but labor disputes kept the sport from attacking it the way ownership wanted to deal with it. It was around that time that new problem in the room began taking root—vocational drug use as the steroid and PED era began in earnest.

Looking back twenty years later, we realize that every one of us dropped the ball during the steroid era, including the media that turned their heads because quite frankly we were fearful an incorrect allegation could end with a lawsuit. I certainly understand that but when I hear media members getting on a soapbox today when they could have reported things as they were happening, it makes me laugh. I can't criticize a media member for not reporting, but don't preach about it now.

I have heard so many writers and broadcasters actually incriminate players as users without any proof, which is totally opposite of the stance in the mid-'90s when there was circumstantial evidence that they chose to ignore. They have taken their power in the Hall of Fame voting to be judge and jury by decling to vote for certain players or making them wait to be inducted.

The bottom line with PEDS and steroids is simple and I know it is not the popular notion—players used them because they wanted better careers. The users did not use them to look better on the beach in a bathing suit, they did it to help themselves perform better and recover quicker from injuries. And despite steroids being banned since 1991, the only thing Major League Baseball did in those years was send a memo to teams reminding them of the fact.

Once baseball returned after a long work stoppage in 1995, the game needed a jolt and as home run totals hit new levels, Major League Baseball turned their heads. Never more so than in 1998 when Sammy Sosa and Mark McGwire began their assault on the single-season home run record held by Roger Maris. They heavily promoted it with ads featuring the phrase "Chicks Dig the Long Ball," understanding that the renewed interest in the game was largely due to the daily home run derby.

During that 1998 season, a bottle of Androstenedione was spotted in McGwire's locker and although that was perfectly legal and available over the counter, it was still strange to see it there in the open. Most media members ignored it but AP writer Steve Wilstein refused to. Here is an excerpt from his story written in 1998:

> Sitting on the top shelf of Mark McGwire's locker, next to a can of Popeye spinach and packs of sugarless gum, is a brown bottle labeled Androstenedione.
>
> For more than a year, McGwire says, he has been using the testosterone-producing pill, which is perfectly legal in baseball but banned in the NFL, Olympics and the NCAA.
>
> No one suggests that McGwire wouldn't be closing in on Roger Maris's home run record without the over-the-counter drug. After all, he hit 49 homers without it as a rookie in 1987, and more than 50 each of the past two seasons.

But the drug's ability to raise levels of the male hormone, which builds lean muscle mass and promotes recovery after injury, is seen outside baseball as cheating and potentially dangerous.

I believe this was the moment the awareness of steroids in baseball began and even though the substance was never tested for at the time in MLB, it cast doubt on what these sluggers would accomplish. In the press box, whenever we saw a player of small stature go deep to the opposite field, we called it an "artificial home run." A year after the home run chase, McGwire hit a home run that defied description at Shea Stadium, breaking lights on the right-field scoreboard 500 feet from home plate.

I had seen left-handed sluggers including Darryl Strawberry, Willie Stargell, Dave Parker, and Willie McCovey hit it that far to right field, but never a right-handed hitter. That day, I turned to fellow reporter Mike Mancuso and joked that Ivan Drago, the Russian opponent of Rocky Balboa in *Rocky IV* could not have even done that.

At that moment, I realized the game had changed forever and really started to believe that if I were a pitcher I'd start using it as well because the advantage for hitters was getting to be too much. And I guess pitchers indeed starting using as evidenced by Roger Clemens's bat-throwing incident in the 2000 World Series. As a result, MLB instituted a testing policy in 2001 but only for players outside of the team's 40-man roster with a fifteen game suspension for the first offense, thirty games for a second offense, sixty games for third offense, a one-year suspension for a fourth offense, and a lifetime ban for a fifth offense. But this was merely window dressing as a real testing policy that would matter was still a few years away.

In 2002, the US government decided they wanted to catalyze that testing plan so it formally told both MLB commissioner Bud Selig and Players Association chief Donald Fehr that a drug testing program plan must be negotiated in the collective bargaining agreement set to expire shortly.

This was the first step that would spin this steroid issue in the next decade as the sport's biggest problem. During these meetings, neither Selig nor Fehr represented the game very well, answering questions from the senators in double talk, blaming everybody but themselves.

It illustrated that baseball needed a culture change from the top of both portions of the organization and it came at a time when the country was a mere nine months removed from the 9/11 attacks. And both Selig and Fehr came off as executives that barely cared about the impact steroid use could have on young people because they cared about only one thing—the almighty dollar—and each of them only wanted to protect their portion of the bankroll.

Eventually, both parties constructed a drug policy that was a step in the right direction but only a small step. They came up with a Major League Baseball's Joint Drug Prevention and treatment program. It was an amendment to the collective bargaining agreement. It called for survey testing among all Major League players with no sanctions against positive tests—it was merely used to assess steroid and PED use. Now keep in mind the players knew this testing was coming and that meant PED offenders had time to clean out their systems prior to the random tests.

The agreement stated that any testing in 2003 where positive tests eclipsed the 5 percent mark of current players would immediately institute punishment for positive tests going forward. Most media members thought the process favored the players because they had time to prepare for the testing. It also was not going to test for THG, the newest banned substance and the test would be anonymous which we later found out was a fallacy when Alex Rodriquez's positive results were leaked a few years later.

The final results showed 5 to 7 percent positive test results among all players and to the surprise of some, punishment for future positive tests began in 2004. A first positive test would result in treatment with no suspension with a second offense meaning a fifteen-game suspension with second, third, fourth, and fifth time offenders moving up in penalty time to a maximum of a one-year suspension.

I was amazed that the amount of players testing positive was at that level and it proved one thing—marginal players and in some cases star players thought it was worth the gamble. This was confirmed as you could continue to see the use of amphetamines out in the open in the locker rooms. But I blame ownership as well here. The 162 game schedule takes place in a 180 day period with day games after night games and excellent on the field performance is demanded. So they decided to use every resource possible.

I am not defending their actions in any way but how can you only blame the players? Owners would have been willing to keep the status quo for years if governmental pressure did not occur. Things only got worse prior to the 2004 season as the BALCO case hit the grand jury.

BALCO was a sports supplement company founded by Victor Conte that provided assistance to athletes. The company began stepping up their product offerings by servicing football player Bill Romanowski, which helped Conte get more athletes as clients. Gregory Anderson was the middle man, providing supplements to players that were viewed as undetectable. One of the staple products was testosterone cream, which could be applied to the skin and be hard to detect.

Once a test had been developed to test for THG, the USADA began an investigation into Conte's business practices. As the BALCO case went to a grand jury, ten MLB players were asked to testify including Barry Bonds, Jason Giambi, and Gary Sheffield. Giambi was by far the most honest of the three as he admitted steroid use prior to MLB testing while both Sheffield and Bonds indicated that they did not knowingly take performance enhancing drugs, saying they didn't know what was in the cream.

The *San Francisco Chronicle* covered the Bonds story like a blanket and provided readers with an inside view including breaking the fact they were in possession of audio evidence that Greg Anderson (Bond's personal trainer) admitted Bonds knew the cream had steroids but he would never be caught. Mark Fainaru-Wada and Lance Williams collaborated the bestselling book *Game of Shadows*, which shed light on Conte's business plan for BALCO but really incriminated Bonds, whose reputation would be tarnished forever.

I don't pretend to know Barry Bonds, but I firmly believe he decided around 1999 or 2000 that his status as the best player in the game was slipping away after the McGwire-Sosa home run race gripped the country. Combine that with the Giants' disappointing loss to the Mets in the 2000 NLDS and I think Bonds knew what he had to do to get back on top. His record 73 home runs in 2001 and his breaking of Hank Aaron's all-time home run record will never be viewed as legitimate despite the fact he was never convicted of perjury or obstruction of justice.

The saddest part was Bonds was already a great player who mastered the art of pitch selection early in his career and coupled that with a talent level that is unmatched. But people will never recognize that no matter how many years elapse.

As time wore on, steroid use continued to take center stage. In 2005, former slugger Jose Canseco wrote a tell-all book titled *Juiced* where he revealed the names of steroid users and the media jumped on it with *60 Minutes* interviewing Canseco. To date, it appears Canseco is the only person that totally told the truth in his book and set a series of chained events that began getting a drug testing program together that had some teeth and would provide results.

Just three weeks after the book was released, commissioner Bud Selig announced that positive test results dropped from between 5 and 7 percent in 2003 to 1 to 2 percent in 2004, so as per the agreement no names would be released. Around the same time, the House of Representatives sent out a meeting request to baseball stars to appear at a hearing of the House Government Reform Committee which, in my opinion, was a rather comical waste of time as the committee was forced to subpoena the invitees who declined the non-legal invite.

The meeting itself proved very little. Both Sammy Sosa and Rafael Palmiero denied steroid use while McGwire simply refused to answer questions. But the political pressure was starting to get to MLB as they instituted the toughest penalties for steroid use the following November: first-time offenders received a fifty game suspension, second-time offenders were hit with a 100-game suspension, while third-time offenders got a lifetime ban. Amphetamines were part of the testing for the first time.

In 2006 federal IRS agents raided pitcher Jason Grimsley's home and secured evidence that he accepted a $3,200 shipment of PEDs at his Scottsdale home. He agreed to cooperate with the investigation but decided against it a week later when they wanted him to wear a wire to incriminate Barry Bonds and other players that he knew.

But on October 1 of that year, the *Los Angeles Times* released the names of the findings—Roger Clemens, Andy Pettitte, Miguel Tejada, Brian Roberts, and Jay Gibbons. More shockwaves occurred as Barry Bonds was indicted for perjury (a charge that he eventually beat with the help of his personal trainer, who served jail time because he refused to testify) and then the Mitchell Report was released, creating more grief for baseball in 2007.

That winter I decided I had to do something to make me a better reporter on these issues. I could tell what was a ball or a strike or when to hit and run but I was having a real problem discerning the legalese I was hearing on a daily basis. So I took online classes on contract law and paralegal issues and it really helped me discern things. It was one of the best investments I ever made in myself.

It proved valuable right away. Based on the Mitchell Report, Roger Clemens had to appear before Congress. He steadfastly denied steroid use even though his trainer Brian McNamee turned over syringes and gauze pads and his teammate Andy Pettitte, who admitted using steroids, concurred with the notion that Clemens took them.

I remember going on ESPN Radio the day Clemens was interrogated by Congress and reporting that I thought the government was constructing a perjury case against Clemens but the show host thought that was highly unlikely. I surmised this because what I learned in my online classes indicated to me the questions lawyers ask to plant the seeds for a perjury case and it matched questions Clemens was asked precisely.

So I was not surprised when Congress announced two weeks later that they were asking the Department of Justice to seek perjury charges against Clemens because "seven sets of assertions by Clemens were contradicted by other evidence." Clemens would eventually skirt past these issues but once again his reputation, much like that of Barry Bonds, would never be the same.

The next big name to drop would be Alex Rodriguez, who was named in Jose Canseco's next book, *Vindicated*, which sent shock waves around Yankee Stadium. The team had already been forced to deal with stories about Jason Giambi, Andy Pettitte, Gary Sheffield, and Roger Clemens, but this one was really troubling. Early in 2009 Selena Roberts and David Epstein revealed A-Rod was one of 104 players who tested positive back in 2003 on those "anonymous" tests, which we now know were anything but anonymous. He would eventually admit what he did but this would forever force people to look at A-Rod differently.

Two days later, Miguel Tejada, who was named in the Mitchell Report, pled guilty to making false statements to congressional investigators, becoming the first ballplayer to be convicted during the PED Era. He only received probation but this conviction was more of a symbol than anything else—the government wanted to show false statements can't always be evaded even though Bonds and Clemens escaped penalties.

A-Rod's problems would resurface again in the Biogenesis scandal where Major League Baseball suspended multiple players including Ryan Braun of the Brewers, who received a sixty-five-game suspension. A-Rod was hit with a 211-game ban after he obstructed the baseball commissioner's investigation. Rodriquez appealed the suspension so he finished the 2013 season but dropped the appeal and received a reduced 162-game suspension, which caused him to miss the entire 2014 season.

Alex Rodriguez is a complicated man to understand but my dealings with him have always indicated he is a kind and generous person who despite his talent has a ton of insecurities. I think people who don't like him pick up on that and make him feel unwanted. There are steroid users who did far worse things than A-Rod, such as Bonds and Clemens but at least A-Rod paid the price by facing up to it and serving his time.

I also discovered that sports fans are tired of PED stories. It has been an issue for the past two decades and they have had enough. Many of them love the game and could care less who took steroids or PEDs. The media handled recreational drugs so differently than vocational drugs and I really can't say why.

I've even heard fans suggest that the amount of injuries we see in baseball today is due to the fact that players don't use steroids or amphetamines and as misguided as that sounds, it might not be off base. But it speaks to the fact fans tune out when they hear a story about drugs.

These issues can be curbed by policies. Even though I was critical of how baseball handled both recreational and vocational drug issues at the outset, I do believe MLB has the best and most efficient drug policy of all the major sports. I think the NFL should come to the table and deal with it much better.

Granted, they've taken on the concussion issue but do you really expect me to believe that in the NFL very few players use performing enhancing drugs? I walk around NFL locker rooms and I find it hard to believe. I would never diminish the NFL concussion issues, but without a PED policy is the sport really tackling all of the major issues a player could experience after his playing days are over?

Alcohol abuse reigned in sports during the '50s and '60s and education helped curb those issues. For the next two decades, recreational drugs wreaked its ugly head and although it will never totally go away, learning about the disease and creating in-depth rehabilitation helped deal with that problem.

But performing enhancement drugs are a totally different issue. For marginal players it could provide them with lucrative contracts. And the users will always be ahead of the testers. The best we can do is create penalties that don't make the risk worth taking for an athlete.

Players such as Ken Griffey Jr. should be held up as examples of stars who let their talent speak for itself.

# CHAPTER 12

# 1994: A Year to Remember

WHILE COVERING SPORTS OVER THE past thirty years, many memorable years stand out. Both the Mets and Giants won championships in 1986, 2000 featured the return of the Subway Series, and 2001 was unforgettable as sports played a huge role in helping to heal after 9/11.

All of those years were special to cover, but 1994 had everything, combining championship moments, the national pastime fighting over the almighty dollar, and a court case that would socially polarize America like no other case had in the history of this country. As a reporter, I covered it all and in many ways, these events symbolized both the end of an era and what was in the offing.

I quickly realized after that year that being a sports reporter had migrated to a job that makes you the combination of a sports expert, legal reporter, economic analyst, and a gossip columnist. Covering the '86 Mets as well as athletes such as Mark Gastineau and Lawrence Taylor gave us a small taste, but 1994 brought it all front and center, changing the sports reporting world forever.

Once we lived through 1994, the game itself began to become secondary as those reporters who cared little about the game became more prominent and in some circles, more valuable than the veteran reporters who stuck to only reporting about what happened on the field.

The seeds for the baseball strike that cancelled the 1994 World Series were planted years earlier as the Major League Baseball Players Association became the strongest labor organization in the country through the hard work of Marvin Miller, whom I feel is one of the ten most important people in the history of baseball. I had a chance to interview him early in my career and I will never forget it. He was approachable and treated me like a veteran reporter but also explained labor issues, to me especially after I told him my dad was a loyal member of the United Auto Workers union.

Miller drummed up support for himself way back in 1966, visiting all the players in spring training and being named Executive Director of the MLBPA. In those days players were treated like cattle by the owners and Miller slowly whittled that away by negotiating collective bargaining agreements that gave the players rights they never had before. He got a 43 percent increase in minimum salaries as well as establishing the framework of arbitration to settle disputes, which would become the framework for years to come.

But these were all small victories with players trying to gain freer movement to go from team to team, ending ownership control. The efforts were not always immediately successful as star outfielder Curt Flood tried to challenge the reserve clause, which inhibited a player's free agency, all the way to the Supreme Court—a fight he eventually lost. Flood's battle ended his career as he sacrificed his entire livelihood to diminish the hold owners had on players with the reserve clause that bound players to their teams. In 1974 Miller used his power to make Catfish Hunter a free agent after Oakland A's owner Charles Finley failed to make an annuity payment and an arbitrator ruled the star pitcher a free agent, giving him the chance to sign a lucrative deal with the New York Yankees.

The following year Miller persuaded Dave McNally and Andy Messersmith, two high profile pitchers, to play out their contracts and not re-sign with their teams. Arbitrator Peter Seitz ruled them both free agents and effectively the reserve clause was obsolete, paving the way for free agency. Miller smartly limited the number of free agents to those with six years of service, creating a smaller pool of high profile players so the limited market would help salaries skyrocket.

In 1980 the players walked out of the first few games of spring training but returned for the start of the season, stating they would strike on May 23 if an agreement was not reached. On the morning of May 23, a strike was averted but the issue of free agent compensation was tabled as a players-owners committee would study the issue.

With that in mind, the owners unilaterally and without any input from the players made free agent compensation the law in the sport. When I think about this in today's world I have to laugh—they said a team signing a free agent would be forced to give up an amateur pick plus a player from their 25-man roster. Meanwhile, the players quickly set a strike date of May 29, 1981, putting the rest of the season in peril.

The owners knew the 1981 collective bargaining agreement would now be a contentious battle so they did two things. They purchased strike insurance, which would allow them to get revenue in the event of a work stoppage and they hired Ray Grebey as a negotiator. Grebey had held a similar role with General Electric when they were faced with labor strife.

It was announced after a meeting between the players and owners that a strike date was being postponed until the National Labor Relations Board had a meeting in which it would ask a judge to rescind the owner's unilateral compensation plan. The request was denied in court on June 10, leaving the players no choice but to strike on June 12.

This was my first foray into covering anything like a work stoppage and it provided me with valuable experience. In this pre-sports radio setting, much of that debate took place in the print media as veteran writers tended to support ownership while the younger ones sided with the players. This was a trend that would continue for the next thirteen years as work stoppages became commonplace in all of the major sports.

Both sides in the 1981 baseball strike started to polarize as talks became less commonplace with both Miller and Grebey using the media to validate their positions. On June 25 the owners began receiving their strike insurance while players missed their first paychecks around July 4. For the first time in over a century we were baseball-less on Independence Day.

For the next few weeks federal arbitrator Kenneth Moffett attempted to get a compromise proposal that both sides would accept. His first effort was accepted by the players but rejected by the owners. Each side then proposed to have certain aspects of the agreement sent to binding arbitration and both parties rejected the other proposal as the word stalemate began to enter into the media's coverage of the impasse.

As the strike plowed on, you could tell the disdain that Miller and Grebey had for each other even as a settlement was reached on July 31. The owners got some free agent compensation as a team losing a player to free agency got to pick from a pool of players from all teams. Play would resume with the All-Star Game while a split-season format would be employed. But the two sides seemed further apart in philosophy even after the agreement was reached and that tension would be around for some time.

Labor peace lasted until 1985 when a two-day strike occurred in August with the main issues being contribution to the pension fund coupled with that old issue–free agent compensation. Owners still wanted to institute a cap on salary arbitration awards. Peter Ueberroth, who had replaced Bowie Kuhn as commissioner a year earlier, brokered a deal that he demanded from both parties but to me this was merely a smokescreen used to shield the public from what the owners were planning to do to combat free agency.

For the next four years the owners got together and decided they would curb free agency by not succumbing to big contracts. The problem was this was illegal—no business can conspire in this fashion to violate a collective bargaining agreement. Yet even owners like George Steinbrenner agreed and stayed away from signing free agents.

Players such as Jack Morris, Tim Raines, and Ron Guidry were forced to take contracts from their existing teams as the market for free agents suddenly dried up. Finally, the union had enough of the owners who were hit with $280 million in damages. The owners really botched this plan as all they had to do was offer a few free agents contracts if they wanted their plan to work, but they could not even do that.

Fay Vincent, who served as the commissioner from 1989 through 1992, tried to keep an objective stance and came out against the owners in public saying:

"The single biggest reality you guys have to face up to is collusion. You stole $280 million from the players, and the players are unified to a man around that issue, because you got caught and many of you are still involved."

Marvin Miller even went a step further, saying that the former commissioner and owners' behavior was "tantamount to fixing, not just games, but entire pennant races, including all postseason series."

This was the beginning of the end for Vincent and final step in a series of events which would produce the 1994 work stoppage, the lowest point in the history of baseball. Vincent was forced to resign when a majority of the owners voiced a no confidence vote for him.

The owners wanted a commissioner who worked for them and not necessarily for the game. So after Vincent's resignation, Bud Selig, the owner of the Milwaukee Brewers, was given the position of acting commissioner. This was the first peg into the plans the owners had going into that point of no return—the 1994 strike.

It was apparent from the moment Selig took over he was the mouthpiece of the owners. After all, he had been an owner prior to being put in this position. And in June of 1994 ownership decided to withhold a payment into the player's pension plan of $7.8 million that was promised, so a strike date of August 12 was set in late July.

By this time in my career, I had covered plenty of labor talks in both baseball and football and this one seemed different from all of the others as the principals involved were not listening to each other and both Bud Selig and Donald Fehr of the Players Association were talking only through the media and not to each other. This was also the latest into any season that a work stoppage occurred and the chasm was so deep that it seemed baseball's worst nightmare would occur—no World Series.

This sport has been through so much dealing with players serving in World Wars and a gambling scandal by the 1919 Chicago "Black Sox," but we never lost the World Series until Bud Selig announced the cancellation of the Fall Classic on September 9, 1994. Fans were in shock and many turned away from the game as a fight between millionaires and billionaires angered them.

That anger continued though the offseason as both sides tried desperately to get their cases heard in a variety of courts. The owners decided to use replacement players but Peter Angelos, owner of the Baltimore Orioles, refused and the Maryland House of Delegates approved legislation banning replacement players from playing at Camden Yards. Many suggested that Cal Ripken's consecutive games played streak made Angelos lobby for this legislation to be passed.

Other issues cropped up, including Blue Jays home games having to move to Florida because Canadian law prohibited replacement employees from working during a strike. Sparky Anderson of the Detroit Tigers refused to manage replacement players and the courts got heavily involved. To this day, I think the baseball world owes Sonia Sotomayor, then a New York District Court judge (and curently a Supreme Court Justice), a huge thank you as she saved the sport by placing an injunction on the owners on March 31, which prompted a settlement.

Major League Baseball has not had a work stoppage of any kind since that 1994 fiasco and I firmly believe both sides paid a heavy price. Attendance slumped but the game survived its darkest hour and with time, fans came back to the sport.

When the players returned, I could see a visible difference in them as well in a number of areas. They were far more talkative than they had been before because I firmly believed they missed playing the sport they loved. Many were not in game shape until mid-season which I am sure catalyzed the use of enhancements we would see in subsequent years, but the game was back. I remember talking to a baseball executive in April of 1995 and he said the smartest thing I heard about all of this. "It is amazing that we could all be this stupid." I agreed and told him, "The only thing more stupid could be letting it ever happen again."

As big as this story was in 1994, it was only one of the stories we covered that year as the two tenants of Madison Square Garden, the Knicks and Rangers, both had unforgettable seasons. The Knicks had built a solid team centered around standout center Patrick Ewing plus some solid complimentary players in Charles Oakley, Anthony Mason, Charles Smith, and John Starks. Ewing was a star in every way—hustling every single moment, scoring like a machine, and becoming a powerful defensive presence at the rim.

Unfortunately, he was never fully appreciated by the fans or the media. He came to the view of New York while he starred at Georgetown University under the tutelage of the man whom I believe shaped so many players in Georgetown Hoya country, John Thompson, one of the greatest college coaches in the history of the game.

Thompson was not revered by the New York media because he represented the antithesis of fan-favorite Lou Carnesecca, who manned Big East rival St. John's bench. Thompson built a program where the development of his players was a rigid system in which he was preparing them for the world they would face after basketball. He wanted to win but also made them aware that young black players would always have to be careful about how they handled themselves and therefore shielded them from the media early on in their careers. Although it made my job more difficult, I understood it and respected him for it.

He knew most of his players wouldn't get the millions that players like Ewing would make, so they had to carve out a strategy that would breed success. During his days at Georgetown, Ewing had been treated terribly by the media as well as the New York fans.

Ewing led Georgetown to three Final Four trips during a four-year period highlighted by a national championship in 1984. When the Knicks won his rights in the NBA draft lottery, he suddenly became a person we would need to talk to every day. I will say this about Patrick—he was never unavailable but he did not cater to any reporter over another. He talked right after the game and if you missed him, you were out of luck. But he always treated everybody the same.

In those years, Patrick was a star in the sport but like many top players, they knew Michael Jordan was the superstar who ran the sport. But even Michael never won till he got a second superstar to play alongside him—Scottie Pippen—and it is not a shock to me that he never won a title without Pippen. Ewing was never afforded that opportunity but made the most of what he was given and benefited greatly from having a great coach in Pat Riley.

The reason Riley was such a force for the Knicks is he changed his coaching philosophy to cater to his team. While with the Lakers, it was "Showtime" with high octane scoring, but the Knicks were more of a defensive team and Riley saw that and coached accordingly. He knew Patrick needed the ball and tailored an offense to achieve that. Ewing's previous Knicks coaches did not always subscribe to that notion in a consistent basis but Riley saw it right away.

Under Riley and Ewing, the Knicks became the biggest show in town and celebrities flocked to the Garden because it was now the place to be. During this period of time, I covered far less baseball as I was told to patrol the Garden because of the success of the Knicks and Rangers.

Hockey was more of a niche sport but this 1994 Rangers team crossed over that line as Mark Messier, Brian Leetch, Mike Richter, and Adam Graves provided a quartet of stars that reached the fans in every way. The media coverage is also very niche in hockey as players and media often deal with each other on a first name basis. This Rangers team was special because Mark Messier made every single player feel like he was a big part of the team no matter how small their role on the squad.

Midway through the season, you could readily see both the Rangers and Knicks were poised in for deep playoff runs and my boss at ABC wanted me to cover both teams, which meant more home games and occasional road trips. It also meant I would be working just about every day from April 17 to June 22, covering games and/or practices for both teams. In those seventy days I managed to get two days off but I never felt tired. The energy of these games were beyond belief and I would not have traded those two months for anything in the world as I experienced what some reporters wait years to get a taste of.

Up to that point I had covered mainly baseball and this gave me depth covering the other sports, which came in handy with a long baseball strike on the horizon. It also made me aware that the landscape was changing, particularly in the NBA. In the baseball locker rooms I had been in up to that time, the writing press had control of the media sessions but things were a bit different in the NBA locker rooms.

There was more of an international flavor and many of these reporters gave us all a taste of the future as they were far more technically advanced than the domestic media. It was in the early stages of the migration to smartphones but cell phones were in full view in the NBA locker rooms even though teams had a rule you could not be on them while in there.

Locker rooms became so crowded with cameras and hangers on that most teams brought their stars into interview rooms that created a wall between the players and the media, not allowing relationships to develop.

Because of this, attending practices is very important since for the most part, far less media attended those sessions and you could get to know players more on a one-on-one basis. For me, it was very helpful as I was able to formulate a solid working relationship with players such as John Starks and Derek Harper. Both were extremely accommodating and would often grant me exclusive interviews

As the playoffs were set to begin, both the Knicks and Rangers had first-round series with their inner-city rival: the Broadway Blues played the Islanders while the Knicks tangled with the Nets. Both teams dominated their cross town rivals as the Rangers swept the Islanders in four straight games, outscoring them, 22–3. For Rangers fans, it provided some redemption for years of hearing that "1940" chant at the Nassau Coliseum.

After the game I remember how businesslike the Rangers were. They knew they still had much work to do.

The Knicks began their playoff run two weeks after the Rangers began theirs, opening their series with a win. I covered both a Knicks and Rangers playoff game in the same day on May 1: the Knicks took a two games to none lead with a 90–81 win over the Nets in the afternoon and that evening was Game One of the NHL Eastern Conference semifinals, where the Rangers beat the Washington Capitals, 6–3. I worked for eighteen hours and the time just zoomed by.

Also covering the twin bill were Mike Mancuso of WFAN and Bobby Grochowski of AP Radio. Bobby was the best hockey radio reporter ever created—he knew the game from top to bottom. I always felt my knowledge of hockey was the weakest of the four major sports I covered. Bobby helped me learn and appreciate the fine points of the game.

Mike controls much of the freelance radio work in the New York area and shares it so everybody gets a piece of the action. He has also brought along many young reporters and honestly cares about them.

Both teams plowed on as the Rangers beat the Caps in five games while the Knicks took five-game series from the Nets, three games to one. Pat Riley and Patrick Ewing would take on the Chicago Bulls minus Michael Jordan, who had retired from basketball and was playing minor league baseball.

That series would have so many twists and turns as the Knicks won the first two contests before the Bulls won Games Three and Four in Chicago, reminding the teams of their series a year earlier that the Knicks lost in six after taking the first two games at home. Game Five in '93 saw the Knicks blow it when Charles Smith missed several layups at the end but in reality, they lost it by missing 15 of 35 free throw attempts that night.

The aftermath gave us a taste of the way our media was beginning to change. It was easier to point to one moment at the end of the game and blame Charles Smith instead of the horrid free throw shooting. It was easier to find a scapegoat—in a sense it was one of the first Twitter moments I witnessed years before Twitter came to be.

I always thought Smith had to be fouled on one of those shots but I understand that's part of the game. I remember talking that night to reporter Dave D'Alessandro, who told me these breaks even out. Little did I know his words would prove prophetic one year later. With the Knicks staring at defeat, Hubert Davis got the gift of a lifetime. Referee Hue Hollins called a foul on Scottie Pippen late in the game, which left us all scratching our heads in the press box as Pippen didn't appear to touch Davis.

Hubert calmly hit the free throws to give the Knicks an unlikely 87–86 win and a three games to two lead in the series. The Knicks would lose Game Six in Chicago but win Game Seven in front of a raucous crowd back at the Garden, putting them in the Eastern Conference finals against Reggie Miller and the Indiana Pacers.

While this series was going on, I was also covering the NHL Eastern Conference finals between the Rangers and Devils, which New Jersey led three games to two heading into Game Six. Little did I know the upcoming two weeks would provide a number of storylines the likes of which we had never seen.

On May 24 the Knicks beat the Pacers in the series opener, but all I could think about that night was the guarantee Mark Messier made earlier in the day promising Rangers fans a Game Six win the following night. The captain of the Rangers was taking all the pressure off his teammates and putting it squarely on his own shoulders. The Devils took a 2–0 lead, but all I could remember watching was Mike Richter making save after save to keep the game close.

And then it happened—Messier set up Alexi Kovalev, who got the puck past Martin Brodeur and the score was 2–1 after two periods.

The Captain scored three goals in the third period—a natural hat trick—to give the Rangers a 4–2 win, forcing Game Seven at the Garden. Once again, Messier was understated in the postgame, knowing the seventh game would be a war and knowing what was at stake—the organization's first trip to the finals in fifteen years. He deflected talk about his his guarantee by heaping praise on both Richter and Kovalev in typical Messier fashion.

The next night I saw the Knicks beat the Pacers to take a 2–0 lead in the Eastern Conference finals, but the big story was the brewing rivalry between Spike Lee and Reggie Miller. Three games later, Miller and Lee really went at it but the seeds were planted in Game Two as Lee began riding Miller from his front row seat. In the present day world of social media, this could have developed into the one of the biggest feuds in history. Sports radio talked about it but the more pressing story the next day was Game Seven between the Devils and Rangers.

This had been a great series with two outstanding goalies, Mike Richter and Martin Brodeur, who were at the top of their game going head to head.

This game had everything you could ever expect from an all or nothing game. Brian Leetch made a spin move on Bill Guerin that defied description and the Broadway Blues had a 1–0 lead that they held onto for dear life until Valeri Zelepukin stunned everyone by tying the game with less than eight seconds remaining in regulation.

In those days, our hockey press box at the Garden was right in the middle of the crowd between the old green seats and blue seats and you could feel the anguish of Rangers fans.

Hockey playoff overtime isn't like anything else in sports because the clock is pointless to look at as the game could end at any moment and in this case, that would mean the end of the season. That first playoff period was complete with near misses for both teams but no resolution. Fans had to sit through yet another intermission.

In that second overtime period, after the Devils nearly scored, Stephane Matteau circled around Brodeur and put the puck behind him, giving the Rangers the win and earning them a trip to the Stanley Cup Finals. This moment was one of the most singular greatest broadcast calls I've ever heard. Much like Bob Murphy found the right words on the Bill Buckner play in the 1986 World Series, Howie Rose made the greatest call I've ever heard in the sport of hockey when he said:

*"Matteau behind the net ... Swings it in front ... He scores! Matteau, Matteau, Matteau! Stephane Matteau ... And the Rangers have one more hill to climb, baby, but it's Mount Vancouver! The Rangers are headed to the finals!"*

It is a call that will live in New York sports history right alongside Murphy's Buckner call and Russ Hodges calling Bobby Thomson's homer to give the Giants the 1951 pennant. It had clarity, emotion, and the precise question every Rangers fan was asking—*can we do this? Can we end this fifty-four-year championship drought?* It is so typical of Howie Rose, capturing the moment as well as anyone who speaks into a microphone.

After this incredible win, the Rangers locker room was happy but not ovefly so. The conference championship trophy was accepted politely but with little fanfare. These Rangers players knew that to make history they had one more mountain climb just as Howie Rose eloquently said the moment Mattaeu scored.

I covered practices the next few days since the Cup Finals would start on May 31 and the Knicks were in Indiana where they lost Games Three and Four, evening that series at two victories apiece. Game One of the Stanley Cup Finals went into overtime but this time the Rangers ran out of dramatic finishes, losing to the Vancouver Canucks, 3–2.

The Knicks and Pacers met in Game Five a night later and the feud between Spike Lee and Reggie Miller really heated up as Lee was in Miller's face most of the night but Reggie got the last laugh with a 39-point game highlighted by 25 in the final quarter, giving the Pacers a 93–86 victory, sending the series to Indiana for Game Six with the Knicks' season on the line. As the game was slipping away, Miller turned to Lee and put his hands around his own neck indicating Lee's Knicks were choking their season away.

The next night the Rangers evened the Cup Finals with a 3–1 win. My bosses decided rather than send me to Vancouver, I'd go to Indiana for the next chapter of the Lee/Miller battle. To Lee's credit, he showed up in Indiana and didn't hide from the negative publicity. This was another one of those moments I realized sports reporting was changing as a celebrity had entered center stage on a night the Knicks could be eliminated. The Indiana crowd followed Lee's every move and I think all that attention took pressure off the backs of the Knicks.

John Starks had an incredible night, scoring 26 points as the Knicks, much like the Rangers did in their Game Six at New Jersey, defied the odds by winning at Indiana, 98–91, setting me up to cover my second Game Seven conference final at the Garden in ten days. Meanwhile, the Rangers took a two games to one lead with a 5–1 win in Vancouver as Alexi Kovalev lit the lamp with a shorthanded goal. Pavel Bure of the Canucks was ejected after hitting Jay Wells in the face with his stick. Remember Bure's name because he comes front and center in Game Four. But first came Game Seven of Knicks/Pacers on June 3.

On my way to the game, I told my ABC Radio producer that so much chatter had been going around in this series about Reggie Miller and Spike Lee coupled with hatred between these two cities that this could be the perfect moment for Patrick Ewing to rise above it all and make his mark on New York forever.

Ewing did not disappoint Knicks fans as he pumped in 24 points, including a tip-in to seal the victory, but I will always remember his 22 rebounds—including 11 on the offensive glass—as the reason the Knicks advanced to the NBA Finals for the first time in twenty-one years. That was a special moment as Ewing hugged fans in the front row, many of whom likely booed him during his early years with the Knicks. It was a great celebration for a man I truly believe is, aside from Walt Frazier, the greatest Knick in the history of the franchise. He put this team on his back in Game Seven much in the way Messier dragged the Rangers into the finals with his Game Six natural hat trick.

I drove home that night feeling like the luckiest guy in the world— in the space of ten days I covered two Game Sevens that put a pair of teams in the Finals that had struggled for so many years to get there. The drama of covering moments like these is why you strive to do this job. But so much more was to come—including a murder case involving a sports legend that would change the way we report in so many ways.

The Rangers won Game Four on June 5 as Pavel Bure was stopped on a penalty shot by Mike Richter in the most pivotal moment of the series. The Rangers took a commanding three games to one lead in the Stanley Cup Finals and were 60 minutes from winning their first Stanley Cup since 1940. Game Five would be on June 9, they day after the NBA Finals began in Houston.

Most experts picked the Rockets to win the championship as they felt Hakeem Olajuwon would neutralize Ewing. Game One belonged to the Rockets, 85–78, as Hakeem outscored Patrick, 28–23.

So as June 9 dawned, Rangers fans hoped this was would be the night they waited for all of their lives. The Canucks had other ideas as they took a 3–0 lead in the third period but almost like a light switch turning on, the Rangers scored three quick goals to tie the game, sending Madison Square Garden into a frenzy. But just 29 seconds later, Dave Babych slipped one past Mike Richter and the Canucks escaped with a 6–3 win, putting the celebration on hold. The Rangers then lost Game 6 in Vancouver, 4-1, setting up the seventh game of the Stanley Cup Finals and putting their fans through a living hell waiting for game time on June 14.

The Knicks proceeded to win Game Two, sending the series to the Garden for the next three games. I covered Game Three on June 12 as the Knicks suffered a tough 93-89 loss to give Houston a two games to one lead

While the basketball and hockey championships were going on, a story emerged from Los Angeles that Nicole Brown Simpson, the wife of football Hall of Famer O. J. Simpson, and Ronald Goldman were found slashed to death with police witnessing a gruesome scene where Nicole was slashed so badly her larynx was exposed and they found a bloody glove.

At that point, detectives went to Simpson's estate to inform him of the attack and found more evidence including a second bloody glove as well as blood on a Ford Bronco belonging to Simpson. Here is where the LA police dropped the ball. They entered the home without a search warrant, providing a loophole a good defense attorney could leap right through with no problem. They decided to issue an arrest warrant for Simpson, who was questioned for three hours after which he hired Robert Shapiro as his attorney. Naturally, we were all curious where this story was going as we assembled for Game Seven between the Rangers and Canucks.

As I arrived at the Garden with my best friend, John Pezzullo, whom I had sat with in the press box numerous times, we agreed that nothing would ever be the same for Rangers fans. If they won, their fifty-four year drought was over and no future playoffs could equal the intensity that this year had held. At the same time, if they blew a 3–1 lead, Rangers fans might have said enough is enough because the pain would never go away.

There was a quiet anticipation in the crowd as this would either be the best or worst night in the lives of Rangers fans. The mood was electric but guarded even after the Rangers took a 2–0 lead on first period goals by Brian Leetch and Adam Graves. Trevor Linden, who played a marvelous game for the Canucks, got a shorthanded tally to make it 2–1 and then scored again to make it 3–2 after Mark Messier had restored their two-goal lead.

For the next 15 minutes and 10 seconds, Rangers fans bit their fingernails, put their head in their hands and generally saw their whole life flash in front of them with Mike Richter making great saves but nothing could calm this crowd. They'd have to live through three face-offs in the final 37 seconds of the game but the buzzer finally went off, giving them the moment they spent their entire lives praying for.

It was the greatest single moment I ever witnessed at Madison Square Garden as it was a massive outpouring of joy. I think only Boston Red Sox and Chicago Cubs fans could fully understand as their teams had similar long-suffering paths to championship glory.

This team will forever be in the hearts of New York and they shared the moment with the fans, spending what seemed like hours on the ice that night. I thought back to Messier's first coming to New York and the fact he was actually booed the year before this run to the Stanley

Cup. But he never wavered—he took accountability, made no excuses, and when the door opened a crack, he blasted right through it.

The next night, June 15, the Knicks evened their series with an impressive 91–82 win as Derek Harper and John Starks combined for an incredible 7-for-15 from three-point range, making this a best-of-three with many feeling the underdog Knicks had a real shot.

June 16 was an off day, but I went into ABC Radio to do some paperwork. The Simpson story was beginning to heat up as Nicole's funeral took place with O. J. front and center. Word began to surface that Simpson was set to be arrested the following day and I talked about it at length with veteran broadcasters Mike Harris and Fred Manfra, who both told me that they must have solid evidence if he was going to be arrested.

I went home thinking about the O. J. case more and remembering this was a guy I met a few times at ABC functions and now he was being charged with a gruesome murder of two defenseless people. Little did I know that the story had just started.

I woke up on the morning of June 17 knowing I had a long day as I was covering the Rangers victory parade in lower Manhattan and then heading to the Garden to cover Game Five of the NBA Finals. An historic day to be sure, but even I could not predict the type of history I was about to encounter. It would be a day where emotions would swing like a pendulum, from the euphoria of Rangers fans at the parade to the horror of the O. J. story, to trying to cover a Knicks game that could put them one game from an NBA title.

The parade was everything you would expect and more as this special group of hockey players bonded with the fans as they had all year long. It had been eight years since a sports parade took place in the city because the football Giants held their celebrations in New Jersey in those days. The 1986 Mets parade was a great event but this parade had a special quality to it because very few Rangers fans thought they'd live to see this moment. One fan held up a sign the night they won the Cup that simply said, "NOW I CAN DIE IN PEACE."

We hear so many horror stories about riots after teams win in other cities but I must say, whether it was the Giants, Yankees, Mets, or Rangers, New York fans always acted in a classy manner and on this day you saw so much hugging you thought you might be in a 1960s love-in. This was the first time a hockey team ever paraded up the Canyons of Heroes and it seemed fitting this was the team to do that.

The 1994 Rangers symbolized what is great about sports—leadership coupled with caring for each other are totally necessary in the sport of hockey especially with the Hall of Fame talent in their locker room.

More than that, they had stars living in the city touching the fan base on a daily basis. Granted there were some that lived up in Westchester County but Messier and Leech lived in Manhattan. They lived every moment as New Yorkers on and off the ice. They immersed themselves into New York and felt what every fan felt and that will forever make them special.

The glee of the Rangers parade was quickly dashed as we all started to hear what was going on in Los Angeles where the O. J. Simpson story was unfolding in a way that could only be described as surreal. He was scheduled to appear at the police station at 11 A.M. (2 P.M. New York time) but never showed up, so three hours later the LAPD issued an all-points bulletin as the world started to follow this story in amazement.

By this point, I arrived at Madison Square Garden to cover Game Five and all the talk was about O. J. with many members of the media getting to a monitor in the press room to watch coverage on CNN. About an hour before the game started, his friend Robert Kardashian read a letter (which sounded more like a suicide note) from O. J. to the media.

I sat in shocked silence, not really believing what I was hearing. Most times when non-sports news comes up that is controversial in nature, sports media types debate it during the pregame meal. At my table sitting with writers and broadcasters, there was dead silence as we all thought O. J. left the scene and wrote this note because he was about to take his own life.

We went to our press box seats because the game was about to begin but my mind was drifting thinking of one thing—O. J.'s children. They lost their mom and might be about to lose their dad in a very short period. I know a murder was committed but for some reason I could only think of his children. I was in a daze but had to snap out of it because ABC was relying on reports from me during the game.

In these days there was no texting or instant messaging and the press box monitors were tuned to NBC's coverage of the game but fans around our seats were telling us the sports bars at the Garden were showing the Knicks on one set and CNN on another other set. As halftime approached, I walked into the media center and everybody was watching CNN, and we could see that police cars were following O. J.'s Bronco at a snail's pace.

There were media members that thought we might witness him commiting suicide on live television. I returned to my seat and my monitor was on NBC, which had a split screen covering the game in a small box while the O. J. chase continued. Fans around us were listening to transistor radios to get news while watching the Knicks win Game Five, 91-84, to go up three games to two. The crowd really got into the game in the fourth quarter. Patrick Ewing scored 25 points, shooting 11-for-21 from the field in a game most of the nation did not see.

As we headed into the interview room, Knicks coach Pat Riley came in to talk to media and given his history in LA, you knew he would get an O. J. question. By the time he began speaking, the chase had ended and Simpson was apprehended while news leaked out that a disguise, his passport, family pictures, a loaded .357 magnum, and $8,000 in cash was found in the Bronco.

In those days, reporters were gathered in a huge room where an NBA media relations representative would hand them a microphone to ask a question. Someone got a microphone and asked Riley if he thought O. J. would have made it if he ran to the left instead of the right. It was an inane question and as MSG security guards charged towards him, he ran away at which point Mike Lupica started to try to chase him as well. Mike came back a few minutes later, being out run by a reporter who worked on the Howard Stern Show.

I finished my work for the night and headed home thinking I saw the full gamut of human emotion that day. The Rangers parade seemed like it occurred ten years before. We saw an American celebrity who was about to be charged with murder have police chase him slowly to try to prevent his suicide.

The Knicks traveled to Houston for Game Six and came within inches of winning an NBA title. They trailed most of the game but 16 points in the fourth quarter by John Starks brought them within two in the game's final seconds. Starks took a three-pointer that to this day I thought would go in, but Hakeem Olajuwon got a piece of it, ending the comeback and forcing a seventh game.

Three days later, Starks had the worst game of his career, shooting only 2-for-18 from the floor as the Knicks lost Game Seven, 90–84. Starks was grilled by the media, which seemed unfair especially that he contributed mightily in the comeback in the previous game. But I think it provided fodder for the new media that permeated sports talk radio. If Starks would have released that shot in Game Six a split-second earlier, he could have had the same hero status as Stephane Matteau of the Rangers. But that's how minute the difference between winning and losing is come playoff time.

As 1994 plowed on, the baseball strike took most of our attention from a sports perspective while the Rangers had to wait until January 1995 as the NHL owners locked out the players in a labor dispute of their own.

Meanwhile, the O. J. trial came into full view as Court TV and other outlets televised it live. Watching it, you could see how the defensive strategy evolved from refuting evidence to making this a racially motivated indictment. The media jumped on this issue and took it to the airwaves as the trial plowed on for months and months.

The prosecution had no murder weapon nor any witnesses but tons of other evidence that Simpson's "Dream Team" of attorneys attempted to discredit in a number of ways, including revealing that evidence was tampered with or that detective Mark Fuhrman was a racist who had a hidden agenda.

Prosecutor Marcia Clark seemed unequipped to handle the case, which, first of all, should have never been in Los Angeles since the crime took place in Brentwood, affecting the demographic makeup of the jury.

Secondly, I never quite understood why Al Cowlings was never subpoenaed to testify—he was in the Bronco and could have been forced to testify. The prosecution could have even offered immunity for the possible crime of aiding a fugitive in exchange for his testimony.

And the fact that Clark made O. J. put the glove on gave defense attorney Johnny Cochran the line he needed in his closing remarks, "If it doesn't fit, you must acquit." The prosecution bungled the case and I wasn't surprsised that the jury found him not guilty based on the evidence.

One thing I've learned from legal classes is there is a huge difference between committing a crime and being found guilty. The prosecution had an airtight case here but simply did not do their homework. They never researched Fuhrman's credibility and their lack of regard in scaling fences to get evidence as well as leaving it unattended made their case shaky.

But the biggest issue I simply could not understand is why none of the evidence found in the Bronco was used in the trial. All of it indicated Simpson was a fugitive who was considering fleeing.

From a media standpoint, the trial changed the way we cover stories like this and made Court TV a big-time cable network while also giving us a glimpse of how news stations would cover legal issues from now on. They all had to hire full-time legal experts and decipher the evidence in a trial that involved famous people.

The Knicks and Rangers continued their successful ways during the rest of the decade, but the Rangers didn't return to the Stanley Cup Finals until 2014, when they dropped the series to the Los Angeles

Kings. Meanwhile, the Knicks returned to the finals in 1999 with Jeff Van Gundy at the helm, after Riley left to run the Miami Heat.

Nineteen ninety-four was unlike any year in my career as it combined covering work stoppages and championship runs in the backdrop of the biggest court case in the history of this country. It made me a better reporter but it also help bridge us to the new world of reporting we were entering. Technology would soon change and sports talk radio would continue to alter the viewing habits of fans.

Covering the Knicks and Rangers runs to the finals was something I will never forget but I had to do it while also reporting on a greedy debate between millionaires and billionaires and following a court case that revealed domestic abuse had become one of the biggest problems we would have to face as we approached the next century.

It illustrated the dichotomy of life in this country—enjoy the fun moments but remember that greed and hatred will always be there.

## CHAPTER 13

# Subway Series: The Media Takes Sides

I STILL CAN REMEMBER MY uncles talking about the Subway Series and how the 1950s featured year after year of October drama in New York. Moments like Don Larsen's perfect game, Jackie Robinson's steal of home, Bobby Thomson's "Shot Heard Round the World," and the 1955 Brooklyn Dodgers reaching baseball nirvana. I marveled at their stories but had to be satisfied with the annual Mayor's Trophy Game between the Mets and Yankees, which did not even count in the standings.

Those exhibition games were well attended and had interesting moments, such as the lowly Mets walking out of Yankee Stadium with a win in 1963 but the games were missing a main ingredient—the result meant nothing other than a day of gloating in the neighborhood for the winner while the loser acknowledged that the game didn't count for anything.

The last contest was played in 1983 as scheduling made it very hard to play the game. The teams would occasionally meet in spring training with the only person actually caring about those games being George Steinbrenner, who actually berated Billy Martin for losing to the Mets. George always had this thing about the Mets because when he bought the team in 1973 all anyone in the city talked about was Tom Seaver and the Mets. He turned that all around by the late '70s, but once the Mets were sold by the Payson family in 1980, he knew the team was serious when they hired Frank Cashen, who was one the sport's premier baseball minds.

Steinbrenner felt he had nothing to gain anymore by playing the Mets, so the game was eliminated. That all changed when interleague play was introduced by commissioner Bud Selig, primarily to increase interest in the game being coupled with introduction of the wild-card playoff spot. The first regular season Subway Series was set to be a three-game encounter at Yankee Stadium in June of 1997. I thought the use of the term *Subway Series* was a misconception because it should be reserved for a World Series, but the sponsorship opportunities with the Subway food chain made the naming convention a reality.

I spent the entire week leading up to the first game interviewing players to set up this historic series. This was prior to social media and smartphone texting, but sports talk radio was in full force. The Yankees and Mets were years away from owning their own regional sports networks, so pregame shows were not yet highly developed. Cablevision, owned by Jim Dolan, had cable rights for both teams—MSG had the Yanks while the Mets were on the secondary MSG Channel, SportsChannel New York.

The Mets started Dave Mlicki in the series opener while the Bronx Bombers went with Andy Pettitte. This game was minus the two main characters that would later make this Subway Series percolate interest—Mike Piazza and Roger Clemens—who would not only divide the city's baseball fans but the media as well. That was still in the future as both players would not be heading to New York until the following season.

The Mets jumped on Pettitte and the reigning world champion Yankees in the first inning, plating three runs including a Todd Hundley steal of home and the blue and orange were never headed as Dave Mlicki tossed a shutout, beating their cross town rivals, 6–0. The postgame media sessions were held in a small room at Yankee Stadium where both managers, Bobby Valentine and Joe Torre, said that they were cognizant of the significance of the moment. The Yankees won the next two games to take the first Subway Series but the real winner was the New York baseball fans. I thought at that moment that our children and grandchildren would find it hard to believe it took thirty-five years for these two teams to play a game that counted in the standings.

As that 1997 season wore on, both teams had disappointing finishes as the Mets faded in the 1997 wild-card race while the Yankees lost their first-round playoff series to the Cleveland Indians. The Mets obtained Al Leiter after that 1997 season and traded for future Hall of Famer Mike Piazza in 1998 while the Yankees, fresh off a World Series title in 1998, added Roger Clemens to their staff. All the pieces were now in place for the reality show that was about to develop—Roger Clemens vs. Mike Piazza.

You could not find two personalities who were more different. Clemens was a loner in many ways while Piazza was a regular guy who you could find having a slice of pizza at his favorite Italian joint. Once traded to the Mets, Piazza was set to become a free agent after the '98 season but instead of testing free agent waters, he asked the Mets to hit his price and when they did he signed a seven-year, $91 million contract. Clemens, on the other hand, pinched every penny out of George's pocket that he could. After leaving New York to spend three years with his hometown Houston Astros, he returned to the Yankees in 2007, waiting until after the season had started to sign with them, receiving full dollars for pitching a little more than half a season.

The Subway Series was expanded to six games, home and away, in 1999. The first matchup in the Bronx in early June was an interesting series of games as the Yankees won the first two contests and after the second loss, the Mets fired pitching coach Bob Apodaca as their season looked to be in serious peril. Bobby Valentine's time as manager seemed to be in jeopardy and the next night Roger Clemens would try to sweep the Mets away. Their record sat at 27–28 and as I left the ballpark, I firmly felt things were getting out of control.

I got to the park early the next day and encountered Mike Piazza in the hallway. He said that the season is still early but this might be one of those games that could tell his team a lot about themselves.

Piazza homered off Clemens as the Mets grabbed a much needed win by scoring seven runs off Clemens. Roger made us all wait so long to speak to him after the game and when he spoke there were scripted answers but you could tell he got tense when the subject of Piazza's homer came up. Meanwhile, the Mets catcher merely talked about how lucky he felt getting a big hit off a great pitcher.

Clemens was getting some heat from the Yankees fans for his sub-par performance during his first year in pinstripes but the interesting thing was the division in the media about Roger. I had covered him during the 1986 World Series where there was a debate as to whether he asked out of Game Six or not. I have always felt he was phony. If you asked him a tough question, he would glare at you and most reporters looked intimidated when they asked him questions after a loss. One night he glared at me after a tough question. I looked right back at him and he gestured for me to go away as if my presence was insignificant. I did not take it personally but that was what Clemens did to people—if you were a reporter in his camp, he'd talk to you.

That win proved to be a watershed moment for the 1999 Mets season as it started a run in which the Mets went 70–38 in the final 108 games, giving them a 97–66 record—their best regular season record in eleven years, eventually earning a spot in the National League Championship Series against the Atlanta Braves.

The second Subway Series of 1999 took place at Shea Stadium right before the All-Star break and that first night Leiter and Clemens battled at even terms until Piazza went yard again off Clemens, giving the Mets the win. Clemens had to once again field questions regarding Piazza and it was apparent to everyone that he was annoyed about it. I recall going on the radio that night with a talk show host in town who was known to be pro-Yankee and he scolded me on the air for talking about Piazza being the best hitting catcher I'd ever seen. My response to him was, "Please remember this conversation when Mike is inducted in Cooperstown."

The media was beginning to take sides and it really surfaced the next day as a reporter who worked on the Yankees broadcasts saw me in the press box and told me that I was far too bold on the air the previous night. He called me a reporter with no baseball acumen and I laughed it off. When he asked why I was laughing I responded, "I'm just a no-name reporter and you've built a great career—why did what I said last night bother you so much? Maybe because it's the truth."

That afternoon, Piazza struck again, walloping a long homer off Ramiro Mendoza to give the Mets the lead in one of the best regular season games I've ever witnessed. The world champion Yankees took back the lead, but Matt Franco's two-run pinch single off Mariano Rivera won the game for the Mets, 9–8. As I entered the locker rooms, the Mets were elated but all the Yankees could talk about was they thought Rivera had struck out Franco on the previous pitch, but home plate umpire Jeff Kellogg missed the call.

The rivalry had officially heated up as Piazza's continued domination of Clemens along with both teams trying to reach the World Series made these games so compelling. But the best was yet to come.

The Mets made it to the NLCS, losing to the Braves in six hard-fought games after nearly forcing a seventh game in a series they trailed three games to none while the Yankees won their third World Series in four years as Clemens finally seemed to find his way.

As the 2000 season approached, the Mets added Mike Hampton to their pitching staff after nearly making a deal for superstar outfielder Ken Griffey Jr., who refused to accept the trade.

The first series was in the Bronx and once again Piazza vs. Clemens took center stage when Mike hit a long grand slam homer as the Mets plated nine runs off Clemens in five innings of work. As Piazza circled the bases at Yankee Stadium and the contingent of Yankees fans booed while the Mets fans hollered, you could tell Clemens was a seething time bomb on the mound waiting to explode. He had tried everything to get Piazza out—fastballs, splitters, and curveballs—but had no answers. I am sure this was the day  Clemens decided he was going to bean Mike Piazza. I have never been more sure of anything in my reporting life.

A rainout forced the teams to play a day night doubleheader later in the season that would put this Piazza/Clemens rivalry in the history books and would also create a debate between the media that covered baseball in this town.  The doubleheader would feature a day game at Shea Stadium followed by a night game in the Bronx. In the opener, Doc Gooden pitched against his former teammates, guiding the Yankees to a win.

In the second inning of the night game, Clemens hit Piazza in the head with a fastball and silence blanketed the crowd. Even Yankees fans stood in disbelief as Piazza lay motionless until he got to his feet. He suffered a concussion, which forced him to miss a few games, including the All-Star Game. In the radio press box, I uttered what we were all thinking, "I guess Clemens had exhausted every way of retiring Piazza and that's all he had left so he beaned him." A reporter who covered the Yankees turned to me and said Roger would NEVER do that on purpose. And a pretty fierce debate ensued.

After the game, Bobby Valentine spoke to us but I cornered him in the hallway to ask what he thought about the incident. He said to me, "You're a smart guy, what do you think?" I replied, "All I know is Piazza stands far away from the plate and this guy can't get him out." He looked at me and gave me thumbs up sign.

As strange as all of this was, things got even stranger. Piazza was being treated for a concussion and the word was that Clemens tried to call him but Mike was being treated. Clemens, took that as a form of disrespect and that was intensified when Piazza commented about the incident.

"I don't want to say he intentionally hit me in the head, but I think he intentionally threw at my head. There's no place for that in baseball.

"Roger Clemens is a great pitcher, but I don't have respect for him now at all.

"I could respect the fact of his throwing inside. Getting hit in the ribs and body are part of the game. But he has very good control; he only walked one guy [in 7 1/3 innings]. If he knew he had to come up and hit the next inning, I think he would have been more careful. I think it was very much an intentional pitch."

For his part, Clemens said the beaning was unintentional: "I'm glad to hear he's all right," the pitcher said. "It was supposed to be in. I wanted it to be belt high."

There was more to come as the teams played a Sunday night game at Shea and rumors of retaliation were flying. The Mets refused to let the Yankees use their weight room and this had now become a full-blown news story.

Radio talk show hosts took to debating this issue and for the first time I actually saw members of the media arguing loudly with each other in the press box on a news story. There were no more on the field incidents but the most interesting thing I took from all of this was the reaction from the Yankees.

Joe Torre and his staff blindly supported Clemens which was certainly understandable, but his teammates didn't exactly give him a rousing show of support. Derek Jeter, who was a victim of Clemens while he pitched with the Blue Jays, had no comment on it and to me that spoke volumes. I say that because the Yankees captain not only played the game the right way but also lived his life the right way.

He knew what Clemens was capable of and refused to blindly support him because he fell victim to it at one point. He was now his teammate and understood his talent was needed to win it all but just could not just agree with what he did.

The Mets' stance was they wanted to move past it but quietly many wondered why Mike Hampton did not retaliate in that Sunday night game. Off the record, many of them said they felt Piazza needed that support. The Mets catcher never said that was how he felt but I have a sneaking suspicion that he did.

The teams went on their merry ways, both making it to the post-season and heading on a collision course to the World Series. The Mets beat the Giants in the NLDS and manhandled the Cardinals in a five-game NLCS series win. Meanwhile, the Yankees beat the A's in the ALDS and the Mariners in six games in the ALCS and so the real Subway Series was finally here.

Naturally, the Piazza-Clemens war was a huge story but there was so much more at stake here. I wondered if the series would be even better if interleague play had never been adopted.

Game One was an exciting extra-inning contest that the Yankees took on an RBI single from Jose Vizcaino after Armando Benitez blew a ninth-inning lead.

The next day, the sports reporting world was knee deep in wondering what would happen when Clemens faced Piazza. Even a Hollywood screenwriter couldn't have predicted what happened in the first inning.

After Clemens struck out the first two batters, Piazza strode to the plate and he fouled an inside fastball off as his bat shattered with part of it traveling towards Clemens. Roger proceeded to pick it up and throw it at Piazza. From my seat in the press box I could not believe my eyes—nor could I believe Clemens was not ejected.

Roger totally lost control, much in the same way he lost it when umpire Terry Cooney tossed him out of Game Four of the ALCS ten years earlier. Piazza had a look of shock on his face but knew retaliating could only hurt his team. As much as I criticized Mike Hampton in that regular season Subway Series game, I just could not blame him here. After all, this was a World Series game.

The Yankees won the game and the postgame press sessions became downright comical. Joe Torre came into the interview room and was asked about the bat throwing. Mark Kreigel of the *New York Post* grilled Torre and the manager kept saying, "Why would he do it?"

Kreigel responded, "That's what we want to find out—why did he do it?" Torre stormed off but was ordered back to the podium by MLB. In a sense, he had to take the medicine for Roger.

MSG did a postgame show and Keith Hernandez was on the air with a reporter known to have ties with both George and the Yankees.

As the reporter went on that Roger did not mean it, Keith finally just said, "Can you take your Yankee hat off just for a minute?" That was classic Keith—he always speaks his mind.

The explanation we heard from Clemens was he thought the bat was the ball so he threw it. I was asked on a national radio show what my perception of that was and will never forget what I said. "Aside from the fact the ball is a different shape or size than a bat, all I can say if he thought it was the ball, why throw it at Piazza? Shouldn't he be throwing it to first base?"

What we saw that night was roid rage from Clemens—the world knows that now but many media members blindly supported Roger. I totally understood Torre doing that but not members of the media. I found it hard to fathom.

One reporter came running up to press box informing me that Mets first baseman Todd Zeile told them that he knows Roger did not intentionally throw the bat. Upon hearing that, I went right to Zeile. He told me that he said he would hope Roger did not do it intentionally but it certainly appeared he did. I had that on tape and asked the reporter to produce his interview with Zeile but he couldn't.

The Yankees ended up winning the Series in five games, but I kept working on a story I heard prior to Game Four. I heard that if the Series moved back to Yankee Stadium, Lenny Harris would be inserted in the leadoff spot to lay down a bunt against Clemens and charge him. I heard the story from two different sources but could never confirm it so I did not go with it. I am thinking in our current social media story this one would have had legs.

This feud would continue for a few more years as Torre resisted pitching Clemens in games at Shea so he would not bat but finally relented in 2002. Shawn Estes took the mound for the Mets and in fairness to him he was not part of the 2000 team, but he had to bear the brunt of retribution.

He threw a pitch behind Clemens, missing the target as Mets fans groaned. They had waited so long for this moment and Estes did not come through. Both benches were warned and then the impossible happened—Estes hit a home run off Clemens and later Piazza did as well, rounding the bases as he would any other home run and finally putting this feud to rest once and for all.

Piazza said after the game, "I don't really know what closure means." And in a way he was right. But he also proved he was the class act in this whole situation and Roger Clemens was not. Media members who dispute that are in my opinion either on the Yankees payroll or so intimidated by Clemens they refuse to criticize him.

I really feel this whole story refuted the notion that sports media is totally objective, myself included. For those who think the media doesn't take sides, think again. We are all people that have opinions about the game we cover and the people we interview. And quite frankly, there is nothing wrong with that.

People like Joe Benigno on WFAN have proven that. But that does not mean their take is wrong even if it is subjective. This past presidential election proved that as both candidates had their supporters in the media.

Sports talk radio lives on that notion as do many of the TV debate shows that have people screaming at the top of their lungs. If the truth be told, sports reporters have always done this. Howard Cosell told me that early in my career that objectivity does not sell and he honestly loved Muhammad Ali so he refused to just follow along with the media that was against him.

## CHAPTER 14

# 9/11: The World Would Never Be the Same

It was Sunday, September 9, 2001 and I had just covered a Jets-Colts game. I got a postgame bite at a local restaurant not far from Giants Stadium with some fellow reporters. I remember us having a few laughs and talking about our careers. Some of these guys are my best friends in the world—Mike Mancuso, Larry Hardesty, Bill Meth, Howie Karpin, Bob Grochowski, and Tom Mariam. Little did we realize that it would be our last night of sports reporting in the pre-9/11 world. We had all been through so much but were about to experience something two days later that we never thought possible—an attack on the mainland of this country from a terrorist group that wanted to see our way of life dead and buried.

The next day (September 10) I spent an off day in New York City meeting with  clients as at the time I was managing ad sales ops for Bravo. I remember walking around the city and having a great client lunch at the Oyster Bar in Grand Central Terminal before returning to my home in Bronxville, where I lived at the time. The next day I was scheduled to be at a meeting in Long Island and after leaving my house, headed for the Whitestone Bridge via the Hutchinson River Parkway.

As I began driving toward the parkway, I heard on the radio that a plane had crashed into the World Trade Center. As reports kept coming in you could readily undertstand this was not an accident—it was an intentional act of terrorism. As I drove over the bridge, the second plane hit the towers and all I could think of was that we were under attack and I was driving on a bridge—Could it be next?

I crossed the bridge and took the Cross Island onto the Long Island Expressway when I heard a report on the radio that one of the towers had collapsed. Drivers beside me were holding their heads and I personally knew many people that worked in that building, including my accountant, and hoped they could escape despite the horrific details I was hearing.

When I arrived in Jericho for my meeting, people were so unsure about what was happening, especially after the Pentagon was struck. Slowly details began surfacing that it was indeed a terror attack. I contacted my family assuring them I was all right, but with bridges all closed, I stayed in a hotel in Woodbury overnight, watching TV and finding out more about the attacks.

I walked around that night in a daze, stopping to eat at a local diner and feeling the pain of people who hadn't heard from their family members who worked in the building. After dinner, I walked around the area thinking the world I lived in the previous day was deep in my rear view mirror, never to be seen again.

Talking to my parents that night, I explained to them much like the Empire State Building was their crowning landmark, the World Trade Center towers were the same for my generation. I honestly felt it symbolized the greatness of life in both New York and this country—two towers that hit the heavens and connected our dreams to reality. Part of me died that day and will never come back. In the days following the attack, I found out I lost four friends in that building including the aforementioned accountant.

Mayor Rudy Guiliani did a marvelous job of trying to keep our city calm and showed why he is a great man—he honestly cared about everything we were going through and refused to abandon rescue efforts until every resource had been used.

The image of New Yorkers fleeing the scene of the collapsed towers running for their lives is something I will never forget and I will always remember the footage on news reports of parts of the Muslim world rejoicing at the news. As a country, we have fought numerous foes but this enemy was beyond dangerous—they did not mind dying, in fact, it was considered a heroic act that many aspired to be viewed as martyrs. At the same time, we were a country that valued life and the freedoms that make our country the most desirable place in the world to live.

The sports world came to a screeching halt and rightfully so. Games were the last thing on anyone's mind. The 2001 baseball season was delayed a week with both the Mets and Yankees set to return on the road with the Mets resuming in Pittsburgh before returning to New York for their first game against the Braves. Prior to leaving for Pittsburgh, the Mets had a practice at Shea Stadium, which I attended.

I was still walking around stunned and sat in the dugout with colleagues and friends I spent most days with in a place I felt was a second home, Shea Stadium. The home of the Mets had become a holding area for the supplies used in the rescue mission that was still taking place in lower Manhattan. Manager Bobby Valentine was front and center in these efforts as were several Mets players, the most notable being Brooklyn-born John Franco.

Sitting in the dugout that day, I remember hearing a plane fly over as I had heard thousands of times in my life as Shea's proximity to LaGuardia Airport made planes passing over it a constant occurrence. But on this day I looked up every time this happened because of 9/11. Omar Minaya, who worked with the team at that time under general manager Steve Phillips, noticed my reaction. We spoke about it and Omar noticed I was struggling with all of this, having lost friends in that building.

I will never forget that both Omar and Bobby Valentine spoke to me and this was not about baseball—it was because they could see I was not the normal amiable person I usually was. And then Bobby said something to me that really helped to begin to snap me back to where I needed to be. He said, "You're a reporter and a damn good one and you need to do what you normally do. If you don't then the terrorists win, and we can't have that." I will always appreciate Bobby for that moment and the fact that he did it in a quiet setting—not for others to see but because he could see I needed it. That's a side of him few people get to see and I will always be in debt to him for that important moment in my life.

The Mets played on the road for a week and as September 21 approached, we knew it would be a night we never experienced before as sports reporters. The game was secondary as the city was still in heavy grief and that entire week I saw the good in my profession as so many out of town reporters I had met over the years called me to see how I was doing.

Sports reporters like Les Grobstein in Chicago, Craig Heist in DC, Mike Luongo in Philly, Carl Beane in Boston, Ed Berliner in Miami, Bruce Morton in Denver, and Kevin Barnes in Atlanta all checked in on me and it spoke volumes of the closeness of the radio reporting industry. These were people I rarely saw (maybe once or twice a year) but there is a fraternity in our business that even makes competitors help out each other in times of need. And this was before social media—we used the telephone to talk to each other—that was social media we used then.

As I drove into the press lot at Shea, I quickly saw ballpark security was ramped up with officers stopping my car and looking underneath it to see if any devices were there. These officers all knew me but it didn't matter as they had to inspect every inch of the stadium parking lots.

Officers at the press entrance were also checking every bag we brought with us. In those days, I had a cassette recorder and they made me hit the play button so that they could determine it was not a machine that could prompt any kind of dangerous device. The officers kept apologizing knowing that we've encountered each other every day for decades but to tell you the truth this made me feel better because, quite honestly, the thought crossed my mind that 55,000 fans might be a great target for terrorists.

The pregame ceremonies were very emotional for me as I lost it on a number of occasions and my best friend, official scorer Howie Karpin lent his support for me to get through it. When the bagpipes were being played, it was such an emotional moment and the national anthem, which I have seen at hundreds of game I have covered, suddenly took on such greater meaning.

Right before first pitch, the Mets and Braves shared a moment I thought I would never see between these two rivals—handshakes and hugs to express solidarity. It brought the theme to my mind that sports is the toy department of the world but it is also somewhere we can lose the problems in our lives for a few hours. The problems will never disappear but we could find solace in our love of sports to help us through it. That was firmly illustrated a few hours later as Mike Piazza strode to the plate with a runner on and the Mets trailing by a run in the bottom of the eighth inning.

I knew from getting to know Piazza over the years that he was never afraid to express how much he loved baseball, God, the country, and the military. I also knew he was having trouble keeping his emotions together before the game. He had immediately embraced New York after he was traded to the Mets in 1998, spending numerous hours in Manhattan experiencing the city.

The best offensive catcher in baseball history totally understood the pain the city he loved was going through. He tried to help the best way he knew how—by hitting a baseball as far as he could to bring a smile to the face of the city he had adopted and truly loved.

As his bat connected with Steve Karsay's pitch, I just knew the ball would leave the park. I had seen that swing countless times in big spots turn the game around and convert a Mets loss into a dramatic win. But this one stands out as a home run that touched people who needed it most. As he was circling the bases, I saw people in uniform smile and cheer. I saw firemen hugging policemen, Mets fans hugging uniformed people who I am sure lost co-workers in the attack. Up in my press box seat, I mentioned to my colleagues that we would see tons of home runs in our careers but not a single one will ever surpass that one because none will ever have a bigger impact.

After filing my stories that night, I walked to my car in the Shea parking lot remembering that same walk after great events like the Bill Buckner game or the Robin Ventura grand slam single. But this one was different as it symbolized why we live in the best country in the world. My love of sports got me through the worst period of my life but more than that, illustrated that my colleagues, even those competing with me in their careers, were there for me in time of need.

The Yankees would continue that era of good feeling with a playoff run that defied description. The 2001 World Series against the Dia-mondbacks included two improbable comebacks for the Bronx Bomb-ers, which unfortunately ended in Phoenix with the home team beating Mariano Rivera in Game Seven to end the Yankees' championship run.

As time went on, the sports world, like life in New York City, started to return to normal. Security checks became the norm and entry in the baseball clubhouses became more scrutinized.

Remembering 9/11 became a concept that would unite the sports world in helping those affected by it. In many ways, no other industry has done more for it and, to this day, I think of September 11 every time I enter a ballpark.

That concept came full circle when I covered a Mets-Phillies game on May 5, 2011, as word spread across the ballpark that Osama Bin Laden had been killed. In this new world (unlike 2001) we all had smartphones and received the news. I slumped back in my chair and did not know how to feel. This would not bring my friends back but it was a rightful conclusion to his life. I knew both political parties would use this for their own purposes but that meant little to me. The fact I heard this news in Philadelphia, where so much of the great history of our country began, felt appropriate.

But I also realized 9/11 changed the way we report on sports as athletes are becoming more involved in political issues. The media demands to get their take on these issues and I always found that to be a bit silly. Athletes, actors, and singers have a voice but that voice is no more important than yours or mine. And social media has changed that. Kneeling during the anthem or explaining why they do so has become a staple theme for the media. We report on sports—not burning social issues. Sometimes the lines cross and editors ask us to cross it even further.

And I think that concept was born during 9/11. I am not saying that is all bad or even wrong but it has changed the industry. If it points out things that socially need to be changed, then I suppose it is a positive. But gone forever is sports reporting being the toy department I described earlier in this chapter. Much like our world was forever changed on 9/11.

# CHAPTER 15

# Women in the Press Box

As I BEGAN MY SPORTS reporting career in the mid 1980s, women still had not yet fully gained the access to the sports locker rooms that they have today. Once the process began, there were so many obstacles these women had to face and I saw firsthand how unfair some of the veteran sports reporters were to them.

Claire Smith and Suzyn Waldman were reporters who were pioneers in breaking down those barriers and bringing much needed diversity into the sports reporting world. I have had a great deal of respect for them both from the moment I first met them.

Claire Smith was the first woman to ever cover Major League Baseball on a regular basis for any newspaper, serving as the New York Yankees beat reporter for the *Hartford Courant* for five years and followed that up by being a columnist for both the *New York Times* (1991 to 1998) and *Philadelphia Inquirer* (1998 to 2007). She currently holds the position of News Editor of Remote Productions at ESPN. Her handprint can be vividly seen on programming like *SportsCenter* and *Baseball Tonight*.

She was the recipient of the 2017 J. G. Taylor Spink Award from the Baseball Hall of Fame, a long-overdue acknowledgement of her contribution to our industry. What Smith brought to the forefront is the fact that women deserved to stand alongside men in the locker room and she did it facing every roadblock you could imagine.

On my very first day covering the Mets in 1984, two well-known writers were chatting about how the presence of women in the locker room must be stopped. I honestly thought I was hearing a conversation in a time tunnel a hundred years earlier and could not believe my ears. In my early years in the business, I had female bosses while at both Lifetime and The Discovery Channel and any chauvinistic tendencies I possessed were knocked out of me. But so many male reporters were still living in this macho world and their worst stereotypes of women came to the surface every single day.

I was alarmed when I heard that Smith was physically removed from the San Diego Padres locker room during the 1984 National League Championship Series. To his credit, Padres first basemen Steve Garvey met her outside the locker room and agreed to an interview that forced Major League Baseball to declare the next day that equal access in all baseball locker rooms must exist.

Think about that for a minute—she was physically removed by some clubhouse attendant and treated like a prisoner. But she knew deep down in her heart she had to stand up for what she believed in and also was very cognizant this could be a watershed moment for all aspiring female reporters.

I talked with her briefly a few times in my early days as a reporter and she gave me solid advice on how to work every corner of a baseball clubhouse. I was impressed that she did this for someone she barely knew and her advice would only help me. To this day, I remember that when a young reporter asks me a question I try to demonstrate the same patience and class that she exhibited to me so I can help someone in the same fashion she helped me.

From a broadcasting standpoint, Suzyn Waldman is someone every one of us should look up to and I believe she is deserving of winning the Ford Frick Award presented by the Baseball Hall of Fame for her contribution to baseball broadcasting. I hope to be in Cooperstown the day she is honored. Suzyn appeared on the New York scene just as

WFAN launched—in fact, she was the first voice ever heard on that July day in 1987 when sports radio hit the Big Apple airwaves. I got to know her in early 1990s as she served in a multitude of roles at WFAN including Yankees and Knicks beat reporter while I was covering baseball and basketball for ABC Radio.

I enjoyed talking sports with her as she always chatted about it in such a conversational way. She also had a great attitude in the locker room as players really enjoyed talking to her and opened up in a much different way than they did with other reporters. When I joined WFAN in the mid '90s, we already knew each other and she always made me feel welcome whenever we worked together on a shift or when I saw her at the ballpark.

We should never forget that she brokered the meeting that brought Yogi Berra and George Steinbrenner together after a fourteen-year period in which the two did not speak to each other and Berra stayed away from Yankee Stadium. Both men might have never gotten around to mending broken fences. And she put that meeting together in her own way.

But I always heard the rumblings from some of my male media colleagues that they thought they were better than Waldman, and even if they were nice to her outwardly, they tried to discredit her at every chance. I noticed it at WFAN's studios in a vivid way one day when I was producing on a super busy NFL/late season baseball Sunday. Content was flying in all day that needed to be edited and Suzyn called in with a voice report that I told her she had to redo since Bernie Williams drove in four runs, not three as she had mentioned in the report.

She revised it and thanked me and then one of the other editors said to me that I should email management about the mistake because the editors always did that. I asked why as they sensed I questioned them with a very perturbed voice. They admitted that they only did that with Suzyn's reports and I said to them I would *never* do that to anyone. The important thing is the listener got the correct info and we are all here to help each other.

At that very moment, I totally understood why she would sometimes be gruff with the people taking in her reports. It reminded me of the idiotic conversations I had with writers who complained about the presence of women reporters. I learned early in my life that diversity is a good thing—and I was so lucky to be around Suzyn because her excellence taught me what I needed to get better at and she always offered advice in a one-on-one conversation—never in a large group. I will never be able to repay her for the help she gave me.

Suzyn was not only a pioneer for women but also for every one of us that serves as a radio baseball beat reporter because she created the need for this position that gave listeners inside information while providing an advertising revenue source for the station. If Suzyn and Ed Coleman hadn't done such a great job on their beats, I would never have been able to carve out my niche as a Mets beat reporter at ESPN Radio.

Waldman also became a radio talk show host at WFAN, later joined the YES Network, and now serves as a color analyst on the Yankees radio broadcast team with John Sterling. There is no woman in New York that has done more for eradicating the awful stereotypes that have existed for years in sportscasting. And she did with hard work along with caring about the young people in the business who will be our future reporters.

Two notable incidents that brought the plight of female reporters to the forefront involved Erin Andrews and Lisa Olson. While working at ESPN, I would occasionally see Andrews and was very impressed by her knowledge of college sports. She was able to break down a game like a veteran while at the same time deliver in-game interviews that were very interesting because she did not ask the typical questions.

In 2009 Andrews was the victim of stalking when an insurance salesman named Michael David Barrett took videos from an adjoining hotel room and was arrested on charges of interstate stalking. But the story got worse when it was revealed that the hotel was involved in the incident as it provided Barrett with dates she was staying at the hotel as well as giving him the adjoining room, granting him the access needed to record nude photos and distribute them on the Internet.

Barrett was convicted of the crime and a civil suit ensued where a jury awarded her $55 million in damages from both Barrett and the hotel. Andrews's personal privacy was violated in a number of ways and to this day, some sports reporters snicker about it, indicating she knew about the photos. Nothing could be further from the truth and I was outraged by the ease in which this stalker gained access to recording her in the nude and distributing it online. I give Andrews credit for seeing the civil case through without succumbing to the public pressure she had to endure—in essence, she became a victim twice.

Lisa Olson's story is just as troubling. While working at the *Boston Herald* in 1990, she was abused by several members of the New England Patriots who taunted her by walking naked right in front of her. Zeke Mowatt touched himself in a private place right in front of her which to me should have generated a season-long suspension by the NFL.

Olsen properly complained, calling the incident "mind rape" while Patriots team owner Victor Kiam called her "a classic bitch" and then told a crude joke in public, asking, "What do the Iraqis have in common with Lisa Olson? They've both seen Patriot missiles up close." Things got so bad for her that she received hate mail and death threats and her apartment was burglarized.

She ended up transferring to Australia to write but returned to the United States in 1998, taking a position with the *New York Daily News*. This is a great writer that was treated horribly by both the people who for all intents and purposes assaulted her while at the same becoming a victim again when both the Patriots and the NFL turned their heads. Meeting her, you can readily see that she loves sports and writes about it so well.

Another trailblazer for women in sports was Nanci Donnellan, "The Fabulous Sports Babe," who was a fixture in the early days of ESPN Radio. She performed the network's first weekday syndicated sports show and was so popular she was heard in more than 500 cities around the country. She was also one of the prime reasons ESPN2 got off the ground as her radio show was simulcast on the network.

She was a trendsetter in two ways: she became the first female sports show host to ever be syndicated nationally and also provided the first real glimpse of a national show combining entertainment with sports. I will be the first to admit her style was brash but it honestly gave us a peek into the future.

Another trailblazer was Robin Roberts, whom we think of today as a newscaster but she did great work at ESPN. However, the courage she has shown goes far beyond her on-air work. Robin has faced so many health issues, including both breast cancer and a disease of the bone marrow, and yet she continues to live her life to the fullest. In many ways, she was the most versatile broadcaster I've ever been around when you consider she excelled on both *SportsCenter* and *Good Morning America*. Her courage has no boundaries and every aspiring journalist needs to understand that she represents a professional that was given tough break after tough break but has never quit.

I firmly believe the trailblazers I have mentioned created an atmosphere where women can be treated equally in the sports reporting business. But there are always slipups and setbacks as we have seen over the years. I've been around so many women in this business I admire and I feel they must be applauded for never backing down.

They include Sam Ryan, Kim Jones, Linda Cohn, Hannah Storm, Meredith Marakovitz, Tina Cervasio, and Anita Marks. I have worked with each of them and their resolve is a direct result of what the female trailblazers did in setting the stage for an equal playing field with the male broadcasters.

The sad thing is every so often even today you see women media people treated badly. Men can never understand what they go through because they never had to walk in their shoes. The best thing we can do is point out these incidents immediately and fight for their rights to the same resources to do their jobs as men receive.

The Olson and Andrews stories bring out a huge point in today's world—stalking can lead to sexual abuse. I have become directly involved with the Joyful Heart Foundation so I can learn more about spotting it as its founder, Mariska Hargitay (star of *Law & Order SVU*) is constantly using her resources to get the word out.

Nobody is ever going to make me believe that the NFL did not have knowledge of the Ray Rice footage before it was publicly revealed. They hid it because they did not want a scandal. I credit Major League Baseball for taking far greater steps than the NFL in a number of ways. They hold players accountable while demanding they take the necessary steps in rehabilitating themselves. And trust me those steps are real—they are monitored by numerous people and commissioner Rob Manfred takes this very seriously.

And I firmly the presence of female reporters have brought these issues to light much quicker than they would have had diversity not been present in the sports reporting world. Sports always mirrors society and sometimes when society has to take big steps, sports needs to lead the parade. They did so in 1947 with Jackie Robinson. But women's rights in this business took years to develop and the sports profession should be embarrassed about that.

# CHAPTER 16

# Bobby Valentine and Rex Ryan: Unfair Media Coverage

BOBBY VALENTINE AND REX RYAN were two personalities I had the pleasure of covering on an everyday basis while watching the media misrepresent how important they were to creating successful teams. I was amazed to see how these two men were disrespected by a media base that really missed how much they meant to championship runs. They both fell short in that quest but I learned so much by being around them.

Let's begin with Bobby Valentine, the most brilliant baseball mind I have ever been around and he was so willing to share that with anyone that would listen. I firmly believe the concept that the reporters failed to see was that in the "media scrum" after games he would really not prefer to have a baseball debate but when you spoke to him one on one he was more than willing to engage in any conversation.

This is a man who possesses 536 wins as a Mets manager from 1996 to 2002 and took his team to two straight National League Championship Series which, by the way, is the only time the Mets have done that in franchise history. He got them into the playoffs in 1999 after trailing by two games in the standings with three contests left in the season, forcing a one-game playoff against the Cincinnati Reds, which put the Mets in the postseason for the first time in eleven years.

When that weekend started the Mets were behind two teams, the Reds and Houston Astros, in the hunt for the lone wild card spot. I distinctly remember being in the Mets clubhouse seeing some players already starting to pack their bags thinking they would be flying home after that weekend series against the Pirates. But Bobby would have none of it as he actually unpacked bags, putting personal items back in the players' lockers because he only wanted positive energy in that room.

Four days later, the Mets were on their way to Arizona for an improbable playoff appearance. The amazing thing is that this man knew how to control a game from the manager's chair. He absolutely took Buck Showalter, Dusty Baker, and Tony LaRussa—all great managers—to school in playoff matchups. Some might say he never found the answer to the Braves but let's face facts—that Braves staff was arguably the best starting rotation ever assembled and he did get the Mets to the World Series in 2000 after that Braves team was upset by the Cardinals in the NLDS.

Bobby V's teams always played with passion and desire, which is how I would describe him as well—an intelligent baseball man who wore his heart on his sleeve but also got every ounce of desire and passion from every one of his players. Marginal players like Todd Pratt, Benny Agbayani, Rick Reed, and Melvin Mora had their finest years at Shea Stadium because they had a manager who always believed in them.

He also understood that star players like Mike Piazza, Al Leiter, Edgardo Alfonzo, Todd Zeile, and John Olerud were not personalities that would jump up and down and get in players' faces. Yet Valentine knew their leadership in the room was important—so for the most part he let their subtle actions lead the group as well.

The beat reporters who covered the Mets in those days disliked Valentine and would jump all over the most minor things. Some refused to talk to him in the pre- or postgame setting, which I thought was so unprofessional. I remember Channel 5 reporter Tom McDonald would always try to get him into a heated debate and most times the

Mets manager would just laugh but one time he really undressed that reporter when he asked a question as to why he always rested Mike Piazza on Sundays and how that is unfair to fans who bought a Sunday ticket.

First of all, Bobby didn't always rest him on Sundays (sometimes he would sit him on Saturday) but the point is he was trying to get him to say something to the effect that winning is more important than what some fan wants. So Valentine proceeded to say, "I see you take most Saturdays off, Tom. Is that fair to your viewers?" It was a great response, and McDonald quietly walked away from the media session.

I also think people failed to get to know the real Bobby V who, to this day, is the most loved man in Stamford, Connecticut, because of how much he helps people. We all know the great work he did after 9/11, but I was around Bobby before he even became the Mets manager. He owned a sports bar in Stamford and I worked across the street as a bartender to generate some extra income. It was kind of an artsy bar and closed around 12 A.M., so I would often go go across the street to unwind with my colleagues to watch a late game after our shifts ended.

Many times he would come by and say hello and never made us pay for anything. He knew we were struggling and starting out in our adult life and he wanted to do something nice. It was not for credit—it was just because he cared about people.

In the dugout, he was a great tactician that was never afraid to try something new. He was the first manager I remember using five infielders in a walk-off situation where the home team had a runner on third and less than two outs in a tie game on the road. Now most managers employ that strategy and it is never questioned. But I remember a veteran columnist coming up to me and saying that it was an insane move. When I asked why he told me it was never done before. My response to him was that he has just described most innovative things in life—none of them were ever tried before.

Bobby was a fiery guy who never backed down from a confrontation but he also knew when players were dogging it and he would call them out. Those players would always run to the media and complain. It sold newspapers but everyone missed the point. As manager, it was his duty to call the player out and he would not be doing his job if he didn't. In those years, Todd Hundley was a core bat in the lineup but Bobby knew his lifestyle off the field could harm his career and some writers criticized the manager for hinting at it in a subtle way.

When Mike Piazza arrived (a deal Bobby begged the Mets to make) we all saw a perfect illustration that the future Hall of Famer was not only a better hitter than Hundley but also had his entire life in order—dedicating every ounce of his persona to baseball. Once again, Valentine's instincts were correct.

Valentine didn't have a great relationship with general manager Steve Phillips but sometimes that occurs with two dominant personalities. After the 2000 World Series, it was apparent that Ichiro Suzuki, a great Japanese player, would be coming to the United States to play in the majors. Bobby confided in some people that he would love the Mets to sign him because he watched him play and called him "one of the best players on the planet" but Phillips resisted his advice. Just think of how the Mets might have done had Ichiro worn their uniform in his prime years.

But it was not only the print media that took on Bobby V. The sports radio world also took potshots at him, constantly referring to Joe Torre as the genius in town while Bobby was the guy that wore a disguise after he was ejected from a game. The truth of the matter was Torre had far better personnel than Bobby did and if the situation were reversed, Bobby could have been just as successful in the Bronx as Joe was with the Yankees. Can you imagine if Bobby V had blown a three games to none lead in the LCS as Joe did in 2004? We might still be hearing about it but Joe got a pass. Those I sat with in the press box could never understand why I defended him. He helped re-awaken the Mets franchise during a period when the Yankees owned the town. A World Series championship eluded him but Derek Jeter contended that the 2000 World Series was as tightly contested a five-game series as you can imagine.

I also think people underestimate what Bobby V did in Japan with the Chiba Lotta Marines, guiding them to their first championship in thirty-one years, sweeping the Hanshin Tigers three years after being let go by the Mets. In typical Valentine style, he issued a challenge to the World Series champion Chicago White Sox for a seven-game series but that never materialized.

That win by the Marines made Bobby a cult hero in Japan and to this day he is a beloved figure for the fans of that team. The unfortunate thing is Bobby had a rough year in his final managerial season in the majors with Boston in 2012 and that's what people mostly remember. The media had a field day reporting on his failure with the Red Sox, but to me Bobby Valentine is one of top managers in Mets history, behind only Gil Hodges and Davey Johnson. As Gordon Gekko said in *Wall Street*, "Those are the facts—the rest of it is conversation."

Rex Ryan remains one of the most interesting New York sports personalities of the past three decades. He came to the Jets in 2009 to take over a franchise that was badly in need of a culture change. And from his first press conference, he made everyone quickly realize he would not back down from anyone—especially the media.

What impressed me the most about Rex was his prowess at building a defensive game plan that struck fear into the hearts of his opponents. He remains in my eyes the smartest defensive mind in the business, which the media never acknowledged because of his blustery personality. I firmly believe that was in some part due to the perception they had in their minds about his dad, Buddy Ryan, whom most felt was a great defensive coach but nonetheless was a substandard head coach.

This illustrates media's total lack of understanding about the complexities of coaching in the NFL. The game is very different than it was even twenty years ago in the sense that head coaches have a specialty—it may be offense or defense—but so much time has to be invested in one or the other that is impossible for a head coach to be great in both areas. That is why he relies heavily on the coordinator of the aspect of the game that is not his area of expertise. Most people simply don't understand that.

For example, Tom Coughlin, who won two Super Bowls with the Giants, was an offensive guru whose teams always moved the ball well but their defense had their up and down years. He was still a great coach because he focused on his best skills and his success depended on whether his defensive coordinators got it done.

I remember covering Rex in that first season and he was direct, blunt, straightforward, and honest with the media, letting them know he had no intention of playing second fiddle in this town or in this league. He was incredibly smart in that he could smell reporters who passed themselves off as experts from a mile away and treated them accordingly.

He was also able to understand how his comments would make headlines. He would say things like he did not come here to kiss Bill Belichick's rings, which angered the media but brought a smile to the faces of Jets fans.

We have become so used to politically correct responses in the press conference settings that a Rex Ryan session seemed so different. To me Rex was always refreshing and I contend when he was asked to tone it down by both the media and even the Jets organization, it turned him into someone he was not and hurt the team in the long run.

This was a man who took the Jets to two straight AFC championship games, something no head coach had ever done in franchise history. And in that second year, he did something I have never seen any coach do in the history of the league. He went on the road and beat teams quarterbacked by Peyton Manning and Tom Brady in consecutive playoff games with two completely different defensive game plans.

He went into Indianapolis and used a bend but not break defensive scheme to frustrate Manning and then devised a plan totally different in Foxboro, putting pass rush pressure right in the face of Brady and it worked perfectly, sacking the great Patriots quarterback five times. That is all I needed to see from Ryan to appreciate his greatness as a defensive mind.

My sense is that there is a little of Rex Ryan in all of us. But it rarely filters out into the real world and seeing him let it not only come out but dominate the conversation often made reporters angry. In many ways, some of the coverage Donald Trump receives reminds me of what Ryan went through. You never know what he would say but the bluster is what was covered, not the substance.

After some disappointing seasons, Rex was asked to tone it down and he complied. At that point, his media sessions sounded like every other one you would hear—boring and without any meat to it. And the reporters covering the team complained about that as well, saying that it gave them nothing they could use. One reporter said to me one day, "That session gave me nothing to write about. What am I going to do?"

I replied, "You guys are unbelievable. You had all your stories written for you by Rex for years and you complained about that and now you still complain when he is the politically correct coach you wanted him to be." I got a dirty look but really did not care—it had to be said.

Todd Bowles, who replaced him, has the persona everyone wants to see in a head coach, right? But his media sessions seem so scripted that I think I am watching a bad TV show—you know what is coming and he never says anything you don't expect, seeming to be on a 140-word Twitter limit in his responses. I don't blame Bowles because it is who he is. By the same token, I always enjoyed Rex's sessions because it was who he was—getting tattoos, giving opponents bulletin board material, and living the life he wanted to live.

After these sessions, we would all return to our work stations in Florham Park and I would hear a bunch of reporters using terms like *bully* or *punk* to describe Rex. I would always laugh because aside from Weeb Ewbank, he was the best head coach in franchise history. He wore his heart on his sleeve and created game plans that beat Peyton Manning, Tom Brady, and Philip Rivers in playoff encounters on the road. Even in years he missed the playoffs, he beat both the Miami Dolphins and his former Jets team in Week 17 games that had get-in scenarios for their opponents.

He was able to get so much out of his players because they know he always had their backs and would take on the media on their behalf. I would hire Rex Ryan to coach my team in a New York minute because his defensive brilliance and passion for the game makes him a winner—no matter what the reporters who covered the team think.

Rex Ryan and Bobby Valentine are two men who deserve far more credit than they received. But in a town where the media gets the last word, that simply won't happen. I enjoyed covering them both.

# CHAPTER 17

# Team and League Ownership of Networks Change the Game

THERE WAS A TIME YOU could count on a few things as a sports fan in New York: the Mets would be on Channel 9, the Yankees on Channel 11, there was the Saturday NBC *Game of The Week* and the peacock channel would also air the Championship Series followed by World Series. Phil Rizzuto was the voice of the Yanks along with Frank Messer and Bill White while Lindsey Nelson, Ralph Kiner, and Bob Murphy manned the mike for the Mets.

Home games for Jets and Giants as well as the Knicks and Rangers were experienced via radio as legendary voices including Marv Albert and Marty Glickman kept us glued to our transistors. Road games were televised with pros like Jim Gordon and Curt Gowdy guiding us through the game. Back then, corporations owned these channels and they paid the teams a franchise fee to broadcast games, keeping every single dollar of the advertising money.

As time went on, teams and leagues began to understand this advertising revenue was extremely valuable and the price tag kept getting higher and higher. The NFL's blackout of home games was lifted in 1973. Before then, many New Yorkers drove deep into Connecticut and booked hotel rooms to watch big home games. The Jets' AFL championship win over the Oakland Raiders that served as a prelude to their Super Bowl III win in 1969 never actually aired live in New York and was aired on tape delay that night at 11:30 P.M.

Public pressure made the government force the NFL to tweak the restriction. If the game was sold out seventy-two hours in advance, then the blackout could be lifted. Still, think about that in today's world—let's say you could not see your team's home games unless you drove seventy-five miles away to a hotel that had the game on TV and it was blacked out on every other form of viewing the game as well. You might have a Twitter revolt.

More than that, advertising was so primitive the networks had not yet developed the dynamic selling strategy we see today. NBC seized the opportunity to bring in the first real cash bonanza in selling ads on live sports.

Throughout the 1980s and '90s, all sports began to see that development and the NFL used their Super Bowl to brand the league in a way that the networks would pay heavily just to be a part of that brand. The executives at the then three major networks (ABC, NBC, and CBS) paid dearly for that relationship mainly because ABC proved in the '70s that pro football was no longer just a Sunday afternoon fall pastime—fans would watch it in prime time and make it a social event.

I can recall discussing this with Howard Cosell later in his career while I was at ABC Radio and he told me that *Monday Night Football* transformed the game into a social event and advertisers flocked to it like wildfire. He would do a halftime show featuring highlights from the previous day and club officials would actually be angry with him if their team's highlights didn't make the cut. Cosell's pregame set-up pieces were always must-see television as he could make you laugh and make you angry all in the same moment. I have always thought Cosell, no matter what you thought of him, helped transform the NFL from a niche sport to the game that resides in the souls of every sports fan.

Many credit the 1958 Colts-Giants overtime championship game as the moment that did that, but in my opinion the two people who had the most to do with it were Joe Namath and Howard Cosell. Both were brash and overconfident but extremely talented and delivered when they entered the biggest stage, Namath put the AFL on the map when he signed to play quarterback for the Jets and engineered, to this day, the greatest upset in sports history, validating the merger between the AFL and NFL. Joe Willie did it at a time when the generation gap was wider than ever but he appealed to both ends of that gap with his talent and a style that the younger generation gravitated towards, bonding dads with their sons.

Cosell did it in a much different way but with the same level of confidence we saw in the long-haired Namath. He spoke slowly, enunciating the right words loudly and pounded into our brains. He made football appealing to female fans as well because he gave us more than the game. *Monday Night Football* is now a shell of its former self and that is sad because Cosell built a foundation I did not think could ever be destroyed.

Sporting events were becoming more expensive to produce each year, and the threat of work stoppages made networks fearful enough to purchase insurance should a strike or lockout take away commercial inventory. And then the three networks were thrown the ultimate torpedo—the creation of a fourth network as FOX hit the scene in the late '80s with fresh programming and a burning desire to be involved in live sports.

By the early '90s, shows such as *Married With Children, Melrose Place, The Simpsons*, and *Beverly Hills 90210* established FOX as a big time network, joining the trio of networks to become a quartet of competitors. All this did was increase the money the leagues could ask for in rights fees. The first pin to drop was the NFL, when FOX outbid CBS for the NFC contract after the 1993 season, while NBC retained the rights for the AFC, leaving CBS without NFL football.

Five years later, CBS, knowing they had to bid out of the sky to get back in the football business, did just that. They signed an eight-year, $5 billion contract to telecast AFC games with FOX returning as the NFC network. This left NBC out in the cold and they tried to wrest *Monday Night Football* away from ABC but the stakes got too high for them. This began a huge decline at NBC Sports, once the envy of the industry, as they also lost baseball rights in 2000 and the NBA rights in 2002. They were so desperate for football programming that they partnered with Vince McMahon's Worldwide Wrestling Federation to launch the ill-fated XFL in 2001, which bombed out after just one season. They acquired NHL rights in 2004 but the league was in a lockout that cancelled the entire season and left a lot of eggs on the faces of NBC Sports executives.

NBC did not recover from this until 2006 when they got the *Sunday Night Football* package but by then the whole broadcasting world had changed. Most notably, the NFL had launched its own network in 2003. By the end of the decade, all four major sports leagues had established their own networks.

Locally in New York, the path was a bit different as teams began to explore owning their own channels because cable operators owned a monopoly, forcing teams to settle for less money in subscriber fees the operator had to pay. In some cases, the cable operators refused to televise games until affiliate agreements were agreed upon at lower rates.

The classic confrontation was between the Yankees and MSG Network. Way back in October 1969, the station that would become an absolute monopoly in New York aired its first event, a hockey game between the Rangers and the Minnesota North Stars. It was carried on cable television in Manhattan on an unnamed station. More than two decades later, after some shrewd deals by Chuck Dolan, MSG became a staple for the New York sports fan by not only airing Rangers and Knicks games but also creating additional deals to acquire Fox Sports New York, giving them the rights to televise the Devils, Islanders, Knicks, Rangers, and Mets. Prior to that, they had owned Yankees cable rights from 1989 through 2001.

MSG was owned by Cablevision, which also controlled millions of cable television homes in the tri-state area and they really tried to play both ends of the court. Cablevision put MSG in prime broadcast positions on their own systems while charging exorbitant fees for other networks like ESPN to share the same luxury, which was solid business negotiating.

When the Yankees decided to start their own network in 2002, Cablevision decided they would make it impossible for Yankees games on YES to appear on their Cablevision systems. Keep in mind they were now a direct competitor because in 2002 Cablevision began airing Mets games on MSG as a result of their acquisition of Fox Sports New York.

The Dolans had attempted to buy the Yankees back in 1998 but those talks fell through, making this story even stranger. Cablevision subscribers were unable to see Yankees games on YES for an entire year until the government intervened by brokering a temporary agreement that catalyzed an actual agreement in 2004.

But this whole situation symbolized the movement in sports broadcasting as teams and leagues began to get the idea that owning their own channels could prove to be a lucrative concept especially with viewing habits of sports fans beginning to change. The fly in the ointment was getting carriage on the local cable providers but once that was solved, the organizations would get to hold onto all of the sales revenue plus give themselves editorial ownership of the content that they provide.

Upon launching in 2002, the YES Network quickly revealed they were as concerned about editorial power as they were with sales revenue. When I first watched the YES Network, I realized what a government-run station would be like—the Yankees could do nothing wrong and if we gave them the time to solve world peace, they could do it in five minutes.

In 2003 Don Zimmer, the Yankees bench coach, publicly criticized owner George Steinbrenner and it became widely known that the YES broadcast truck was ordered not to show him on camera during their telecasts. I covered George in his heyday of being in the media eye every day and he had a way of proving his point in the strangest of ways.

In the '90s, the media parked their cars on a street near Yankee Stadium and were provided with yearly passes that were placed on the windshield. But this was the same time George was trying to hoodwink the city into paying for a new stadium complete with infrastructure that would alleviate parking issues.

One day to cement his point, he stood outside by these press spots directing traffic on a 100-degree July day as if no one else know how to do it. By the next day, those press parking spots were abolished because he decided that they were the cause of traffic. Typical George.

Covering the Yankees boss was a process in which you always thought, *Why does a guy who has so much act like this?* After many years, I realized it was just because he could. This new network provided George with his ultimate toy—he could create the news and control it all by himself and people would need to run to him to get it. More than that, he now had a stable of talent that would produce telecasts to his liking, stroking his ego in every way.

YES Network, to its credit, pulled in big advertiser numbers because the on-field play was compelling. But George loved the control, which was quite obvious when manager Joe Torre, a patient man, got regularly grilled by reporters who I am sure were told to act in that fashion. Again, typical George—*I pay top dollar so if I ask someone to jump, their only concern should be how high.*

In 2006 the Mets launched their own channel, SNY, and from the start you could see that from an editorial standpoint it was the total opposite of YES. To begin with, they covered the entire New York sports scene—not just the Mets—and I know for a fact from working at SNY.tv there was absolutely no interference from Mets ownership.

The channel hit the ground running but clearly had some things they had to tweak. Matt Yaloff did a great job handling the studio pre- and postgame shows but they didn't have a strong on-site reporter until the following year, when they hired Kevin Burkhardt, who manned that position flawlessly until 2014 when he left to join FOX Sports.

The Mets telecasts are flawless from a production standpoint for a number of reasons but the biggest of those is the best teamwork I've never seen in my thirty-plus years of covering sports. Unlike the YES broadcast team, the trio of announcers in the booth—Keith Hernandez, Gary Cohen, and Ron Darling—take on all issues honestly and directly even if ownership might cringe a bit when they debate a serious issue. Their production team melds a game plan into each and every broadcast that has no hidden agendas.

First Kevin Burkhardt and then his successor, Steve Gelbs, provide solid insight, but never at the expense of what's going on during the game that day. They both developed solid relationships with players and that enhanced their broadcasts.

The other aspect of the SNY broadcast that gets underreported is the work on-site producers like Matt Dunn do every single night. Other regional networks have people who do this but Matt stands on an island by himself. He knows quickness is important but is also aware that accuracy is as well and must be adhered to at all times. I travel around the country and have not seen another on-line producer do the job as well as he does.

I honestly believe the YES Network has similar levels of talent but corporate strategies limit their effectiveness. Jack Curry does a fantastic job on their studio shows and I have noticed that they have become a bit more critical in the past few years, which is a good sign.

The best illustration I can give you of how SNY covers a tough event was the night the Mets fired Willie Randolph in 2008. Earlier in Randolph's tenure as manager, Ian O' Connor wrote a story about how Willie felt racism could be an issue for him with the media. SNY tackled that story head on and got to Willie and members of the organization quickly, but the night he was fired was a little different story.

The organization did not handle the firing well and SNY pulled no punches, theorizing how it could have been executed in a much better way. I can only imagine how YES would have handled a similar story during the Steinbrenner years.

SNY makes a point of covering all the area teams and gives all of them their proper due including the Yankees, who receive regular coverage from the talented Sweeney Murti. The programming around the Mets broadcasts are different as well—they are certainly not puff piece productions as both *Daily News Live* and *Loudmouths* are unlike anything we see on the other local sports stations.

I am not claiming there is only one way of running a local sports channel, but the SNY model has longer staying power because it has swung with the times having programming which reflects the social media theme that permeates the sports culture we reside in today.

The other sports channel in town, MSG, tries to live in the middle, but I am sure Jim Dolan's bravado got in the way of that. The best illustration of it was the fact that Bob Page, one of their greatest talents, was underutilized. He was the antithesis of what Dolan wanted on the air—biting, unapologetic, and totally had no filter—he always said whatever came to his mind. In fact, my boss at ABC Radio hired him in 1991 to replace Howard Cosell on his *Speaking of Sports* show.

In my opinion, Bob Page would do very well today in this social media world. MSG looked down at his bravado but he'd be a star on a program like *Loudmouths*. Timing is everything and if Bob hit the scene in 2005 instead of 1988 he might have been as big a star as there is in our business.

On the national level, the real wave of the future is league-owned networks. The NFL Network and the MLB network are classic cases of leagues wanting the best of both worlds. They are charging exorbitant sums of money to networks for TV rights and still putting some games and other content on their stations making them must-carry channels on all systems at the price they want to pay.

Both baseball and football have great historical resources with NFL Films owning a legendary library of programs while Major League Baseball is the most historic and stats-oriented form of entertainment ever created in this country. These leagues know it and they present it in a style that fans of all ages can enjoy.

From an advertising standpoint, they also live the best of both worlds. They don't have to worry about reaching huge ad sales revenue numbers to eclipse rights fees but they do have a dual revenue model for themselves as they can charge subscriber fees for their network across the country with a myriad of cable providers while at the same time pulling in ad sales dollars because they own commercial inventory on the network. This is the model that the newspaper industry could have executed with the advent of the Internet. Luckily, the NFL and MLB thought this through in a much more intelligent fashion than the print industry did.

Viewing habits will keep sports on the TV screen because fans want to see live games. But the other sports programming we have today, on topics such as fantasy gaming and the trade deadline rumor mill are just beginning to percolate. For that reason, the industry needs to learn from past mistakes.

They need to be careful what is labelled as "free programming" because they will never be able to charge fans for something they can get for free. Television providers should make sure to negotiate digital and Video on Demand rights early in the contract talks as these platforms will continue to rise in popularity.

They should use all the resources available to them as the digital platform can not only be provided for viewing or listening pleasure but also to bring in advertisers by making embedded messaging available within programming. Sports viewing habits have become more and more interactive so those needs need to be catered to as well by promoting their direct input into every broadcast and placing ad sales dollars on that interaction.

Some of these ideas may not really seem pertinent to broadcasting a sporting event, but as the stakes go higher, they become crucial steps in monetizing every single broadcast minute. Deals like the one ESPN signed with the NBA need to be scruitinized. Maybe the worldwide sports leader does not need to own *every* piece of broadcasting rights in the four major sports. Maybe an MMA deal or one with NASCAR might be more cost-efficient.

The more networks spend on broadcasting rights, the better they have to be at thinking out of the box to make the most of the deals. I have heard too many programming executives say they must have the rights to a particular event, but if there is one thing I learned over the years, it is that any major sporting event can be covered as a news product—with no heavy broadcasting rights fees. The way to do this is to set up ad sales deals promoting news coverage a week prior to event with ad-tagged promos (*Our NBA playoff coverage is sponsored by...*), cover it like a blanket complete with billboards, in-program messaging, and spots, and then produce a recap show with more embedded sponsors.

I learned how to do this at ABC Radio when we covered the Olympics. The only thing we couldn't do was use the Olympic name so we referred to them as "The Summer Games." We provided our affiliates with exclusive content and were able to produce a myriad of pieces that even the rights holders did not have. These packages can be sold for for huge sums of money and the only overhead is talent and production—not exorbitant rights fees. I did the same at IFC with major film festivals like Cannes, Tribeca, and Sundance.

Sometimes you have to pay those fees because it fits your brand like a glove but those are special instances that should be the exception, not the rule.

Once change arrives, the normal reaction is, "Where did this idea come from?" In the case of leagues and teams owning their own channels, it was a combination of factors, but the creation of FOX, the fourth major network, got the ball rolling that created an avalanche of change.

# CHAPTER 18

# The "Los Mets" Era: Stereotypical Sports Reporting

WHEN OMAR MINAYA TOOK OVER control of the Mets after the 2004 season, he quickly elevated them to contender status by making a big splash in the offseason by signing Pedro Martinez and Carlos Beltran as free agents.

In my opinion, the New York media never gave Minaya the respect he deserved. He vaulted the Mets from also-rans to a final four team just two years after taking over a 71–91 team and was responsible for ending the Braves domination of the NL East. He also left the organization in much better shape than he is given credit for. Their 2015 World Series team was loaded with parting gifts from Minaya, including the likes of Jacob deGrom, Matt Harvey, Jeurys Familia, Daniel Murphy, Juan Lagares, Lucas Duda, and Stephen Matz, just to name a few.

In addition, Minaya made the move for R. A. Dickey, who his successor Sandy Alderson used to obtain both Travis d'Arnaud and Noah Syndergaard.

Clearly, Omar made some mistakes and my overall point is not to canonize his tenure in New York but it was clear to me from the day he arrived that there were members of the media that made sure the term "Los Mets" became a negative description of how he built the team. Many of them would mimic his Spanish accent and some radio hosts would edit his interviews to poke fun at the way he spoke. It was a disgusting display of childish behavior from people who obviously did not understand that marketing Hispanic players was a smart business move.

And the ironic thing was Omar was a totally accessible executive who always returned phone calls and made the Mets a championship caliber club with the help of his managerial hire, Willie Randolph, who was also disrespected by the media.

During Minaya's first spring training in charge, I readily noticed how the core media felt about this issue and I honestly thought it would just run its course but it never did. My feeling was it was up to me to learn about the Hispanic player's culture, not the other way around. So I spent time with them in that first spring training learning about their journey to the big leagues. Both Martinez and Beltran opened up to me so much that I began to understand how pure their love of the game was. Sure, it put millions of dollars in their pocket but these stars had it in their souls and that is what many of my colleagues just could not understand.

So many Hispanic athletes lived in poverty and baseball was a blessing even though the fields they played on were primitive and their equipment substandard. I visited some of these places in the offseason and saw firsthand the environment they grew up in. But I also saw the passion that these communities brought to the table every single day. Knowing this made my skin crawl every time I heard a beat reporter make fun of the accent a player had.

One veteran reporter noticed my dispeasure and would routinely ask me what my problem was but most times I would just ignore it until one day when I finally had to say something. I shot back, "You guys do this every time a different culture comes into your baseball world and I will never understand that." He gave me a death stare and we never spoke again.

I knew that once Carlos Delgado came to the Mets, he would never tolerate what the media was doing and quite frankly I loved it. I developed a great relationship with him and I believe to this day he spoke highly of me to his teammates, which helped me in a myriad of ways. At the time I was working at ESPN Radio and we had a show *New York Baseball Tonight* where I had to do a one-on-one pregame interview and I was one of few reporters Delgado would agree to that with, which angered my colleagues, even those that worked with me at ESPN.

Delgado once had a poor performance in a Subway Series game in the Bronx and I asked him about it. He reacted viciously to me and one reporter came up to me expecting me to trash Delgado, which I refused to do. My thought was he just had a bad day and he snapped. That is OK as he is entitled to feel frustration after a tough loss.

Before the next game at Shea, he called me over asking to speak to me in a corner of the clubhouse. A fellow ESPN reporter followed us, but Delgado asked him to leave, letting him know this was a personal conversation. He said, "Rich, I want to apologize—you have always been fair to me and I snapped at you the other night. You are the last reporter that deserved that."

I give him so much credit for that as most players would just let it go but he did not. It is also an example of why you develop a relationship with a player based on trust. We talked about so many things over the years and I learned so much about his culture. He is also a shining example of how writers sometimes get a preconceived notion about a player and refuse to ever adjust that opinion.

Delgado came to New York with an on-field résumé defining him as clearly one of the best power hitters in the game. He was an RBI machine. He showed that time and time again and nearly carried the Mets on his back in their failed 2008 playoff bid. And I firmly believe if he had been a white player, his entire Mets career would have been viewed very differently.

One veteran writer said out loud while we were in Philadelphia, "Delgado is a punk and I wish him and I could go one on one." At that point, I proceeded to laugh and when asked why I said, "That would be the shortest fight in history. But if you are determined, let's alert the hospital emergency rooms in Philly."

As time went on, every time the Mets would make a player move the quips in the press box would start. If a Hispanic player was added to the roster you'd hear, "Los Mets strikes again." If the player was not Hispanic, you'd hear, "What's going on? Minaya must have been told to do that."

That was an awfully stupid comment as Minaya simply picked the best player available with Paul Lo Duca, Billy Wagner, Shawn Green, and J. J. Putz being some key acquisitions during his tenure. But never let facts get in the way.

Which brings us to the Tony Bernazard story, which became the defining moment that led to Minaya's downfall. Bernazard was not the most politically correct executive I have ever been around. The first time we met, I introduced myself saying that I was the 1050 ESPN Mets reporter. His response was, "Big fuckin' deal." But there were times he was more talkative and I must admit he was a huge Daniel Murphy supporter, telling us one day he would become a dangerous hitter that could win a playoff series.

There were a litany of incidents in the Mets minor league system detailing times he had threatened players. After a series of these incidents were written about it in the *Daily News*, I ran into Adam Rubin, the writer who reported the story, while waiting for a postgame cab outside of Nationals Park in DC.

I mentioned to him that it must have been quite a week for him but he retorted that most don't understand that Minaya and Bernazard should both be fired and he should be working inside the Mets organization. I thought I was hearing things so I asked him to repeat it and he did.

A few days later, Omar Minaya announced that the team was terminating Bernazard's contract and I witnessed the weirdest presser I've ever seen. During the media session, Omar indicated the reason this issue took so long to resolve was that Rubin had been campaigning for a job inside the organization and he had to evaluate the merits of the report.

Immediately, I thought of the conversation we had earlier in the week. We had all heard Rubin ask the Mets about working for the organization in a number of positions and I thought Omar was telling the truth especially based on what he told me in DC. But I did think this was certainly not the time for Minaya to reveal this.

Right after the presser, Rubin conducted an impromptu interview session and I asked the first question. "I just want to be totally clear: did you ever ask for a job inside the Mets organization?" His response floored me. "It is no different what you are doing, Rich. Can I tell them?" At that point, I said yes because even though I had no idea what he was about to say, I thought saying no would indict me with a topic most thought I did not want to share.

"You are taking the LSAT these days, Rich." It was totally true but there was a basic difference—I wasn't asking Jeff Wilpon for a position nor was I trashing a Mets employee whose termination would create a vacancy in that department. Rubin repeated his claim during an SNY show in which he was a guest.

This created a tough position for me because my ESPN bosses had no knowledge of this and I think it put doubts in their mind about my longterm future. Ironically, Rubin would take a job with ESPN that had been promised to me.

And let me be perfectly clear—I would *never* blame Adam Rubin because he was just trying to carve out his future but I'd be lying if I said I wasn't bitter about it. Since then, we've become pretty good friends and I totally respect his work ethic.

The whole incident just brought out more hatred for Minaya despite him apologizing to the reporter twice, which I personally thought was overkill. But that disdain for "Los Mets" began to show its ugly face after this incident more than ever before.

Minaya was now in his fifth season on the job, and I knew things would not end well for him after everything that had transpired.

He left the organization in a much better state than he will ever be given credit for but the thing that infuriates me the most is the disdain Mets fans still have for the term "Los Mets" and that is so out of line. The collapses of 2007 and 2008 were hard to swallow but Minaya remains, in my opinion, one of the best GMs in franchise history.

Whenever I say that, people look at my last name and ask if I am Hispanic, which I am not. But it is downright insulting to think that only a Hispanic writer could give him any credit. I certainly criticized him when I needed to but his overall report card is a good one (not great but good) and saying anything other than that is nothing but Los Mets hatred.

But treatment of Hispanics was not the only issue with covering the Mets in those days. Manager Willie Randolph was often treated in a disrespectful manner by certain members of the media.

I enjoyed being around the man who put an end to the Atlanta Braves' run of fourteen consecutive division titles in 2006 but who never gets credit for it. Early in the 2008 season, Ian O'Connor wrote a story that Willie felt racism could be an issue in New York and even cited the media's treatment of former Jets coach Herman Edwards. Willie later rescinded the comments but I wish he hadn't.

If you think there aren't journalists in New York with racist tendencies, think again. It is a only a small faction of the press, but I sensed it during Willie's tenure as both Minaya and Willie had to deal with it. I covered Willie as a player and he was a great guy with a terrific sense of humor who was always available to chat after the game. When he became manager, most wrote he deserved the chance but I started to hear some comments that made me wonder such as, "Willie is a smarter manager than I thought he would be." What exactly did that mean? That a black manager can't be smart?

Early in his tenure, his pre- and postgame press conferences could sometimes get a little tense, but one day I had the opportunity to chat with him one on one and I was able to see the same side of him I enjoyed while he was a player. We talked about a variety of things other than baseball and from that moment on our relationship was great.

When I shared that experience with other reporters, most snickered, saying that it was up to Willie to reach out to them. Are you kidding me?

A few weeks later, Willie was sitting in the dugout joking with a group of reporters and trying to figure out what celebrities each of us looked like and when he came to me, I stopped him, saying, "C'mon Willie, don't say Tom Cruise—I get too much of that." He replied, "Yeah, you're Tom Cruise so I guess I'm Denzel." At that point, a writer mentioned to me that he thought Willie was being a phony. I started to think about the closet racism I witnessed twenty years earlier covering Strawberry and Gooden and thought that although two decades had passed, not much really changed.

Willie did a fine job in his first year as the Mets stayed in the playoff race until falling out of it in September, but he never let the team quit as they posted their first winning record in four years. In 2006, with more reinforcements obtained by Minaya, he led them to a 97–65 record—the team's best winning percentage in eighteen years. However, injuries to Pedro Martinez and Orlando Hernandez weakened the starting rotation when the playoffs began. Nonetheless, the Mets swept the Dodgers in the NLDS and forced a seventh game in the NLCS against the Cardinals.

This is where the media started to turn on him and I think they were totally off-base. In that Game Seven, he chose Aaron Heilman to pitch the top of the ninth of a tie game rather than his closer, Billy Wagner. He did it because Wagner had faded in this series, giving up a homer to So Taguchi that gave St. Louis a win in Game Two as he was starting to have difficulty getting right-handed batters out.

After Yadier Molina's two-run homer off Heilman gave the Cardinals a 3–1 lead, the Mets put their first two runners on base in the bottom of the ninth and rather than sacrifice them along, he had pinch-hitter Cliff Floyd swing away. Floyd struck out and we all know the rest, including Adam Wainwright striking out Carlos Beltran to end the series. After the game, the media piled on Willie and although I may have bunted there, I firmly believe it was one of those decisions that you could defend going either way as Floyd was certainly capable of getting an extra-base hit.

The 2007 season was different from the start as the media began questioning every move Randolph made starting in spring training. Behind the scenes, VP of player development Tony Bernazard was also criticizing him. He would make snide remarks about his decisions and that was feeding the media fodder for their stories.

Despite all of that, the Mets were 83–62 with a seven-game lead on September 12, but over the next three weeks they would win only five games and miss the postseason. Willie took the collapse very hard but never used one excuse the entire time, taking full accountability although you could feel Bernazard's hand wreaking havoc with Mets players. My sense is he wanted bench coach Jerry Manuel at the helm and knew if players challenged Willie, it would hasten his departure.

Omar Minaya went to bat for Willie after the collapse but a poor start in 2008 sealed his fate. Mangerial firings are a part of baseball but the way Willie was let go was hanndled very poorly. The team split a Sunday doubleheader and we all waited hours to see if Willie would board the team plane to the West Coast. When he did, we all thought he was safe for now. But after winning a game in Anaheim, Willie was fired, one of the strangest nights I've ever spent as a reporter.

Randolph helped change the culture in the Mets clubhouse and a break here or there might have given him a more successful tenure in Queens. For him not to get another shot at managing makes me think some of the things I've always thought—that racism does exist and like it or not, it will affect the perception people have when minorities are put in position of authority.

I heard the racist comments in the press box, so I know what Willie was feeling was real and not contrived. I lived through a period where reporters would say Magic Johnson is a great athlete but Larry Bird is such a smart player. I know what they were saying—the white player is smart but the black player is athletically gifted. I realize that these stereotypes will probably never leave the minds of some reporters.

In spite of the way they were treated by some in the media, it should never be forgotten that Omar Minaya and Willie Randolph were important reasons the Mets came within an eyelash of reaching the 2006 World Series.

# CHAPTER 19

# Fantasy Sports and Sabermetrics Enter the Mainstream

When I was a young fan, it was crystal clear that baseball was more numbers oriented than any other sport. You simply knew certain figures that stuck in your mind such as 714 being Babe Ruth's career home run total. The number 56 represented Joe DiMaggio's all-time top hitting streak. A total of 300 career wins or 3,000 hits were important milestones.

The other three major sports were simply not structured that way. If you wanted to talk about the top totals in touchdowns, rebounds, or goals scored you needed to take a trip to the library to look it up, whereas in baseball they were on the tip of your tongue.

Numbers began to appear more prominently in the 1980s as primitive forms of sabermetrics began to find their way into baseball press boxes. In my rookie year of covering the Mets, the team began using computers to track players and Davey Johnson was the first manager I could remember that began using computer printouts to help him put together his daily lineup. .

He would occasionally refer to this in his pregame sessions explaining some moves made in the previous night's game or relaying to us why the lineup looked a certain way. In many ways, Davey was a pioneer in using numbers but he also made it fit into his philosophy on managing a team. From the beginning you could see he hated the sacrifice bunt and despite having players who could run such as Mookie Wilson and Lenny Dykstra, the Mets were a power-based team. Much like Earl Weaver, the manager he played for with the Baltimore Orioles, Davey felt the three-run homer was the big weapon.

The term *sabermetrics* was not yet part of the mainstream baseball vernacular but so many of Johnson's philosophies would become the mission statements of people who would eventually bring that term front and center in the sport. As time evolved, stats like OBP (on base percentage), WHIP (walks and hits per innings pitched) and OPS (combination of on-base percentage and slugging percentage) replaced categories that had ruled player evaluations for years. Some began saying that RBIs, batting average, pitcher wins, and ERA were statistics that were no longer useful in baseball evaluation.

The sabermetric concept would gain even more steam as Bill James, who first coined the term, wrote many books taking this approach to evaluate players in a way that many baseball people had ignored for many years. After self-publishing his first few books, his *Baseball Abstract* hit bookstores in 1982 and I bought these books annually.

I have studied baseball statistics for many years and feel sabermetrics can be a useful tool but I do have a few problems with it. It has become a crutch for both the media and general managers to validate moves. I have always felt it is a tool but like the tools you keep in your shed at home, not every tool should be used to complete every task.

My point is that this concept has made everyone forget how to use their eyes to analyze a game. Pitch counts dictate so many things in a manager's decision making on when to go to their bullpen. But pitch counts are not created equal as a hurler could actually be more tired with an 85-pitch high impact outing than a 110-pitch effort that has very few of those high impact at-bats. But it is almost like managers attach this magic number to a starting pitcher and never deviate from it.

Another example is this attachment to WHIP as an end-all stat to evaluate pitchers. I do think it aids in the analysis but to totally discount ERA makes little sense. Let's say a pitcher has a high WHIP (1.5-2.0) but has a low ERA. Doesn't that tell you he has the strength to get through tough situations? That's why watching the pitcher perform is important—not just looking at his stats. Again, stats should contribute to decision making but should never totally replace actually watching a player.

One sabermetric figure I do think has helped in the analysis of hitters is OPS which combines two things that in past years were viewed separately—on-base percentage and slugging percentage. I also think the fielding metrics are helpful but again it should not replace the intrinsic things you miss on a stat sheet.

The best example I can give for that in recent times is Asdrubal Cabrera, the shortstop the Mets signed as a free agent prior to the 2016 season. All I kept hearing was that fielding metrics proved he was an average defensive shortstop at best. I only needed to see him play every day for three weeks to see that analysis was way off base.

The biggest on-field impact sabermetrics has had on the game is the defensive shifting that teams now do on a regular basis. Year ago, you only saw shifts when sluggers like Willie Stargell and Dave Kingman were at the plate.

We've gotten to the point today where not shifting is the exception, not the norm. As with most things in baseball, a new innovation gets overkill and some team will find a way to combat it. But until then it will be yet another crutch. By that, I mean if a player gets a game-winning hit because of the shifting you will always hear the losing manager say that the percentages dictated using the shift.

Sabermetrics came into full view of the media in the mid-'90s when Oakland A's general manager Sandy Alderson gave former player Billy Beane a position as chief scout and the two of them took analytics to a new level. Ironically, the A's had the highest payroll in the majors after appearing in three straight World Series from 1988 to 1990 but that changed when new team owners ordered a slash in payroll.

This duo found a way to get players who fit into their sabermetric system mostly because a limited payroll made them measure the construction of their rosters in a very different way. Beane had been drafted by the Mets but never quite made it, amassing a .219 career batting average despite being a first round draft pick of the Mets in 1980, the same year they picked Darryl Strawberry with the first pick of the draft.

Beane eventully became Oakland's general manager and built a team that was eminently successful, qualifying for the postseason four consecutive years starting in 2000. His success was explained in the book *Moneyball,* which became a Hollywood movie that explained his philosophies in a vivid fashion.

Beane never got to a World Series with his unique management style, which he once compared to how the financial world changed when he said:

"It's all about evaluating skills and putting a price on them. Thirty years ago, stockbrokers used to buy stock strictly by feel. Let's put it this way: Anyone in the game with a 401(k) has a choice. They can choose a fund manager who manages their retirement by gut instinct, or one who chooses by research and analysis. I know which way I'd choose."

The Red Sox tried to hire Beane but when he decided to stay in Oakland, they brought in Theo Epstein, who had far more money to spend than his counterpart in Oakland. Theo made some tough decisions that had sabermetrics written all over it, like dealing away Nomar Garciaparra for players whose salary and moneyball tendencies fit better on his roster than the hard-hitting shortstop.

Epstein is one of the smartest baseball men in the business and not just because he ended two long "curses" in both Boston and Chicago. He totally understands that "moneyball" is a concept that could help in the development of your team but he also knows there are times you simply have to overpay for talent knowing that contract is likely going to be trouble toward the end of the pact. In fairness to Beane, he did not have the cash on hand to take that approach but my sense is he was tied to his philosophies so much that might not have made a difference.

I firmly believe that Sandy Alderson used these concepts in building the Mets when he arrived in 2011 but not to the extent he used it in Oakland. As I stated earlier, it's a tool you use—but not the only tool.

The real positive part of sabermetrics has been that ownership in the sport has become more cost conscious than ever, which I think has assisted in the labor peace we've seen in the sport since 1995. There are still owners who will empty their wallets for free agents but the big difference is that it does not always create the bidding wars that were common in the past. Players have used the opt out clause to increase earning potential as a response to this, but I firmly believe owners are more cost sensible than they been in years.

I do think the media uses sabermetrics far too much in their analysis. With all of these statistics readily available, why does any fan need the media to recite them over and over again? I think most fans want a different take from us. They desire to hear the things they can't get from a stat sheet because we watch these players from spring training through the end of the season.

For example, at a recent Mets game I proposed in the press box that teams should bring their closer into the game in the eighth inning instead of the ninth inning if the middle of the lineup is coming to the plate in the eighth. I was actually told that they'd never bring in the closer that early at which point I asked, "Don't you want your best pitcher facing the other team's best hitters?" They responded that the manager would never do it because defying the formula could get them in trouble if it did not work.

Get them in trouble with who? The media? Managerial moves need to be executed based on situations and occasionally a hunch could bring great results. During the 1996 season, Yankees manager Joe Torre sometimes went with hunches deciding whether Cecil Fielder or Tino Martinez would be in the lineup at first base. And they weren't based on spreadsheets—they were based on his years of experience plus knowing the temperature of his players. That's what I miss the most with the advent of sabermetrics—those hunches that managers made in the past. Those days are gone forever.

The stat that annoys me the most is WAR (Wins Above Replacement) which might sound cool but do we really need it? If Yoenis Cespedes is missing from the lineup do I really need a number to show me that the Mets are not the same without him?

To me, it's pretty simple. You have a core group of players on every team—three or four hitters, two solid starters, a closer, and a set-up man in the pen. Those eight plus complimentary players that perform on an average level will dictate your season. Do you really need to see the WAR of those eight players to understand their importance?

I also think the numbers crunch has limited two offensive stats I still deem very crucial— batting average and RBIs. I understand that driving in runs can be dictated by many other factors, but if you have three or four players in your lineup with 90-plus RBIs, you should have enough to win if your pitching is above average. But I understand some saying that stat is not always an indicator because you need players on base in front of you to score runs.

But turning your back on batting average stats makes little sense to me at all. I always look at the on-base percentage but a .300 batting average stills holds serious weight to me no matter what the on-base percentage reads. This is another example where you must use the combination of your eyes and a stat sheet—not just one but both.

I know most sports reporters do not agree with me on this because in their articles you can't go five or six sentences without a sabermetric stat to validate their take. But there are people in the business that combine the old and new way of analysis. Kevin Kernan, John Harper, Andy Martino, Joel Sherman, Ken Davidoff, Mike Vaccaro, and Wally Matthews all do it very well.

The baseball/sabermetric marriage is here to stay but I hope as time passes, more people analyze players with a combination of eyes and stats. They did it for years in the sport and it worked. Let these new stats help you but remember what the great Vin Scully once said:

"Statistics are used much like a drunk uses a lamppost: for support, not illumination."

While sabermetrics have had a huge impact on baseball, the sport of football has changed in the eyes of their fans because of fantasy sports. Much like people who are not sports fans become bracket mavens in the month of March, it is equally hard to find a football fan who does not own a fantasy team. And sometimes they care more about that team that the squad in the league they actually root for every week.

Fantasy sports allow fans to draft a team among all players in the league and based on their combined stats they come up with a total amount of points which ranks them based on what their opponent's team does. There are many types of games and here are some of those:

Head to Head leagues where you play another team each week.

Total Point leagues where the annual point totals dictate the winner.

Salary Cap leagues—where players are auctioned off and teams must adhere to an overall salary cap.

Individuals put money into a pot and depending on the size of the league, the top finishers win money. Fantasy football leagues have become commonplace over the past twenty or so years whether it be in offices, family parties, or even among the media.

These leagues also allow you to trade players between teams and even pick up undrafted players off waivers just like any NFL general manager does. It has given football fans the inherent thought that they own their own team. Wide receivers, quarterbacks, running backs, tight ends, kickers, and even defensive metrics for teams make up your team's scoring with so many different derivatives used including yards gained  as well as touchdowns, with longer TDs getting more points than shorter ones.

The interesting thing about these leagues is that it does educate the casual fan on the personnel on teams. We've gotten to the point where a fan can tell you the third-string wide receiver on every team but I bet they can't tell you the top five offensive linemen in the league.

That's because offensive linemen don't have a fantasy stat. However, we all know the play of an offensive line can often dictate the success of a team. And that is sad because fans are missing one of the most important aspects in the game of football.

The NFL has received a huge financial impact from fantasy football as TV ratings remain solid in that fans watch until the end of the game. That's because their fantasy team may get yardage or a touchdown from a player late in the game even though the results of the contest they are watching is no longer in doubt.

The media began to cover the sport so differently as fantasy football became a staple crop in this country. Injury reports became important as fans need to revise their lineups.

The networks all began having fantasy pages on their websites which could be tailored to personal leagues monitoring all of their stats. Sites like CBS Sportsline provided leagues their own website pages and would keep live updates on NFL Sundays that would instantly update your team's stats.

In 2006 the NFL partnered with Sprint in a $500 million deal that would allow subscribers to draft and track their teams on their cellphones. And starting in 2011 the NFL started posting fantasy stats on the video scoreboards in all stadiums around the country. Sirius XM, which has an ongoing relationship with the NFL, launched a 24-hour radio network devoted entirely to fantasy sports.

Companies like Fan Duel and Draft Kings came into prominence the past few years and created organizations that became profitable quicker than any new companies I can remember in recent memory. Draft Kings received $304 million in fees from fans in 2014 and negotiated deals with both MLB and the NHL as well as a $250 million advertising deal with ESPN where they receive integrated branding on the channel through 2017.

As the money earned from all sides continued to increase, the government began to become involved and a debate ensued in New York. The companies did not view fantasy gaming as gambling, they called it a game of skill. The big issue in New York seemed to be that some upstate casinos wanted these games outlawed in the state because it indirectly took customers from them while the fantasy gaming companies refused to call these games gambling.

The issue was resolved on June 16, 2016, when the New York legislature issued a bill allowing fantasy gaming in New York. Five months later, Fan Duel and Draft Kings agreed to merge.

Sabermetrics and fantasy gaming have become such a big part of the sports fan experience. When either topic comes up in my reporting I try to find a positive in it. Fans know more about the sports they like because of fantasy sports and sabermetrics can be a useful tool if used the right way. What the media must now remember is fans generally care about two things—how did the team they root for do and how did their fantasy players perform? Not necessarily in that order.

# CHAPTER 20

# The 140-Character World: Social Media and the Internet

I SPENT THE FIRST TWENTY-FIVE years of my reporting career without social media—how did I ever survive? I often wonder how the industry became knee deep in social media without understanding the repercussions, but I think complaining about it just makes me sound like an angry old man. The truth of the matter is I resisted joining Twitter until May of 2009, which means I never used it while covering the Mets until they left Shea Stadium. Somehow that seems appropriate.

At Shea, we sat in the press box and actually watched the game while covering it, something you rarely see today. Twitter and Facebook have made each and every one of us think we are celebrities and here's a news flash—we aren't no matter what anybody thinks. When I bring up this topic, I think of one of my favorite movies, *The Paper*, with a star-studded cast including Marisa Tomei, Michael Keaton, Robert Duvall, Glenn Close, and Randy Quaid.

There is a scene in the movie where Close's character, Alicia Clark, is asking Bernie White, played by Duvall, for a raise and he tells her a story about covering the Olympics and overextending their credit in a bar drinking to all hours of the night. A famous person bailed them out and Duvall used that story to illustrate the point that they might cover celebrities but that does not make them one. I think about that every time I hear a reporter crow about their number of Twitter followers as if it validates them.

But the blame for that needs to be shared with our bosses. They demand that we spend time on Twitter and tell us even in our personal time, we must sign in and try to get more followers. They say we need to do it even if we are off the clock and tell us if we get beaten on a story on social media, it is our you-know-what. It makes us all fearful of getting beaten so much that beat reporters tend to all leave the postgame locker room at the same time, fearful they will get scooped on a story.

I was once chatting with Jose Reyes of the Mets after a game and could tell I was keeping the other reporters in the room from doing their jobs. We were not even talking about the game—we were talking about the best places he knew to eat Dominican food. He gave me the name of a place I wrote in my notebook and I quickly realized I was in a brave new world—beat writers were afraid that I might have scooped them on something. As soon as I left the clubhouse, everybody followed me.

Beat reporting is a long day as it is but this new Twitter world has made the job a 24-hour position and that was a change we all had to get used to because now it was becoming the biggest part of our job. When I began tweeting, some reporters still did not have access to Twitter. In 2009 the Mets PR department asked us not to tweet during manager Jerry Manuel's press conferences during spring training and most complied but two reporters were renegades and that actually made their fellow reporters much angrier at them than the Mets' PR team was.

There were arguments among reporters in the media dining room in Port St Lucie, but it didn't matter to me because as a radio reporter I could be put on the air and didn't have to wait until a report was printed on a website or in a newspaper. That spring training there were plenty of big stories as Citi Field was opening but I was not even on Twitter until May. The only reason I joined was my boss demanded it and little by little I used it more to promote on-air appearances on ESPN than to break stories.

The change was becoming evident as reporters in the clubhouse starting used phones to send Twitter messages and most were looking down on their phones more than they were talking to players. Again, I resisted as long as I could but now I had to comply with management. Some of the older beat writers just refused to do it and eventually got angry with those who did. It created a generation gap chasm between the old-school writers and the younger ones, which was interesting to say the least.

Words like tweet, retweet, followers, and hashtags became staple words in our world as fans began following beat writers and sports talk conversations started via Twitter. My take on all of this was this was I wouldn't let Twitter and its often negative approach make me sound snarky because it just wasn't me. But many of my fellow reporters (with a few exceptions) adopted a negative tone.

What began to happen was my takes brought out both the best and worst in my followers. Most of them are fine people who are passionate about sports, but some are downright scary and I have received some threatening tweets and messages over the years. One said they knew where I parked my car at the Citi Field press lot but I just ignored it. Nothing ever happened and my sense was that giving it attention would just fan the flames even further.

But at the same time, I am grateful to have great followers like Miss Met, Too Gooden 16, Robert Z, Michele Gladstone, Cindy Moskey, Kelly Betts, and the 7 Line just to name a few.

I try to answer as many tweets as I can but when it gets vicious I generally just ignore it. In 2013 someone using the twitter handle Dan X Tanna was arrested in Connecticut for stalking and harassing Mets players via Twitter. In one tweet, he threatened a girlfriend of a Met, illustrating that social media can be scary and dangerous.

From a professional standpoint, Twitter is a great vehicle to promote content by getting people to click on your writing or even an audio interview. It creates a great dashboard to get people to get to your content.

The issue I have with that concept is so many people put stories that merely are used to get clicks with things that are simply not true. That is extremely troubling. I don't appreciate the fact that some of my fellow reporters look down on all of the tweeters who really study the game from afar. There are so many young bloggers that I follow on Twitter and I love their research. In fact, it has helped me on a number of occasions.

A blogger named Michael Mayer (@themainemets) broke the Michael Cuddyer retirement story in 2015. He happened to be looking at the Mets official website and relayed via Twitter that Cuddyer was listed as retired. Most Mets beat reporters scoffed at it and called it a false tweet. But I decided to research it and when I heard blatant "no comments," I knew the story had legs. A few hours later, it all leaked out and Cuddyer went on to announce his retirement on the *Players' Tribune* website.

At that point, many others took credit for breaking the story but I just could not—this belonged to Mayer and I acknowledged it on Twitter. While I was vilified by many of my colleagues, I knew it was the right thing to do—the young blogger did the legwork and rather than steal the stoplight I decided to point it on him because his hard work needed to be recognized.

The funny thing about social media that all of us simply do not acknowledge is that our followers couldn't care less who broke the story, they just want the information and want to hear from the athletes or team management personnel that the story concerns.

But social media makes us all think we are stars and this becomes a tug of war. Normally I don't get involved is this "he said, she said" debate but this was a young reporter whose tweets about Mets prospects has always been dead on correct and he could use my support.

I really believe that my fellow colleagues don't quite get social media—it is an information vehicle, not a place where the negativity of their jobs and lives should reside. I have a theme of staying positive on social media which leaves me in the minority on Twitter. I refuse to disrespect those who might be critical of my views or attack me. If people believe these awful views of me, then they are not my close friends, and if they are my close friends, they will not believe these awful things. It is that simple and always will be.

Over the past decade, social media has merely intensified what started all of this personal branding—the Internet, which first hit the scene in the mid-'90s. The concept was a great one but the media made one big mistake—they lacked one single plan how to create revenue from this new method of communicating to their fan base.

The electronic media made a small effort to do it but the print industry simply did not and mostly that was because the newspaper ad sales professionals were not equipped to handle that. Daily newspaper advertising had been relegated to mostly car dealerships on Sundays and some even resorted to carrying ads for phone lines that participated in sex messaging. These salespeople lacked the ability to sell to bigger advertisers because they were door to door salespeople—not corporate account executives.

In fact, most newspaper advertisers migrated to signage on highways, train stations, sides of buses, or cab tops. Even the sideboards at Madison Square Garden during a Rangers game became more attractive places to advertise than the *Daily News* or *Post*. As advertising revenue continued to take a nosedive, the ironic thing is the Internet could have saved the newspaper business but because their senior management was ill prepared, they failed to take advantage of the opportunity.

They were even unequipped to develop an ad sales budget. As newspapers created websites, they allowed all of their content to be viewed for free, which made no sense to me because as the Internet grew, why would anyone buy a newspaper when they could read it for free? The revenue from newsstand sales would eventually disappear. Newspaper management contended they would make it up by advertising on their websites.

There was a plethora of problems with that concept as they failed to realize that advertising agencies set up totally independent contacts for each client that decided on digital advertising. The newspaper sales people did not know them and once they contacted them, the agencies quickly realized they didn't know what they were doing.

One ad sales vice president at a major ad agency told me that a *Daily News* salesperson informed him that all spots on a website would be valued by size of the ad, much like in newspapers. The problem with this was that certain pages would be more popular than others and should be priced accordingly. They also had no way of tracking amount of web visitors and would not guarantee anything on their deal.

The television industry was so far ahead of the print industry in this regard because Nielsen ratings showed numbers and validated the guarantee that advertisers needed to see in terms of viewership. This is why TV websites can actually make money while the print industry could only cite circulation but could never cite what pages people did or did not visit.

However, there were ways of tracking this but it cost money and the print industry refused to pay for them. Meanwhile, the TV industry had a way of tracking it and so digital advertising took off on broadcasting websites.

I remember having a meeting with the head of ad sales at the *Daily News* back in the late 1990s where I presented him with a plan to monetize the website. I used the TV model where you gave them a chance to build to revenue by making the first three years of the plan optimizing revenue for the website by charging a user fee. That fee could be 50 percent of the newsstand price used to develop website visitors and by the time three years elapsed, your ad sales revenue would grow. At that point in time your subscriber fees would begin to level off and then the ad sales revenue would take over.

When I brought up promoting various columnists on their own pages creating subscriber rates just to read them, he laughed me out of the room. His laughter turned to anger when I asked him a simple question: *If you're giving content away for free, how could you ever make money?* He called me a dope and asked me to leave his office.

As I headed down in the elevator, I realized the newspaper business was in big trouble. It might take time but this guy's take was as bad as the television industry not accepting the fact that pay TV would take off, creating a cable television concept that would allow viewers to get an unlimited amount of channels, and thinking giving viewers all of those channels for free would be a good idea.

Once sales revenue began to plummet, the newspapers tried to begin charging web visitors to view their online content, but the horse was already out of the barn—you can't start charging people for content you were giving out for free.

Right after that meeting at the *Daily News*, I met with my radio brethren and we decided to start a website called Sportsvoices.com, which would house audio content from every postgame locker room across the country in the four major sports. We were able to get an investment banker to give us seed money to start the business and had an office near Madison Square Garden.

We used the concept of the TV dual revenue strategy and started by encrypting the audio so that only subscribers could hear it. To attract visitors, we allowed them to access one or two designated games a night to give them a taste of what it sounded like. Later we set it up so it could be heard but not downloaded so fans could hear it but companies could not steal it. We made a few affiliate deals including some team websites and one of the largest radio networks in the country.

Once this got some momentum we started to try to get ad sales deals but knew this would take time because we had to get thousands of unique visitors before that could become a reality. Some of the top radio sports reporters were involved in this and each brought a skill set to the table.

Mike Mancuso of WFAN handled all of the scheduling, Mike Farrell ran the overall operation, Andy DeNardo of WCBS handled the technical aspects, Bill Meth of AP Radio handled day to day operations, and I took care of ad sales while Todd Ant of ABC Radio brought name recognition to the group.

We did well through the year 2000 but the investment banker went through a messy divorce and unfortunately we had to abandon the project. As with most things on life, the timing was off as I firmly believe if we had started this business a few years earlier or if the investor had come through, it would really have worked out for us. What we were hoping for was the business would survive for a five-year period and then we would sell the project to a bigger website.

Website content changed the industry in another significant way—long, detailed articles were no longer what sports fans would read. Social media has shortened their attention span and the game analysis became highlights on SportsCenter as they needed all their information in a neat little package. My generation watched or even listened to the game on the radio and viewed highlights on local television newscasts, making stars of sportscasters such as Warner Wolf.

We grew up understanding the game because reading newspaper columnists and watching sportscasts taught us the nuances of sports. That is missing today because young fans want the Cliff Notes version—who won matters but why a team won is not really important to them. And because of that I miss newspapers. In New York a great part of the summer was spent running to the corner to buy the paper, reading the sports pages, and debating it with your friends. This also taught you about the game within the game.

For the most part, today's columnists talk about their take on the game on Twitter world and maybe a five-paragraph column on their websites. It does not allow them to be who they really are—great writers who have a wealth of knowledge and the ability to tell the story within the story. Their editors want them to promote people clicking on the story rather than teaching young fans about the game and how little things sometimes win games.

The other casualty in this new Internet world was magazines that were such a part of my young life as a sports fan. Two magazines would never leave my side, *Sports Illustrated* and *The Sporting News*. One would explore the big story of the week in detail while the other became my baseball bible—giving me every stat and story I needed for every team in my favorite sport. I always looked forward to setting time aside to read them.

As time went on, the publications grew thinner and thinner due to lack of advertising and because the Internet kept narrowing the attention span of readers. *The Sporting News* eventually shut down the print publication and it is now merely a digital offering while *Sports Illustrated* still exists but many people read it on the Internet.

There is a website called *NY SportsDay* (www.nysportsday.com) that stands out as it was built with a grass roots effort by a reporter named Joe McDonald. He built a site where fans can learn about sports as he hired seasoned reporters who get to the root of the game within the game. Joe does not demand exaggeration of stories to increase visitors, he just asks us to be ourselves. I contribute articles for the site along with writers including Rich Mancuso, Wally Matthews, Howie Karpin, and most recently, Dwight Gooden. Another pro that really understands the concept is Matt Cerrone, whose efforts with MetsBlog has grown the site to a point that it is part of the very fiber of New York sports. Matt always understood how to grow it much better than some of the bigger bosses in the Internet industry.

On the other hand, Leon Carter was the poster child for how not to build a website when he was hired by to be the executive editor of ESPNNY.com—spending money without thinking about how the revenue could be accumulated. Joe McDonald and Matt Cerrone leave the ad sales to people who are experts, not uneducated salespeople.

The press release announcing his hiring stated that the only sports story in New York that would be bigger than Leon Carter coming to ESPN would be LeBron James coming to the Knicks, but Carter overpaid personnel and then abandoned the project when times got tough.

Carter wanted to reconstruct the business plan he used at the *Daily News*, which has become an advertising graveyard. The problem with hiring a newspaper executive to an Internet position is that most newspapers don't do a good job of branding their personnel but it is vital for an entity like ESPN New York to do so—a concept that Carter did not understand. He brought some great writers with him from the *Daily News* but left behind the best reporter on his staff—Frank Isola who, to me, is Mr. NBA.

At the time ESPN New York launched in 2010, the NBA free agent class was deep and Isola covered it better than anybody so I wondered why he did not make the cut? The answer was simple: Carter ran out of money and like the general manager who overspent without landing his big free agent he was stuck. He should have realized that he had radio personnel who could have doubled as writers, giving him more money to spend on the product or even save some for the future when he might want to reallocate dollars.

But like a child using his parents' credit card in college, Carter emptied the bank account and we now are seeing the havoc it caused. There were plans to also launch similar sites in Philadelphia and Washington, DC but those plans were thwarted by reckless spending. And when parent company Disney had poor annual reports, losing money on bad movie deals, we all knew where the ESPN casualties would surface. I remember explaining to Leon how the ESPN NY website could make revenue by partnering more with the radio station but he thought they were two distinctly different entities. He may have known how to put together a newspaper's sports section but he had stuck in his mind the old newspaper sales strategy of only relying on an archaic way of selling. That site could have sponsored individual pages of their talent like Wally Matthews, Andrew Marchand, Ian O' Connor, Adam Rubin, Rich Cimini, and Ian Begley—all of whom were very marketable writers. But it never happened and much like the newspaper websites, ESPN NY has become a cash drain on the company. ESPN.com will always exist but their city sites (also including Boston, Chicago, Cleveland, Dallas, and Los Angeles) will continue to be torn apart as the number of writers diminish each year and it did not have to be that way. The ironic thing is the company has Tim McCarthy—a real sales wiz in my opinion—and never let him take the reins from Carter.

CBS decided to launch an interactive portion of their company and hired people who worked at ESPN to manage it the right way, including two great programmers—the late Anthony Mormile and Kieran Portley.

Mormile, who left us much too early at he age of fifty, had led the a sports group at ESPN.com that created the first Emmy Award-winning football show called *Fantasy Football Now*. Once Mormile and Portley joined CBS, they fully understood that breaking stories was nice but Twitter makes that a fleeting victory and realized content and not necessarily having big names was king. There was a prominent writer working there whose contract was ending and he wanted a big pay increase but Mormile knew this would not be money well spent.

Mormile clearly understood how to be successful—create the content, make it valuable, provide it for a small fee, build loyalty in followers, and let ad sales evolve into building a long-lasting revenue baseline. Don't overspend for big names—spend on people that work hard and are hungry to combine job security with a long-range plan that provides salary growth with management that cares about improving their quality of life.

Simply put, build a foundation, create realistic budgets, and you should be successful in this digital world.

Organizations that bear watching as we head into the future include Deadspin, The Players' Tribune, and TMZ. Each has the potential to be a major player.

TMZ is a celebrity website that launched in 2005 and by 2013 was airing a program on every one of FOX's owned and operated stations across the country. They provide exclusive content that advertisers like Revlon and Chrysler gravitated to immediately despite some of their stories being outright fabrications like the "exclusive" photo of John F. Kennedy that was later proven not to be him at all. They continue to break story after story including the deaths of both Michael Jackson and Prince and have also broken major sports stories other outlets either ignored or simply failed to do their homework on.

The first of those came in April of 2014 when they exposed the entire story of Los Angeles Clippers owner Donald Sterling, who allegedly told his girlfriend not to associate with African Americans, causing a stir that resulted in NBA banning him for life. They followed that up later in the year by posting video footage of Baltimore

Ravens running back Ray Rice punching his wife in an elevator. Rice was indefinitely suspended after the report as the NFL botched the original investigation. It is hard to believe that nobody in the in the core media knew anything about these stories.

Unlike many broadcast outlets, TMZ doesn't have financial commitments with the NBA or the NFL and didn't have to worry about alienating the leagues.

Much like TMZ, Deadspin has broken stories that nobody else had, such as when they reported on Brett Favre's sexual misconduct towards Jenn Sterger. The strangest story was about Manti Te'o, the Notre Dame linebacker, who claimed the death of his girlfriend inspired his rise to star status. Deadspin discovered that the girlfriend never existed and a firestorm developed.

What was interesting is that all of this occurred on the heels of the Notre Dame's BCS championship game with Alabama that was televised by ESPN with hundreds of staffers and reporters at the event. Not one of them came up with this story, and I was told by people inside ESPN that the organization was furious about this and could not understand how Deadspin— which has a fraction of the resources ESPN has—could scoop them on this story.

Deadspin also made news in November 2013 when they "bought" a Baseball Hall of Fame vote from writer Dan Le Batard, who did not receive a cash payment and instead the money went to his favorite charity. As a result, Le Batard had his voting rights revoked permanently by the Baseball Writers' Association of America.

Deadspin and TMZ are both known for taking a number of potshots at players and on the other side of the spectrum is The Players' Tribune, which has become a vehicle for players to break news without the middle man—the media. It was founded by Derek Jeter and was an absolutely brilliant concept as he has already brought in advertisers like Porsche, Powerade, Red Bull, and Toyota—a quartet of heavy hitters.

The athletes that have come to the table read like a who's who list: Kobe Bryant, Matt Harvey, Richard Sherman, Steve Nash, David Ortiz, and Kevin Durant just to name a few. With names such as those, the content sells itself and more importantly, connects the fan directly to the player.

# CHAPTER 21

# Covering the Resurgence of the Mets

OVER THE PAST FEW YEARS, the Mets have returned to prominence in New York much in the same way they did in the mid-'80s. You would think the media would have seen it coming because of the similarities, but their dislike for the Wilpons clouded their objectivity. I saw this transformation coming and it was an easy observation to make because Sandy Alderson is a current-day Frank Cashen in terms of his baseball intelligence and ability to look at things both short- and long-term.

The Bernie Madoff scandal made reporters think that could force the Wilpons to sell and even after getting help from Major League Baseball most of them thought they would eventually be forced to sell the team. I knew that would never happen but also realized the team would be forced to take an unpopular way of rebuilding the franchise— not spend on free agents in a way the fan base desired but instead build a foundation by developing the excellent core prospects Omar Minaya gave the organization as a parting gift.

I must admit that in the beginning I was hesitant to think this plan could succeed until I went down to spring training and saw the young arms develop year by year, starting with Matt Harvey, whose stuff was so electric I watched him every time I could.

As each year passed, I saw more pitchers arrive and each impressed me but the thing that really stood out was the yearly evolution taking place, which was a testimony to the organizational restructuring in the team's minor league system.

But the mood covering the Mets in those years during spring training was that they were headed nowhere and that the ownership was holding on to a business they could not afford to maintain in a way New Yorkers wanted to see from a major market team. I saw it differently because I covered the team during the '80s and understood that building a solid foundation had to take priority before any major financial commitments would be made.

Frank Cashen looked to add pitching prospects at every turn and Sandy did the same with his big deal being trading R. A. Dickey for Travis d'Arnaud and Noah Syndergaard. I distinctly remember that night as the moment I knew this team was headed in the right direction much in the way I knew it years earlier when both Ron Darling and Sid Fernandez were obtained to fill out a rotation that would be headed by Doc Gooden.

But the media for the most part took the stance that the Mets traded their Cy Young Award pitcher because of money. However, this deal was a simple one—trade someone at the height of their value and get a maximum return, much like when Cashen traded Lee Mazzilli (a former All-Star) for Ron Darling and Walt Terrell and later traded Terrell for Howard Johnson. I remember Cashen got criticized back then as well. I laughed about it then and laughed about it when Sandy traded Dickey.

The night Alderson made that trade, I called a bunch of scouts who all said they figured the Mets would get d'Arnaud for Dickey but obtaining Syndergaard as well was outright larceny. I went on ESPN Radio the next day to talk about the trade. The talk show hosts made up their minds that it was another example that illustrated Mets ownership had no clue what they were doing. When I contended otherwise, I was scolded by station management, accusing me of bias.

My reaction was simple—I said to watch this guy Syndergaard before you castigate me. I recalled seeing him with the Jays in spring training and I was overwhelmed by his stuff. I knew he was still a prospect but the pieces were beginning to be put in place. Station management said that take did not fit in with the afternoon show host's take on the Mets and the Wilpons.

Alderson had earlier traded for Zach Wheeler, who along with Harvey, would provide a trio of stud pitchers on the way. Jacob deGrom and Steven Matz were prospects lower on the radar because of injuries, but you could see the Mets development skills take root in these two pitchers as I saw a marked improvement watching them in spring training camp in March of 2014. The Mets were loaded with arms and in successive years Harvey (2012) and Wheeler (2013) exploded on the major league scene.

In the case of Harvey, he is a shining example of how the media works—first build up an athlete and then do everything you can to tear him down. He exploded on the scene in his 10 appearances towards the end of 2012 season which can only be described as dominating. The media quickly started calling the days he pitches "Harvey Day."

To be honest, I hadn't seen a Mets pitcher have such anticipation for his starts since Doc Gooden. Harvey had a similar "it factor" I saw in Gooden. He demonstrated a very unique personality and thoroughly enjoyed the spotlight, appearing on magazine covers as well as being a regular front row fan at New York Rangers games.

Some criticized him for that, but what I saw was a pitcher who was well prepared for every start and according to the Mets coaching staff, worked tirelessly between starts getting ready to perform at the most optimal level. Some beat writers felt that he was a diva. Again, you could see the transformation brewing but to me he was a dominating starter who was an ace in every way.

He got a chance to start the All-Star game at Citi Field in 2013 but a month later was diagnosed with elbow discomfort that evolved into Tommy John surgery. To this day, I think his injury delayed the team's rise to a playoff contender by a year. It was a terrible blow to Harvey and his team but there were reporters who actually blamed his injury on his lifestyle, which I thought was totally out of line.

Tommy John surgery is prevalent throughout the industry but I never heard of this said about any of those other pitchers. And the weird thing is most reporters did not write it or broadcast the notion. Instead, they leaked it out with subtle messages on social media. They never even asked Harvey about it—they just sent it out into the atmosphere and let it percolate.

When he returned in 2015, his numbers and stuff were better than any pitcher I could ever remember recovering from Tommy John surgery. His success was due to the fact he worked tirelessly in his rehab but that was underreported because it did not fit into the narrative that Harvey was a diva.

When the innings limit issue surfaced in September, Harvey was straightforward and honest saying that Dr. James Andrews had advised a 180-inning cap. The Mets were clearly heading to the playoffs and this became a burning issue. Quite frankly, Harvey could have handled it better but the media jumped all over him and questioning his competitive fire.

There are two things I never question about him: his talent and competitive fire. After the controversy was put to rest, Harvey took the ball in the playoffs and put together a fine performance—hurling 26 innings to the tune of two wins and a 3.04 ERA. But all the talk was about how Harvey demanded to stay in Game Five of the World Series and there were those who said that was a selfish move.

I want a pitcher to always show the will to stay in and finish a big game. You could say after the leadoff walk he should have been pulled but to blame it on Harvey is just insane. I do not pretend to have a great one on one relationship with Harvey but the way the media tried to tear this guy down was enlightening to me. I saw the press try to do it with so many stars like Darryl Strawberry and Patrick Ewing, for instance, but this one was done with the help of the negative undertones of Twitter.

It continued through the 2016 season and in spring training the reporters embarrassed themselves even more when it was revealed that he had blood clots in his bladder which he tried to address with a press conference after he was treated for the ailment, but many talk show hosts made jokes about his condition. Later in the year when Harvey had season-ending surgery for thoracic outlet syndrome, many suggested the team was better off without him.

It was a classic illustration of the media building the brand of a player and then tearing it down. What got me was they did it with a level of glee that I can only describe as classless.

Despite some of the media's best attempts to minimize their accomplishments, the Mets won the NL pennant in 2015. They did it because they created a clubhouse chemistry that ignored outside attempts to minimize the closeness of this group. Outfielder Yoenis Cespedes was the final piece as his addition put the team over the top offensively, even though the press attempted to bring him down as well.

Cespedes had the biggest impact I have ever seen a mid-season acquisition have in my thirty years of covering baseball. His at-bats became must-see television as he carried them to six straight wins over the Washington Nationals, burying their NL East chances with three resounding come-from-behind wins in DC in early September.

He had become an icon in New York in short order and the media seemed to be concerned more with his off the field activities than with his dominating on the field performance. But they failed to understand a simple thing: His voyage to freedom from Cuba is something none of us could understand because we take ours for granted. He was living under a despotic ruler who killed people without an ounce of guilt and destroyed families at a drop of the hat.

Getting his freedom was something he did at risk, so he has earned the right to live his life to the fullest. That could mean playing golf on game day or riding a horse into spring training. He lived in a country where he had to worry about walking up the street so he was going to explore life in a way he never could in Cuba. I respect and admire him for this. I could understand it. The Mets could understand it. His teammates could understand it. Why couldn't the media? It beats the hell out of me.

Cespedes has re-signed twice with the Mets because he loves playing for them and Terry Collins is a huge reason for that. The manager has been a big factor in the success of this team by understanding that every player needs to be managed differently. Some need encouragement, some need discipline, while others need a little of both. He was not always like that in previous managerial stints but has illustrated to us that we all have the power to change no matter how entrenched we are in our lives.

The Mets clubhouse is among the best I've ever been exposed to. There are divergent cultures coupled with players competing for playing time, but they all possess a level of caring for each other which translates into winning. Granted, you need talent but once that is present, clubhouse chemistry can pull at team through tough times. Like one of the strangest nights I ever spent as a reporter.

Two nights before the August 1 trading deadline, rumors were swirling that shortstop Wilmer Flores would be traded to the Brewers along with Zach Wheeler for former Mets outfielder Carlos Gomez. It created a Twitter firestorm so intense that fans at Citi Field sensed it was happening and gave Flores a classy ovation as they thought he could be wearing his Met uniform for the last time.

But when we went down to the clubhouse after the game, both Terry Collins and Sandy Alderson indicated no trade was made and the next forty-eight hours were surreal. The following day, the Mets blew a big lead and lost a tough one to the San Diego Padres, and with the trade deadline less than twenty-four hours away, most felt the Met season had reached Defcon 5.

The next day Cespedes was headed to town and that very night Wilmer Flores, still a Met, hit a game-winning homer in extra innings, starting the Mets' climb to the top. It was an astounding transformation for a ball club that has had some miraculous moments, but this story would have made a great Disney movie.

That was the night the Mets fans began to believe and the media followed suit as the team began to put distance between themselves and the Nationals. In late August, David Wright returned to the lineup for a series in Philadelphia and once again one of those surreal moments occurred. He had missed most of the season with spinal stenosis but a fierce rehab put him back in the lineup and in the first at-bat of his return, he launched a home run into the left-field seats.

All the pieces were falling into place and on a cool Saturday afternoon in Cincy, the Mets clinched their first division title in nine years. The clubhouse was a crazy scene as this team that was never supposed to win under the present ownership took the NL East. Their division series opponent was the Los Angeles Dodgers and many felt the 1-2 pitching combination of Clayton Kershaw and Zach Grienke would end the Mets' dream but somehow the Mets did not get that memo.

The interesting thing about the Mets' playoff run was not only the pitching which we'd all know would be solid, but nobody saw Daniel Murphy's home run outburst coming. Murphy was a Met for years and could never quite find a position before he ended up gravitating to second base.

As the regular season was ending, you could see Murphy was starting to hit the ball with more authority as he made a minor change in his batting stance. Murphy always had a strange relationship with the press and I knew him pretty well. He matured as a person and as a player over the years since joining the team in 2008 and I genuinely liked him. We shared the same religious beliefs and talked about that on occasion, but most reporters stood clear of him unless he had a big role in the outcome of the game.

His postseason performance was off the charts and it is hard to think the Mets could have won a pennant without his Game Five NLDS performance in Los Angeles hitting a home run, alertly swiping an unoccupied base, plus driving in a first-inning run en route to the Mets advancing to the NLCS.

The media kept scratching their heads as Murphy continued his home run tear (he homered in six consecutive playoff games) and he walked off with NLCS MVP as the Mets won their first pennant in fifteen years. But the media and broadcasters kept insisting that Murphy would not be back the following season and had a good reason for that contention.

Actions speak louder than words and I knew Murphy would not return way back in spring training after the team reached out to first baseman Lucas Duda to talk contract but never did with Murphy. Ironically, Duda never signed a long-term deal but the present leadership thought Murphy was an incomplete player. I can safely tell you Terry Collins did not agree with that contention, nor did I.

That feeling by the organization was further proven when they set their sights on free agent Ben Zobrist, only to lose him to the Chicago Cubs. Instead of reaching out to Murphy once that occurred, they went shopping for Neil Walker. I do believe the switch-hitting Walker was a good backup plan but not even reaching out to Murphy was pure proof they had soured on him.

Whenever I cover World Series or Super Bowls, I always marvel how the losing team is covered. Every time a team fails to win at that stage you always hear "they were exposed." In 2015 we heard it about the Mets and then in February of 2016 we heard it about the Carolina Panthers.

I've always believed that is a crock of nonsense. Winning a league championship is a tremendous accomplishment and in a two-week period this Mets team beat a great quartet of pitchers—Clayton Kershaw, Zach Grienke, Jake Arrietta, and Jon Lester.

That is what we should remember about the 2015 postseason. Give all the credit to the Kansas City Royals but the Mets accomplished what many thought could never happen—they wrested the city away from the Yankees.

The previous year, I said on an ESPN talk show the Mets were coming and the transfer of power in New York had begun. I was laughed at but that's OK. I had history on my side for the people who doubted it. Twice in my life, I saw the Mets do this—in the late '60s and mid '80's. And they did it with pitching and great management both on and off the field. Like Cashen, Sandy made mistakes like trading Angel Pagan. Don't forget that Cashen traded Jeff Reardon for Ellis Valentine, which turned into a disaster and he got same amount of heat in his first three years from the media that Alderson received.

But Sandy knew he had to stockpile pitching and that would get you to the promised land. The organization has a solid foundation and these pitchers are under financial control—and those years of control are staggered. Matt Harvey won't be a free agent until 2019 and none of the other young starters until the next decade. This will allow the Mets to spend money on offense while their competitors will be forced to spend the multi-year contracts on pitchers that never quite work out in the back half of those deals.

It was a brilliant plan and gave the team the best shot at winning given the financial constraints. It also speaks to the Wilpons making the best of an unfortunate situation.

My gut tells me this team will be the next New York team to go up the Canyon of Heroes because this organization believed in their game plan. They tweaked it along the way but never wavered from it despite all of the detractors. And they made themselves the baseball team in New York after spending fifteen years as the other team in town.

# CHAPTER 22

# The Top 15 Sports Columnists

WHILE I WAS GROWING UP in New York, there were two things I did when I picked up the newspaper—looking at boxscores and then reading a columnist's take on what was happening that day in the world of sports. As their jobs have evolved, these columnists have become more multimedia celebrities because they are called upon to break news stories more than review ballgames.

I took that all into account when putting together this list but also wanted to recognize some sportswriters that made column reading a must for me in my formative years. So here it is—my Top 15 list of the best sports columnists.

1. Kevin Kernan, *New York Post*—He is simply the best columnist I've ever been around for a multitude of reasons. First of all, he breaks down the games he is covering by using his eyes, not statistical analysis that many of today's columnists use as a crutch. He also spends time with players in the best settings to converse with them. Nobody utilizes spring training better than Kevin and you can see it in his writing. During interview sessions, he always asks the questions that get to the root of the issues and uses follow-up questions very well—always being respectful but directly to the point he needs. I've learned

so much being around him on how to conduct an interview and he has given me direct feedback on my work that is honest and helpful. More than that, he finds out what is in the hearts of the fans and constructs columns that touch the things they care about and tries to make sense of illogical situations. In my opinion, this guy would be a perfect sports radio talk show host who'd never talk down to the fans but would inform them the right way.

2. Wally Matthews, formerly of *Newsday* and *ESPN.com*—Wally wears his heart on his sleeve but never lets that get in the way of a totally objective viewpoint on sports. His radio show, *Wally & The Keeg* with Tom Keegan on ESPN New York, was short circuited much too quickly as it was gaining steam and I would love to have the opportunity to tweak it to be *Wally and the KERN*—featuring the above mentioned Kernan and Wally. Matthews demonstrates a great sense of humor in his columns but also hits on those acid-dripping stories that must be reported. I appreciate the fact that he always treats broadcasters with much more respect than some other columnists.

3. Joel Sherman, *New York Post*—He does a great job covering baseball and has contacts in every nook and cranny of the sport. He used to look down on broadcasters but now understands it completes his multimedia portfolio as he frequently appears on television. He has broken numerous stories over the years and realizes that social media can be utilized to break stories. Unlike some reporters, Joel fully recognizes when others break stories first. He understands the baseball organizational budget process better than anybody and is able to look past a transaction to predict or theorize the next move far quicker than his competitors do.

4. Bill Madden, formerly of the *New York Daily News*—When I think about baseball, I think of Bill Madden. He has seen it all and realized that being on good terms with ownership creates better columns for the reader. Nobody had a better relationship

with George Steinbrenner than he did and I firmly believe that is because George knew he would not twist his words and that he would always get a chance to respond when Madden wrote something negative about him. This Hall of Fame columnist also perfected the style of engaging managers and team executives in a great dialogue around the batting cages. Security limits that access somewhat these days but Madden moved those talks to hallways or even by the water cooler in the dugouts. A credit to our profession for sure.

5. Dick Young, formerly of the *New York Daily News* and *New York Post*—He was a columnist who hated electronic media because it represented the future, but what he brought to the profession is undeniable. I think Young would do just fine today even though his hatred of broadcasting would probably limit his chances to be on-air. Young spent most of his career with the *Daily News* but moved to the *Post* in 1980. That is when I first met him and by then, he had become a surly veteran columnist. But historically he had seen it all from the days of the Brooklyn Dodgers and New York Giants to all of the baseball championship moments in New York. His most famous tirade was against Tom Seaver in 1977 when he was largely responsible for the Mets trading him to the Reds. In those days Jack Lang and Dick Young both covered the M. Donald Grant-Tom Seaver dispute from opposite viewpoints. Bill Shannon, a respected writer, told me the whole story of what transpired many years later. Once a new collective bargaining agreement was signed, Seaver wanted to renegotiate his contract which Grant refused to do. Grant even called Seaver names in public through Young column's as he championed the Mets management's cause. Young's son-in-law worked for the Mets, raising eyebrows as to the columnist's true motives. Day after day, Young took potshots at Seaver and Tom Terrific decided, at the advice of others, to go over Grant's head and speak to team owner Lorinda de Roulet about the situation. He then agreed to a contract resolution,

which must have angered Young because that day he wrote a scathing column indicating Seaver's wife was upset that Nolan Ryan made more than Seaver did. It was the first time I could ever remember a columnist making it personal and involving a player's family. At that point, Seaver demanded a trade, starting a Mets demise that lasted until after Fred Wilpon and Nelson Doubleday bought the team. In many ways this was the precursor of sports talk radio and social media before it ever existed. It was the harbinger of things to come—exposing fans to off the field controversy to sell papers, improve TV ratings, or today, provide website click-through. The Billy Martin-Reggie Jackson-George Steinbrenner conflicts reinforced that notion because it all happened in the same era and sports reporting would never be the same. Like him or not, Dick Young was a pioneer in that transformation.

6. Chris Mortensen, *ESPN*—Simply the best NFL columnist in the industry who made the transformation to a multimedia professional sooner than most. He could see that fantasy football was becoming a big part of the experience for pro football fans and he tailored his reports to make that a huge part of ESPN's NFL coverage. But where Chris really excels is at the NFL draft, where he not only knows everything about the top prospects but also the hidden value of small school "no names" that can make an impact in the league. He makes every viewer feel like they are part of draft process as he breaks down the options for their team and gives honest appraisals on whether that pick is a sure thing or a gamble.

7. Peter Vecsey, formerly with the *New York Post* and *USA Today*— Nobody in our industry broke more stories than Peter Vecsey. Whether he was covering the Latrell Sprewell choking incident, Julius Erving's trade from the Nets to the 76ers, or the tragic death of Drazen Petrovic, Peter always came through. He was also a master on getting the real story behind coaching changes. He was the first columnist to recognize the NBA was

a player's league, not a coach's league by pointing out that star players could demand coaching changes. Peter was the first to see it and have the courage to print it. He realized toward the end of his career that the world was turning politically correct and some of his takes would be censored but that did not stop him from speaking his mind. In the social media world we live in, Peter would be a megastar—I honestly don't think the basketball world ever appreciated him while he was patrolling the NBA with a sharp wit and a nose for breaking the real story. The term *breaking news* is so overused in today's vernacular but Peter did it better than anyone.

8. Ken Rosenthal, *FOX Sports* and *MLB Network*—Both FOX Sports and MLBN have a terrific "face of their franchise" when it comes to Ken Rosenthal's baseball coverage. His aptitude for the sport is off the charts and much like Vecsey did for basketball, he breaks news at the speed of light. But he also makes sure to check his sources—never taking a chance without multiple confirmations and never jumping the gun when he's not totally sure. He also handles the whole multimedia part of the job better than anyone. He looks so comfortable on TV whether he is a field reporter or in the studio and that is also the way he is off-camera. He looks for the good in people and has always been a tremendous help to young journalists, not to mention being very active in charitable activities within the sport. His real value is both during the winter meetings and the trading deadline  His views on the game are never about him—they are about providing the fan with the most current info possible.

9. Jay Glazer, *FOX Sports*—A former columnist at the *New York Post*, Glazer is a shining illustration of  how the games are becoming almost secondary to Internet reporting. Jay lives with the notion that fans relish info about how NFL players really feel about issues and has the ability to have a conversation with them with no filter. He also does a great job of taking on issues that most reporters steer clear of. Glazer also became the first

journalist I know of that participates in workouts with players based on his MMA expertise, which provides him with great access .

10. Larry Brooks, *New York Post*—He is the only hockey columnist I read because he gives me all the news that I need. In fact, when I am at a baseball game he is covering during the NHL offseason, I make sure I eat dinner with him so I can catch up on what's going on in the NHL. He never follows the herd of sheep that repeat the same old storylines. Larry is never afraid to take on issues directly even if coaches like John Tortorella, formerly of the New York Rangers, try to publicly abuse him. Larry is like that running back using all of his resources to get to the goal line and he always gets there. He informed readers days before both Mark Messier and Wayne Gretzky joined the Rangers that those moves were coming. It is my firm belief that if Larry were not a columnist, he could have been a hockey coach. That's how well he sees the game.

11. Bob Raissman, *New York Daily News* and Phil Mushnick, *New York Post*: I group them together since they have both been influential with their respective critiques of the sports broadcasting business. There was a time when it was common to spot on-air talent in the press dining room checking out their columns. Phil did a great job (and still does) exploring the conflicts Cablevision created with several stations because they owned monopolies that forced fans to be without televised games of their favorite teams until agreements were reached on fees. He is never afraid to take on the leaders in the industry who abuse their power. Raissman coined Chris Russo's "Mad Dog" nickname and should have asked for royalties from him since that branding landed him millions from Sirius XM. His appearances on SNY's *Daily News Live* have brought him front and center and his name recognition puts him on this list.

12. Phil Pepe, formerly of the *New York Daily News*—He was yet another columnist from an earlier era that had a profound

impact on the business. Think about this— Pepe wrote the lead story for the *Daily News* for every World Series game from 1969 through 1981. During that time, he also covered most of Muhummad Ali's fights, both of the Knicks' championship runs in the '70s, and was a beat reporter during Roger Maris's assault on Babe Ruth's home run record in 1961. He wrote close to fifty books with the likes of Mickey Mantle, Bob Gibson, Whitey Ford, and Gary Carter. In addition, Phil was the first writer to cross the broadcasting line as his "Pep Talk" segments were heard on WCBS-FM for over fifteen years beginning in 1989. Even back in the days when broadcasters were at odds with writers, he was one of the few who never placed a barrier between the two groups. Sadly, he passed away in December of 2015.

13. Jon Heyman, *FanRag Sports*—Jon is an accomplished writer who understood the role agents have in breaking story far earlier than most other writers. He has also branched out into electronic media, serving as a frequent guest on talk radio as well as television with breaking stories about player movement. He has been on MLB Network since it launched in 2009. What lifted his career more than anything was his *SI.com* column called The Daily Scoop. He joined CBS Sports in 2011 but a contentious contract dispute resulted in his migration to Fan Rag Sports Network five years later.

14. Ian O'Connor, *ESPN.com*: From pure writing skills, Ian is hard to beat. He is never afraid to tackle issues that need to be explored, including racism and big business aspects of sports. I feel he is underutilized as his award-winning writing style has no boundaries.

15. Claire Smith, formerly of the *Hartford Courant* and *New York Times*: No list of sports columnists would be complete without mentioning the pioneering work of Claire Smith, the first female baseball beat reporter, although I remember her mostly for her fine work as a columnist for the *New York Times*. Claire

is a shining example of what is good about the business and her being honored with the J. G. Taylor Spink Award by the Baseball Hall of Fame was long overdue.

It wasn't easy limiting this list to the fifteen I chose. Peter King, Buster Olney, Jayson Stark, Mike Lupica, Ken Davidoff, Andy Martino, Dave Lennon, Chris Broussard, Peter Gammons, and Mike Vaccaro were all worthy of being included. The biggest change for columnists over the years has been the crossover into electronic media, which has increased their revenue and saved their careers in many cases. Social media has altered things for them and most have accepted it as part of their jobs.

Some have branded themselves well but others that have not, leaving their careers in serious peril. That is unfortunate because the newspaper business is dying out and they can either embrace multimedia or be left behind.

## CHAPTER 23

# My Favorite Athletes to Interview

OVER THE YEARS, I HAVE had the opportunity to report on a wide variety of athletes. Some stand out as genuinely understanding how we could help each other while others resisted that concept. Quite frankly, there are far more players who are cooperative but these fifteen stand out as the best. This is not a ranking, just a list, and I will also mention the handful that made my sports reporting life miserable.

David Wright—David Wright is one of the most honest people I've met. Win or lose, he always speaks to us. During his rookie season with the Mets, he spent time with such veteran players as Mike Piazza, John Franco, and Joe McEwing, learning the dynamics of media interaction. He not only provides us with constant access but creates an atmosphere of good feeling when you talk to him. When he asks, "How are you?" he genuinely cares and gives you his undivided attention. I noticed that from the day he arrived in the Mets clubhouse and you can see he understood the process of both a one-on-one interview as well as having thirty reporters crowding around his locker. He is a player that loves wearing the orange and blue and understands Mets fans want to hear from him.

Bernie Williams—He was a player that was as classy as they come. He played on a Yankees team that had massive personalities but always stood out to me as a player you could talk to at any time, and not just about baseball. He is a brilliant person who has so many interests and on the rare nights his team lost, he always understood what we needed—a fact many of his teammates chose to ignore. Bernie kind of gets lost in historical discussions about that great Yankees era and I never quite understood that. I firmly believe that it was because he possessed an understated personality, but he was as important as any player on that team, commanding center field in a way no Yankee had since Mickey Mantle.

Adam Graves—The 1994 New York Rangers Stanley Cup championship team was a great team to cover and Adam Graves would never say no to a reporter. In fact, if he were late he would apologize, saying that he knew we were on deadline. But you really saw what kind of person he was with all of the time he spent with charities—never merely just spending time but getting to know the people he was helping. Forget his hockey skills for a moment, the world needs more people like Adam Graves.

Chad Pennington—His time with the Jets did not end well but this is a man who wore his heart on his sleeve and never skirted a tough question. As a collegian, he was a quarterback at Marshall and you can see he had a great mind for the game. When he was drafted by the Jets, you could readily see that he understood how to deal with people as well. There was one incident in his Jets career in which he lashed out at media, claiming it was a privilege to cover football. I remember the media going crazy about the comment but I honestly understood where he was coming from because so many media members need to be reminded of that fact. Pennington had the heart of a lion, the mind of a computer, and leadership skills that are rarely seem in this sport. Quite honestly, when he left the team he was never given the accolades he deserved because the Brett Favre show strolled into town.

Jose Reyes—In all of my years covering him, I have never seen him turn down an interview request from anybody even after he was suspended by MLB. This is a man who helped my career evolve because he gave me so many exclusive interviews while I was reporting on ESPN's

*New York Baseball Tonight.* I remember so many days traveling with the Mets I was exhausted, but somehow talking to Reyes energized me and one thing about him—when he is your friend it comes with the notion that that relationship is unbreakable. The domestic abuse incident he was involved in was totally his fault and he has taken responsibility for it. I can confidently tell you his efforts to make himself a better person through counseling is something he takes very seriously and appreciates his second chance with the organization. In 2016 I saw the old Jose Reyes, the one we enjoyed dealing with every day. Not a day passes when we do not talk during the season and we stay in touch during the offseason as well.

Mike Richter and Henrik Lundqvist—Playing goaltender for the Rangers is a high-profile position in New York and I put both of them together here because they are so similar in personality and how they treat the media. Richter was a big reason why the team won the Cup in 1994 but also endured some rough moments in his career including a playoff series in 1992 against the Pittsburgh Penguins where he gave up some questionable goals. It gets forgotten in the 1994 hysteria but it is important to note that the media access he gave us was consistent no matter what the outcome. He was entirely humble after a win and totally accountable when he lost. And he did it all with dignity and grace. His successor, Henrik Lundqvist is in some ways, an even better netminder than Richter but has exactly the same relationship with the media. Both Mike and Henrik made our jobs so much easier.

Gary Carter—The former Mets catcher was one of the finest people I have ever dealt with in this industry. He loved the game, was a devout Christian, and cared about others more than himself. He was so accessible and one time early in my career redid an entire interview when my recording device malfunctioned. The moment I remember most was the night the Mets won the 1986 World Series. Carter showed compassion for the Red Sox, knowing how it felt to fall short. Even in his final days before succumbing to cancer, he was accessible to us and talked about positivity. He was a fiery competitor on the field but off the field he always showed his heart in helping others. I spoke to him after he retired about a variety of things including dealing with my dad's lung cancer. He gave me solid advice and I will always remember that. God puts people in our lives at certain times for a reason. I firmly believe Gary Carter had a positive impact on so many people and showed his love for others in the most tangible way—caring how the people around him feel and as a consequence, helping the media was just second nature to him.

Eli Manning—This is a man who is super talented and has two Super Bowl rings with the Giants but is above all else a regular guy. He does not have to be the loudest voice in the room but he commands the respect of both his teammates and the media. And the reporters have not always treated him well, overanalyzing his demeanor. In my opinion, how do they know what his demeanor is inside the huddle? I've asked players and they all speak highly of him whether they are current teammates or ex-teammates. But the interesting thing about Manning is all of this media criticism really did not change him—he gives us pretty much unlimited access and that speaks volumes about him. It also explains his greatness—never let perceptions bother you because they can change in an instant. The perception of the people close to you—teammates and family—means much more. Eli is giving us all a life lesson.

Chipper Jones—He is the only non-New York player on this list but I had to include him. The former Atlanta Braves third baseman, a certain Hall of Famer, was always honest and accessible no matter what the situation. And there was a lot to talk to him about, including the "Larry" chants, teammate John Rocker's antics, and the first game after 9/11. Each time, Chipper gave thoughtful and truthful responses to tough, direct questions. He was not happy with Rocker's comments about New Yorkers and at same time laughed off the chants from Mets fans. I had spent time with Chipper during spring training, and got to understand him even better, but at the first game in New York after 9/11 you could see his human side vividly—something he always showed the media every day.

Mike Bossy—I dealt with Bossy early in my career while covering the Islanders and understood going in what a great goal scorer he was. But I quickly found out he was also very accessible to the media. Hockey players are well represented on this list as I discovered early in my career they were the most talkative people in the business. Bossy would break down his goals but also was very open to discussing the shots he missed. At the same time, he was very much an ego-less interview and given his record-setting goal scoring pace, that was amazing to me. He stood out in that locker room as a go-to guy along with Denis Potvin and Billy Smith.

Mark Messier—Yet another hockey player, but he stands out above the rest of the players who hit the ice in this town. He came here to do something that had not occurred in over half a century and he responded in every way. People sometimes forget in the year before the Rangers won the Cup, they failed to make the playoffs and Messier was booed at the Garden. But he never ducked the questions and made himself available. Many players might have hidden from the questions that year but not him. And he put his neck on the line throughout the '94 season. You never felt he was talking down to you in media sessions. He learned many of our names and would always stop to chat with us in the hallway by the locker room.

Allan Houston—He came to the Knicks with a big free-agent contract but never big-timed any member of the media. He was readily available after every game and many times he had to face negative questions. He always answered them and even on the day he won a playoff game in Miami with a last-second shot, he had to field a question that I could not believe—was it disappointing it took a last-second shot to beat the Heat? That might be the dumbest question I ever heard, but Houston actually answered it well, saying that he was happy with the win but even in winning there is always room for improvement. But the conversation I remember the most I had with Houston was on Martin Luther King Day at Madison Square Garden one year. We talked about the legacy of King and Houston said the most brilliant thing I ever heard in a locker room: "You know an illustration of what

King gave us is right now you and I are talking and have total trust in each other. It has nothing to do with color or politics, it has to do with talking about a common interest—basketball. We respect each other and can learn from each other. That's why I love him." I was floored by the conversation but it also rang true in my mind that sports can bring people together, even a no-name reporter like myself and an NBA star. To this day, I often think of what Houston said to me and when I see racism in the media I try to fight it by acknowledging it.

Mariano Rivera—The former Yankees closer is the best I've seen in terms of his talent and his will to win. He is also one of the best players in terms of media interaction in Yankees history. There was never a day he didn't answer every question and on the rare days he blew a save, his mindset was crystal clear—credit the opponent and take accountability for the result of the game. It diffused the line of questioning because unlike most closers he would never say subtle things which indirectly cast blame on others. He would also very polite with us, frequently asking if there were any more questions and he would always answer questions from reporters who were late for the session. It is my hope that Rivera becomes first unanimous first ballot Hall of Fame inductee.

Carmelo Anthony—This one might surprise all of you but to me this player is misunderstood in a myriad of ways by the media covering the Knicks. He has a good heart and always answers questions honestly and directly. Who could ask for more from a player? This is my take: great pure shooter, perennial All-Star, and always available to the media. That's why he is on this list.

Carlos Beltran—The outfielder spent nearly a decade in New York and never ducked a question the entire time he played here. As a Met, he gave thoughtful responses in spite of the fact that some reporters questioned his desire as a player. Carlos and I spent a lot of time talking about that and he told me his biggest concerns were his family, God, and his teammates. And there are days that he has to concentrate on one of them more than others. Despite the fact the media misunderstood him, he still always answered their questions. In fact, the same night catcher Paul Lo Duca complained that the Mets' Hispanic players rarely spoke to the media, Beltran spoke at length as he always had. The media did not report that because it did not fit in the narrative of the story. To Beltran's credit, he couldn't care less and when I hear comments from people saying he was selfish I point to him stepping aside from center field and helping Angel Pagan in his last years with the Mets.

This was a tough list to limit to fifteen players and some who just missed the cut were John Franco, Al Leiter, Jeff Francouer, Darryl Strawberry, Ron Darling, Mookie Wilson, Freeman Mc Neil, Wesley Walker, Marty Lyons, Victor Cruz, Brian Leetch, Martin Brodeur, and Mike Piazza.

Those who were not easy to deal with include Barry Bonds, Bobby Bonilla, Vince Coleman, Roger Clemens, Mark McGwire, Lenny Dykstra, and Jayson Williams.

The truth of the matter is that it is up to media professionals to deal with each and every athlete but some make it easier to do than others.

# CHAPTER 24

# A Game Plan for Aspiring Sports Journalists

I FIRMLY BELIEVE THAT YOUNG journalists have it much harder today than when I started in the business. The main problem is that most of them lack proper training in the skills needed to be a reporter. Social media has only exacerbated this situation and young people who take up journalism in school are given so many mixed messages. I will give you a clear message—learn the game you are covering inside and out because it will always be beneficial to your growth.

Resist shortcuts no matter how tempting they may be and understand job rejection is part of this business because evaluating sports reporters is such a subjective process today. Use rejection as a positive and do not waste time blaming others for your rejection. Use it as a way to figure out your areas of development and how to improve your prospects of getting better. Blaming it on EEO regulations or other factors will merely drag you into a negative mindset and that will curtail your development.

If a colleague gets the position, do not burn a bridge with them or the manager who made the decision. And *never* share your innermost thoughts on social media. If you lose out on a job, spend the next day on other things. Treat yourself to some new clothes or take your significant other away for the weekend. Immerse yourself into hanging out with people you love—not whining about your lot in life.

I speak from personal experience here. If you waste too much time on things you can't control, two things will happen: Nothing will change and you will not be spending time focusing on the things you can control, which makes this tough moment in your career doubly troubling.

If you have a bad day, perhaps being scolded by your manager or being disrespected, you have earned the right to feel sorry for yourself for exactly one minute, not a second longer.

Try to stand out in your reporting as a pro who speaks their own mind and even if the world disagrees, stick to your guns. If you do, you will begin to learn that dealing with adversity makes you stronger and at the same time you will develop a fan base. I can almost guarantee there are people that feel the same way you do but might be afraid not to follow the public stance for fear of being criticized.

When I worked at ABC, Howard Cosell would always say, "What is popular is not always right and what is right is not always popular." When I took unpopular stances, I always remembered that.

Preparation time is so vital to solid reporting and so many reporters just don't do enough of it. Part of that is spending time with players but also being familiar with the history of the game, which is so accessible in a number of ways today. I shudder when I hear young reporters' lack of knowledge on the history of sports because it really defines them in a negative way. The real distressing part about it is this is an area of development that can easily be improved. It is just flat-out lazy not to do it.

Today, sports reporting is like an investment portfolio—you need to diversify because putting all of your eggs in one basket is for much later in your career. Get involved in reporting, writing, blogging, tweeting, and networking every single day.

And believe in yourself. It may sound corny but start every day by looking in your bathroom mirror stating your name with the job you want your name attached to—I am John Doe, SportsCenter anchor (to use an example). You will never become what you want to be unless you can say it.

Early in your career, get your foot in the door anyway you can and do that by taking the right internship in your college years. Do not go for the big name company—go where you can learn the most. Things like video and audio editing, ENG camera work, writing press releases, and on-air promos as well as improving your announcing skills can often be done by interns in a smaller TV or radio station rather than at a major network.

Employers will always look at what you did at an internship rather than where you did your internship. In addition, learn non-broadcasting skills that could translate into becoming a multi-faceted applicant that could fit into many possible entry-level positions.

When I was looking for work right after my college years, I got a position at a major cable network but I learned traffic software as well as having a working knowledge of invoicing ad sales clients. It opened doors for me that I have used every moment of my career.

Once you get in the door, you can explore other things but be careful. You always want to perform the duties you were hired to execute and if you do them well, a good manager will help you explore those avenues. However, if you underperform at your role managers will feel like they were being used and that is a mark that will follow you in your future job opportunities both within that company and other organizations.

Sports journalism is a very small fraternity and word travels fast. If you are the victim of losing your position due to a downsizing, take the high road. Most companies offer job placement plans for those affected by mergers that are so common in today's world. Utilize those benefits and never criticize your employers because most times they are just victims of decision-making made high in the food chain of an organization and secondly, this manager may end up later in your career in a place you might be applying for a great position down the road.

Be very careful in the way you use social media. Many organizations observe an applicant's presence on social media as part of their background check. Photos or comments that may be politically incorrect could take you out of the running for a position you desperately want. Graduate schools use it in determining prospective students and will never cite it as a reason for rejection. But trust me, every business looks at it so be aware of that.

Use this as a guideline: Do not tweet anything unless you feel it could be a *New York Times* front page headline. Simply put, everyone will see it. Use it to promote your content and enhance your brand in a positive way but resist the air of negativity that lives in the Twitter brand.

Sports reporting is a demanding profession and many don't really understand it until they are deep inside it. Friendships and relationships will take a beating as many of the people in your life work 9 to 5 and most simply won't understand that you work mainly nights and weekends. When your college friends are off to the beach on a Saturday, you will be covering a game. You have to love it because if you do not, it will eat you alive.

The travel can also be extremely taxing and have an impact on you both physically and emotionally, especially in baseball where you cover games from spring training in February through September and longer if postseason play is involved. I've seen so many young reporters over the years leave the business because the pressure it exerted on their personal life was just too much.

I've always said this is something you need to consider before deciding to be a beat reporter. The first few trips are exhilarating and fun but as time goes on, it becomes a grueling part of the job.

You must know this going in—like most things in life it has plusses and minuses. I would never discourage any young journalist from doing something they love but I want to be crystal clear—the money will not be what you expect (especially in the early years) and the hours will be demanding.

But I will say this—I have had the privilege of covering great events but there are things I had to give up to do that. I would not trade those moments of reporting for anything in the world.

Obstacles only become debilitating if you let them and once you decide never look back. Diversify your skills, get better every day, and never waver from your mission statement. People may try to discourage you. When we hear those comments, just smile and walk away. Pretty soon those same people might be following your every move.

# CHAPTER 25

# Where Do We Go From Here?

IN THIS BOOK, I HAVE examined how sports reporting has changed over the past three decades with technology, sports radio, the demise of the print industry, social media, and fantasy sports being just some of the factors that created this revolutionary shift in the press boxes across America.

It begs the question: Where are we headed? Clearly, social media and the Internet will continue to try to oversimplify sports analysis and analytics will remain a crutch that will continue to be utilized. But I remain an eternal optimist and firmly believe there are veteran reporters and a plethora of young talent in this business that can save the day.

When I cover games, I spend countless hours talking with my colleagues. Young reporters such as Laura Albanese, Anthony DiComo, Marc Carig, Steve Gelbs, and Kimberly Martin give me great hope for the future. Each of these professionals stands out to me as media members that love the game with a passion and don't rely on just numbers—they use their eyes as well as their stat sheets.

There are also veterans such as Mike Puma, Steve Popper, Rich Mancuso, Rich Cimini, and Mark Feinsand that can provide a base of knowledge we can all learn from in how we analyze the game. Radio reporters abound in this business, including Mike Mancuso, Howie Karpin, Marc Ernay, Bill Meth, and Tom Mariam.

Sports talk radio is here to stay and with the additional possibility of live streaming coupled with TV simulcasting it will continue to grow. What worries me is that so many talk show hosts parrot each other and more precisely just repeat what they see on social media.

Fans I talk to are desperate to hear things they can't get anywhere else. They sometimes feel the media is too negative.

I really hope sports radio hosts gain a better understanding of what the fans want. I know that some fans of today care more about the off-the-field news than I ever did when I was growing up. It has taken me a long time to understand this but I've come to the point that I accept it as the new breed of fans. I also think the modern fan is much more interested in the history of sports than the media gives them credit for.

I say that because programs such as ESPN's *30 for 30* documentaries capture the young fan's attention and I get plenty of questions from Mets fans on both 1969 and 1986. It is very similar to the interest my young friends had about the 1940s and '50s when we begged our older relatives to tell us about Jackie Robinson, Joe DiMaggio, and Willie Mays.

Sports talk radio and TV debate shows will go hand in hand in attracting sports fans to the news of the day. I do hope the yelling can be toned down on these shows because the louder voice is not always the correct voice. People like Marc Malusis and Chris LoPresti give me hope that these TV debate shows could be more civil, which I believe will actually make them more useful. But I am a realist and know that the louder voices will usually get the bigger paychecks.

I am very concerned about the demise of the print industry. We have already seen so many great writers lose their positions because of nothing they've done wrong—but merely because print media executives are clueless how to create revenue in any tangible way.

I have cited numerous examples of poor management decisions that have hurt so many writers. To their credit, many have developed their own brands and diversifying their portfolio by entering the electronic media. But some either have not been given the opportunity or are not very comfortable on the air. So where do they go? I have an answer to that but it may appear outlandish at first.

In an earlier chapter, I cited a couple of news sources, Deadspin and The Players' Tribune, that I believe will be big money makers. They will do it in totally different ways and their mission statements will be as different as night and day.

Both of these organizations will be core resources fans will use to get information. Deadspin will be out to get the story that will shock us while The Players' Tribune simply wants to give the player's point of view directly to their fans. At first glance, writers would not want to write for The Players' Tribune because they do not want to be a mouthpiece for the players and I certainly understand that.

However, this is an organization that has capital the newspapers just don't possess and their advertising and revenue progress has been amazing—much bigger than any newspaper or website in the industry. And their presence could eliminate the need for the current middle man—the media. Once enough athletes utilize this form of communication, why would the print media be needed?

For them, the answer is simple—you can't beat 'em so join 'em. But the fly in the ointment is once a few writers (maybe just a handful) jump ship, the party is really over. Ghostwriting is the last thing any sports reporter wants to do but at least the capital is there to pay you long-term—unlike your current employers.

We've already seen major stories broken exclusively by The Players' Tribune and the frequency of that happening will only intensify. I even believe it could become a great concept for a sports talk radio network or a cable network. If you think that is impossible, think back fifteen years or so.

Would you have laughed at me if I told you that cell phone you were carrying in your pocket would be all any sports fan would need? How about thirty years ago? Could you have imagined four major networks (FOX, CBS, NBC, and ABC) instead of three?

In a five-year period (2002 to 2006) both New York baseball teams created their own networks, creating successful business models in very different ways. YES was strictly a Yankees channel (at least at first) while SNY covered all New York sports.

My point here is that things that look impossible now could be very possible a few years from now. My advice to writers is to market yourself one way or the other because living in the middle will never provide you with long-term job security. The daily newspaper executives will continue to shave sports budgets—some no longer even have sports desks as they rely on news people to track sports.

Broadcasters have their own issues. In years past, you could count on networks remaining solvent. Today, mergers and sellouts occur at a moment's notice and the first reaction in these situations is to cut cost and salary. So, tell your agents to get longer term contracts even at less dollars per year because that will at least buy you some time when the inevitable occurs—your employers selling or merging.

Of course, if you are one of the bigger names, you will always land on your feet in any situation. But most do not fall into this category. So make sure your agents take this into consideration when negotiating a new contract. I've been on the other side of that desk in my career and trust me, broadcasting contracts are all about control—when you have it, take it to the mat. When you don't, react accordingly.

I am firm believer that talent and hard work can get you through whatever the future holds. Over the past three decades, those who succeeded were the ones who were able to adapt to the changes in the industry.

This press box revolution has created some challenges for those working in the sports media but also opportunities. Like most revolutions, there are those who benefit and those who do not. The next few years might just give us a clearer picture of where the reporters of today might stand in that equation.

# Acknowledgements

I WOULD FIRST LIKE TO thank my family: my dad, Tony Coutinho, sister Lisa Scarano, and her husband Nick, who consistently inspire me as well as my two wonderful nieces, Genevieve, who has joined the ranks of journalism, and Roma, who is perfecting her acting abilities at Carnegie-Mellon. Also my cousins Rose Scalera, Fred Napolitano, Ted and Linda Pernicano, as well as the trio of Mattos sports stars—Keith, Donald, and Elaine who were very instrumental in supporting all of my career goals.

My upstairs neighbor, Michele Herrera, deserves my thanks for putting up with the long hours of hitting my keyboard at all hours of the night.

From a career standpoint, there are so many people to thank: Kevin Burkhardt, Gary Cohen, Mike Mancuso, Ed Coleman, Bill Daughtry, Chris Majkowski, Howie Karpin, Bill Meth, Matt Cerrone, Don LaGreca, Todd Ant, Scott Wetzel, Anita Marks, and Steve Gelbs have always been there for me. Bosses like Eric Spitz, Mark Chernoff, Pete Silverman, the late Shelby Whitfield, "The Chief" John Martin, Tim McCarthy, Ed Carroll, Evan Shapiro, and Christian French have taught me a great deal about how this business works and how to tap dance around the roadblocks.

The WFUV alumni: Michael Kay, Mike Breen, Charlie Slowes, Doug Mittler, Jack Curry, John Pezzullo, John Gianonne, Bob Papa, and Paul Dottino are friends for life because of how the station will forever identify us as family while shaping our careers.

Special thanks to Marty Noble, Suzyn Waldman, the late Chip Cipolla and Howard Cosell, Johnny Holliday, Bruce Morton, Janet Spaulding, and Bob Klapisch who helped me in my early years plus a heartfelt thanks to the New York Mets Media Relations team of Jay Horwitz, Ethan Wilson, and Melissa Rodriguez, who are always there to make covering the team easier. I would also like to thank my editor, Ken Samelson, who kept me driving to the goal line on this project from the time he suggested the idea of the book right through to the final manuscript.

Donald and John Spano, my Edson Avenue buddies growing up, as well as close friends Dan Brokowski, Andy Barberesi, Johanna Fessler, Amy Nyikos, Tiffany and Ken Grosso, Andrew Whitman, Hilary Russo, Rob Petrone, Kevin Cirrito, Tara Perucci, Kate Horvath, Kelly Betts, and Mary Felder are also people who I look up to and admire because they've been with me at different stages of my life providing inspiration by always believing in me.